PROGRAMMING NATIONAL IDENTITY

PROGRAMMING NATIONAL IDENTITY

THE CULTURE OF RADIO IN 1930s FRANCE

JOELLE NEULANDER

LOUISIANA STATE UNIVERSITY PRESS BATON ROUGE

Published by Louisiana State University Press
Copyright © 2009 by Louisiana State University Press
All rights reserved
Manufactured in the United States of America
FIRST PRINTING

DESIGNER: *Amanda McDonald Scallan*
TYPEFACES: *Whitman, text: Franklin Gothic and Manhattan, display*
PRINTER AND BINDER: *Thomson-Shore, Inc.*

Portions of chapter 3 first appeared in "Family Values and the Radio: The 1937 Radio Elections and the Miniseries, France," *French Politics, Culture, and Society* 24 (2006): 26–45, © Berghahn Books. A portion of chapter 5 first appeared in "Radio and the Fiction of Single Working-Class Women in 1930s France," *Proceedings of the Western Society for French History* 29 (2001), and is reprinted by permission. Portions of chapter 6 first appeared in "Exotic Listening: Colonial Landscapes on French Interwar Metropolitan Radio," *Historical Journal of Film, Radio, and Television* 27 (2007): 311–32, and are reprinted by permission.

Library of Congress Cataloging-in-Publication Data

Neulander, Joelle, 1971–
    Programming national identity : the culture of radio in 1930s France / Joelle Neulander.
       p. cm.
    Includes bibliographical references and index.
    ISBN 978-0-8071-3494-8 (cloth : alk. paper) 1. Radio programs—France—History—20th century. 2. Radio broadcasting—Social aspects—France. 3. Radio broadcasting—Economic aspects—France. 4. Radio broadcasting—France—History—20th century. 5. Radio broadcasting policy—France—History—20th century. I. Title.
    PN1991.3.F7N48 2010
    791.440944′09043—dc22

2009019998

The paper in this book meets the guidelines for permanence and durability of the Committee on Production Guidelines for Book Longevity of the Council on Library Resources. ∞

To Colette Lambert, Martine Mitchell, and Ken Cmiel

CONTENTS

ACKNOWLEDGMENTS ix

INTRODUCTION 1

I: FINDING AN AUDIENCE: MARKETING TO FAMILIES

1. THE PUBLICIS ANTENNAS
Markets, Advertising, and the Rise of the Private Station 23

2. OPENING UP THE STUDIO DOORS
Fashioning Loyal Audiences from Markets 45

3. FAMILY VERSUS LIBERTY
Popular Front Programming and the Radio Elections of 1937 71

II: FAMILY VALUES AND FRENCH IDENTITY ON THE RADIO

4. AROUND THE CRADLE
Family Portraits for the Family Audience 99

5. THE PERILS OF THE SINGLE LIFE
Marginalized Working-Class Men and Women at Radio's Fictional Center 128

6. BOA CONSTRICTORS, MAN-EATERS, AND *LE CAFARD*:
Colonial Landscapes on Metropolitan Radio 160

CONCLUSION 185

APPENDIX A: Educational Classes, Week of March 7, 1937 193

APPENDIX B: Lectures on Public Stations, Week of March 7, 1937 195

NOTES 201

INDEX 235

ACKNOWLEDGMENTS

When Steven Ungar first handed me a cassette tape of French film music in a graduate class in 1995, I little imagined it would lead to a book on interwar radio. And I cannot conceive of having written that book without a tremendous amount of help, friendship, and encouragement from others.

At Iowa, Sarah Farmer gave me the insight to work through tough ideas and the space to let them grow. She challenged me to push my ideas to their limits and kept me moving forward with my work. Steven Ungar and Rosemarie Scullion took in a green historian, helped show me the ropes in cultural studies, allowed me to attend their classes with French graduate students, and, with great patience, plowed through my research papers and offered thoughtful critiques of my work. My fellow graduate students helped me at every turn. Members of several writing groups always had inspiring ideas after careful readings of my chapter drafts: Michelle Rhoades, Nat Godley, Paul Young, Bridget Williams-Searle, John Williams-Searle, and John McCurley. Lawrence Sohner, Lars Peterson, Erin Jordan, Sara Kimble, and Andrea Gayoso offered advice and great friendship to sustain me through the long Iowa winters.

Since coming to the Citadel I have had generous research and presentation fellowships from the Citadel Foundation that have allowed me to continue work on my project. The support and advice I received from my colleagues has been remarkable. I wish to thank them all, but especially Bo Moore, Jeff Pilcher, Keith Knapp, Blaine Roberts, and Kathy Grenier, who read drafts, gave feedback, and made my progress on the work so much easier. At Louisiana State University Press, Alisa Plant has guided me with aplomb.

I have many people to thank in France. Cécile Méadel at the Ecole des Mines gave her time to a curious graduate student searching for documents on her topic. Rosanne Lelièvre and the staff at the Inathèque de France allowed me the honor of listening to interwar recordings at the Maison de la Radio. I will never forget the unexpected joy, after hooking up a reel-to-reel, of hearing Maurice Chevalier joking about riding a bicycle along the Riviera. Friends and colleagues I ran into at the Café des Temps at the Bibliothèque de France made my trips to Paris an intellectual and cultural highlight: Paula Lee, Rachel Fuchs, Philip Whalen, Becky Pulju, Sarah Hanley, and Shannon Fogg among others. I thank also the numerous friends and colleagues who, at every stage, provided advice and support: Brett Bowles, Robin Walz, Jeff Horn, Jen Popeil, Vanessa Schwartz, and Jonathyne Briggs. Rachel Bohlmann, since our first days of graduate school, has always let me bounce ideas off her and led me to think imaginatively about the role of gender in my story.

My two families deserve special thanks. First, my French family, Jean Lambert, Karine and Olivier Dufour, and Claire Collet, whose love and care gave me a real home in Paris and in Suze. And my parents, Pris and Alan Neulander, who kept me flying ahead, knowing there was always a place I could land.

And, most of all, to Kurt Boughan. There is no measure of gratitude that could ever be enough.

PROGRAMMING NATIONAL IDENTITY

INTRODUCTION

Two stories to begin.

The first:

One night at a house in Neuilly, in the bourgeois outskirts of Paris, Hélène begs her husband to stay home from the theater because she can sense, in innate feminine ways, that something awful will happen to her that evening if she is left alone. Jacques laughs off his wife's fears, calling her "hysterical" and in need of a psychiatrist's care. He tells his friend Roger that his wife is "afraid of everything" and has "a nervous condition" and so must be taught a lesson to prevent her outbursts in the future. They lock Hélène in her bedroom and pretend to leave the house. That night, their maid's lover sneaks into the house to rob it and murders Hélène because he expected to find himself alone and everyone at the theater. Sitting in the living room, Jacques and Roger hear Hélène's screams but do nothing, as they assume she is exaggerating her fears. They realize she has died only when the screaming stops and the murderer has escaped out of her bedroom window.[1]

The second:

One morning at Radio-Cité, a radio studio on the Champs-Elysées in Paris, the mail arrives full of boxes of throat lozenges. A few nights before, worried listeners had heard one of the announcers coughing and speaking with a frog in his throat. They send their good wishes, medicine, and home remedies for his speedy recovery. In response, the announcer thanks his loyal audience on the air.[2]

These two stories, one fictional, one allegedly true, speak to the rising audio culture in interwar France. The first story is the plot of a 1937 radio play by Jacques Cossin and José de Berys titled *Fear*. The authors, regular radio playwrights and actors on *Jacques Cossin's Half Hour of Crime Drama and Adventure*, a series that could be heard on French public radio between 1936 and 1939, assumed certain female behaviors. They created, and a woman performed the role of, a character whose innate female traits both allowed her to sense danger and ultimately put her in its path. A hysterical woman, upsetting her husband too often, could be murdered in her own home, within earshot of her own family. The authors and actors had to suppose that interwar French radio audiences would understand their characters and their play and at the same time would be frightened by the action.

Central to the plot of this radio play are suppositions about the sanctity of the home. For the payoff—a frightening murder that would shock listeners—the audience had to understand the home as an inviolable domestic space in which carnage and mayhem should not have ensued. The popularity of the play and the whole adventure and crime drama series depended on the idea that radio listeners wanted a "safe" shock. Plays could frighten or astonish them for a moment, but audiences had to be assured that after the play their own homes remained secure spaces for their families and domestic life. Audiences would listen only if the stories were exciting and unusual and if they felt safe while being scared: the stories had to contain a reassurance that such atrocities would not actually occur.

The response to the announcer with a cold shows the extent to which audiences embraced radio and its attendant personalities and brought them into the warmth of their homes and lives. Radio programmers, working for either businessmen or the state, envisioned French listeners as family groups, located squarely inside the home. They had good reason for doing so, as our second story tells us. Radio listeners thought solicitously of those they heard on the radio. They wished (or the radio owners wanted them to wish) to treat them as family, to take care of them as they would their relatives, neighbors, and friends. As ownership statistics show, listeners had listened in intimate groups and thought of programming in domestic terms. Individual families and households owned the majority of radios. At the end of the decade, only about fifty-four thousand of 5 million radios taxed in France were located in public spaces.[3] The idea of the family audience drove radio's cultural production and the plays and songs on the airwaves. The radio programs and their sponsoring advertisers spoke directly to the French people—families, in particular—through songs, comedies, dramas, and news.

By the end of the 1930s, sharing an auditory culture became second nature to listeners. Radio stations had gained demonstrably faithful audiences who related and responded intimately to their programming. As devoted listeners, they began to privilege sound over vision inside their homes—as a daily source of entertainment, news, and other information. Sound and intimate spaces were linked together, and, within the comfort of these spaces, worlds were opened to French people explicitly defined by sound, and sound alone. Until television joined radio in postwar households, audio culture reigned supreme in dining and living rooms.

The following pages propose a detailed analysis of radio programs, including plays and songs, a project that offers another point of entry into the history of audience and taste in France in the 1930s.[4] Audio culture, as the mass medium of the living room, deserves a more central place in the cultural history of interwar France.[5] Radio was created for an audience different from that of visual culture. If museums, movies, and posters were created for mass audiences to enjoy in a crowd, radio programming was designed for intimate spaces. Building on important work done by Lynn Spigel on domestic life and television, this book seeks to transplant and reperiodize the postwar idea of family viewing to the realm of interwar family listening, because radio owners, programmers, writers, and actors thought of the radio audience as being in its living rooms, made up of imagined traditional families.[6]

In spite of the imagined domestic audience, radio necessarily challenged traditional notions of separate spheres because it was a public medium that spoke its message in the private space of the home.[7] Because of this hybrid quality, radio programmers had many choices in how they would exploit the gender-confused impact of the new medium. They could question outdated notions of gender and attempt to change them by using new images of men and women on the radio. By fully injecting public politics into the private sphere they could alter what people believed the model French family, and France as a whole, looked like. Programmers could also simply reflect fundamental shifts in interwar gender roles by creating shows and characters that acted like the typical people who listened: diverse in class, gender, age, outlook, and experience. Most comfortably and, as we shall see, profitably, they could attempt to obscure the innovative and destabilizing nature of the new public-private medium by reifying traditional notions of the home in programs that idealized notions of separate spheres. The choice was uniquely French. Kate Lacey, in her work on German radio, examined how different governments could coopt state radio to either challenge or defend women's place in the home. The former case proved true with Weimar but was quickly overturned with the Nazi accession to power.[8] In the late 1930s, with no strong lasting government to play a decisive role, France's competing public and private interests would shape radio in their own way.

Overall, then, the notion of the home as a protected and celebrated space was central to the programming choices that French radio directors and owners made in the 1930s. *Fear*, the play that constitutes our first story above, was doubly conformist. Not only did it reflect normative gender roles; it also obeyed the rules of other popular forms of entertainment. The shocking murder in this story, as well as the entire weekly Jacques Cossin mystery and adventure series, mirrored the kinds of stories listeners had probably read in the penny press, serial fiction, and pulp or paraliterature.[9] This reliance on customary fictional tropes helped programs find an already established audience of readers who would feel comfortable with the stories on radio.[10] And radio needed an audience for its programming—either to sell products or to spread political messages. Ultimately, a paradoxically new and old radio culture appeared on the air: new because it offered a mass auditory experience and old because it was conservative, or domesticated in style, easily conforming to the nation's households in dining and living rooms.

To understand the impact of the new programming, one must be aware of France's unique radio system. French radio was exceptional in the West in two important ways that affected its programs. First, radio developed later in France than elsewhere in Europe and the United States. Because France remained more rural than its industrialized counterparts, Germany and Great Britain, radio's appeal remained smaller for longer, because the spread of radios suffered from geographic rather than class barriers. Radio reached urban centers first and then spread into the countryside and, subsequently, into mountainous areas, where stations were harder to tune into.[11] As late as 1937, areas such as the Massif Central and the Alps had fewer than one radio per twenty inhabitants. Two departments, the Lot and the Cantal, had only national stations, when they could tune them in, and no dedicated regional broadcasts at all. By contrast, urban centers such as Lyon, Paris, Bordeaux, Marseille, and the industrialized north had almost one radio per household and at least two or three regional stations to listen to in addition to national commercial and public broadcasts.[12] Second, France, unlike Germany, had no governmental impetus to get radios into citizens' homes. The Germans subsidized radios and required that all households have a means to tune into state broadcasts.[13] German radio, by 1933, was integrated into state propaganda with a centralization of all programming. The French had no such program. As government after government swept into and out of power, the state made no concerted effort to place radios into French homes. Households were on their own, and until programming tempted individuals to buy radios, they could easily have spent their money elsewhere. Radio historian Cécile Méadel has demonstrated that it was only in 1935 that radio became more than a fancy for hobbyists and, instead, became a true mass medium that millions of French people heard on a daily basis.[14] Owing to radio's late expansion, the French could draw from other nations' systems and ideas in devising their own.

Throughout the 1920s and early 1930s, with only a small minority of citizens as radio owners, the French government remained unconvinced of radio's importance to politics and the cultural landscape of the nation. With an unswerving devotion to the exclusive use of print media, the state did not pass its first legislation concerning the airwaves until 1928, when it limited radio's expansion to thirteen public and thirteen private stations and placed all state radio under the control of the Ministry of the Post, Telegraph, and Telephone (PTT). This number would stay consistent through the next decade, although some stations would change hands and one, Radio Beziers, its location as well, in its move to Paris as Radio 37 in 1937. (The maps show the stations as they stood at the end of the 1930s.) Only in 1933 did the Chamber and Senate install a nationwide system that regulated the public stations. The new arrangement, called the Ferrié Plan, combined the stations into a nationwide network that relayed important entertainment and news broadcasts from antenna to antenna. It also established a central Parisian news service and maintained Radio-Paris as the flagship national station that would represent France to its own citizens and to the rest of the world. Most important to this story, the government instated a yearly radio tax of fifty francs on every privately held machine, creating a new source of revenue to run its public stations. At the same time, the government outlawed advertising on its own stations. In spite of the immediate intention to tax radio listeners, this regulation would be implemented only two years later when, in 1935, the energetic and slightly autocratic Georges Mandel took over the PTT and made it a powerful and active ministry.

In tandem with the new plan, and because of new and exciting programming coming from public and private stations, French radio expanded rapidly in the 1930s. The number of citizens who listened to the radio each day went

Private Radio Stations in France, 1938

from, at most, 2 million in 1930 to more than 20 million by 1939.[15] With a larger public to reach, radio stations increased their broadcasting hours exponentially over the course of the decade. For example, Radio-Cité, a private station, started its on-air life in 1935 with only six hours of programming, but by 1939 it broadcast eighteen hours each day. Radio-Paris, the premier government station, increased its airtime from twelve to sixteen hours a day during the same period.[16] Paris-PTT, another public station, the regional station for the capital, had seventeen hours of continuous programming in the 1938–39 radio season.[17]

The French system was different from that of the rest of the West because France was the only nation (apart from Australia) to have both public and private radio systems. The United States had only privately owned stations, while most of Europe, including Italy, Germany, the Soviet Union, and Great Britain, had only state-controlled stations. This dual system meant that in France alone the corporation and the state competed for the ear of the nation's citizens. The two radio systems vied for real control over the product of the radio, each with

Public Radio Stations in France, 1938

its own political and commercial agendas. Each also competed with its own unique lineup of programs to entertain or instruct the French public. The first two decades of French radio were, as radio historian Frank Tenot shows, a time of a "pirate" system, when, in order to gain advantage in the marketplace, radio station and programmers pushed the limits of the law and had the ability and desire to put almost anything on the air.[18] Through constant competition and innovative programming, by the end of the decade the more savvy and wealthy private stations would control the culture of radio, forcing the public stations to follow suit or lose their audience almost entirely.

While free to push the limits of the laws governing radio, French programmers, working within the unique dual public-private system, still had many outside strictures on programming choices. These came from various government policies, new market forces created by the radio audience, the ideals of republican democracy, and, most important, the assumed expectations of the imagined radio audience listening as families inside the home. Ultimately, it was the conservative and commercial voices that controlled the cultural product of the radio. Even if French society was changing in people's working lives, with massive unemployment and a rising percentage of women in the workplace, the home represented a safe space, a place where citizens could escape from the crises outside their doors. Within that space, the belief in an idealized family seemed inescapable. In 1936, one conservative radio critic reminded listeners and programmers alike of radio's patriotic and patriarchal responsibility: "It is important that [those] who control our radio understand what the wireless in the Home means: . . .To try to entertain the great mass of listeners who demand nothing from the Radio but to remember that, in a home, you will find a woman, so often at housework, so little celebrated, and children, the future of our nation."[19]

Most radio programmers had a conservative, bourgeois notion of family based on an ideology of separate spheres. Wives and mothers were to be in the private space of the home and fathers and husbands in the workplace and public realm. In these imagined families, patriarchal heads held the power, ultimately controlling their political and cultural vision. This notion of the individual family audience was well supported by both the prevailing political gender ideology and the new market forces created by radio. Because many politicians worried about the declining birthrate, the 1930s were a decade of traditional ideas of the family.[20] Stable families with mothers free to take care of multiple children at home, government officials believed, would help to build up the French state. Advertisers, too, liked the idea of women at home, listening to the radio and then buying the household products advertised over the air. Homebound women during the day and families in the evening—all captives of the radio—constituted a perfect new target market for their wares.

Radio programmers also chose their schedules by envisioning the home in temporal terms: they thought about who was home and listening to radio at certain hours of the day. Programmers tried to make their radio stations full-time home entertainment. They began the day with wake-up music and news, scheduled programs for women during the day, featured shows for children on their days off from school, offered news for fathers as they returned home from work, ran family broadcasting until eight or nine in the evening, and played adult-oriented shows later at night. Parisian station Radio-Cité, in its advertising campaign of the 1938–39 season, claimed that its eighteen hours of daily programming, full of variety and excitement for everyone in the family, made it "the station you'll never leave again."[21]

Public and private systems both helped regulate the cultural and consumer product that eventually went over the air. They had different methods of program selection. The programming choices on state radio were made by government-appointed ministers. Radio was controlled through the Ministry of the PTT and regional program directors, but by 1936 many other high-ranking officials wanted a part in selecting shows. Even the president of the Republic became part of the radio board. Both Edouard Daladier and Léon Blum, as party leaders and prime ministers, served at least limited time on government radio committees.

Owners of the private stations hired program directors to make choices reflecting the hottest trends in theater and music. The idea was to balance cost with an ever-expanding consumer audience. The more expensive and popular the star, the bigger the advertising budget, which would translate into a larger listening public. For example, Marcel Bleustein-Blanchet, owner of Radio-Cité, hired Jacques Canetti, a successful recruiting agent for Polydor Records, as artistic director at the station. As director, Canetti was able to recruit great singing talent and songwriters from his former pool of recording artists. By providing the newest and best talent available for radio, private stations offered French citizens sophisticated daily variety entertainment unlike any they had heard before in their homes. France's biggest stars of theater and record performed "private concerts" each evening in France's living rooms.

Both public and private stations played a tremendous amount of popular music during their time on the air. An analysis of programming minutes indicates that over 60 percent of private radio's airtime consisted of the latest artists' popular songs, both recorded and live versions.[22] Private stations gave exclusive contracts to the day's biggest music-hall stars, who sang their hit recordings and debuted new music weekly. Public radio dedicated at least one evening a week to similar light music, usually current hits sung by in-house performers rather than by the original recording artists. Popular singing stars rarely appeared on public stations, as the fees for a single appearance were much too high.

Radio plays were also exceedingly popular on all broadcasts, and for public stations they were a mainstay of programming, as they were a cheap form of entertainment. Program guides from radio print weeklies reveal that all the stations filled hours of airtime with adventure stories, crime dramas, variety shows, and radio adaptations of novels and plays. Radio-Paris, the flagship public station in France, introduced a police-crime series that aired one evening every other week, reflecting a popular interest in crime drama. The most successful plays were often rebroadcast by other public stations across

France.²³ Private stations abounded with homey soap operas, including *La Famille Duraton*, a daily fifteen-minute chat around the family dinner table that brought fame to its actors and money to its parent station, Radio-Cité. Lise Elina, the teenage star of the series, claimed in her autobiography, *Le Micro et moi*, that when she accidentally burst out laughing live on the air, all Paris talked about it the next morning.²⁴

Given radio's critical importance to cultural life in the 1930s, it may seem surprising that historians have generally overlooked these radio programs and the overall picture of France and families that they transmitted. But radio's importance was short lived, and much of what was heard was ephemeral—live, unrecorded broadcasts that disappeared into the ether as soon as they were aired. By the late 1930s, moreover, experiments in television had begun, and creative efforts in live television programming started soon after World War II. By the mid-1950s, television had supplanted radio as the creative center of broadcast media. The importance of radio fiction and the centrality of radio in people's lives were soon forgotten—thus the almost black hole of radio studies in the nexus of cultural historical work. We know much about Pagnol and Renoir, Cocteau and Carné, and little about Henriette Charasson, Saint-Granier, and Georges Colin. And yet, during their heyday, most citizens knew just as much of these radio writers and actors, daily entertainers in their homes, as they did of their favorite film stars and directors. In fact, many of those stars, like Jean Gabin, Fernandel, and Arletty, used the radio as another medium for selling their songs and publicizing their films.

Although film has been studied because of existing collections of prints that are easy to access and understand, many historians of the interwar years have ignored the culture of French radio because the available material is limited and its study is difficult, at best.²⁵ Minutes of meetings of radio programming boards are located at the archive of the Office de la Radio et de la Télévision Française (ORTF) in Fontainebleau, but they are now inaccessible due to mishandling and a fungus that has attacked the paper. Moreover, few radio plays exist in aural form, as they were often performed live and never recorded. Of the few that can be heard in recorded form today, most were produced on soft wax records that archivists consider too fragile for audition.²⁶ This leaves few auditory sources for the historian to study.

While some histories do explore the content of interwar radio in other countries, none has done so with the radio of France. Most histories concentrate, instead, on British and American radio shows. These interpretations pose other problems. Until recently, radio histories have been more nostalgic than critical, appealing to an older general audience that can remember the days before television and reminisce about live radio programs from years ago. These books offer anecdotes about programs and radio artists but do not analyze broadcast content to make a historical argument about the social implications of radio and its programs.[27] Recently, new scholarship on auditory culture, especially in the United States, has opened up radio to the same kind of analysis already offered for film, television, and literature.[28] In French history, a new generation of historians of auditory culture has begun work.[29] My book joins this new work, with an attempt to link radio to its politico-cultural setting and an analysis that uses programs and articles about programs as texts worthy of critical study. French radio listening was more than a minor pastime for its audience: it created an auditory culture that helped citizens to interpret their world.

While one can look at many of the programming choices made by station owners and directors, a close analysis of audience response is impossible for radio in France prior to World War II, as the government did not systematically begin polling its listeners until 1945. The popularity of individual programs is thus impossible to calculate. The only clues to listener response come from fan letters printed in radio publications and newspapers. Because of this, French histories of interwar radio tend toward the administrative—showing how stations were set up in various locales and used the law to their advantage.[30] Because one cannot catalog who was listening to individual French radio stations and programs, demonstrating what was on the radio and exploring the gendered politics of programming may be the only way to analyze what messages audiences heard and enjoyed and, in the end, who those audiences were. That the French did enjoy radio is indisputable—listenership increased tenfold over the course of the decade—but a better understanding of the audience for radio and its makeup and tastes would go a long way in helping us to understand interwar France.

Radio plays constitute many of the primary sources in this book. Because I could not listen to radio broadcasts, I read scripts; from 1936 onward, every play on public radio and a small number from private stations were automatically deposited in the national library collection. All of the radio plays featured sound effects, many of which the playwrights wrote directly into the scripts. The most elaborate plays were accompanied by musical scores, sometimes with live orchestras and sometimes with recordings. Imagining the sound of the plays takes some creativity, but the scripts themselves included the pauses in dialogue, and generally the plays were driven almost entirely by dialogue, not by foley, or sound effects—which meant that background sound provided context and was integral to the décor and helped listeners follow the action but did not directly affect the plot.[31]

Radio plays often also had a "voice-off," or narrator, to help establish the scene, describing the physical decor and sometimes the characters themselves. Because it could not be seen, the action of the play had to be communicated through dialogue to guide the listener. For example, instead of moving to the door, a character would say, "I'll go to the door to see if he's coming." One can presume that this might have been followed by the sound of shoes moving across a wood floor and the click of a doorknob. Action could also be described with exaggerated entrances. *The Variety Revue*, a play that anthropomorphized different kinds of programming (lectures, conferences, symphonies) into speaking characters, had singers and comedians enter the studio by horse, motorcycle, flying carpet, and car, all accompanied by appropriate foley. The play even went so far as to mock the limits of radio programming by staging a "Russian ballet" in the studio, with only the comic effect of the slapping sounds of toe shoes on a dance floor.[32] Sound descriptions also took the place of scenery, which was especially important for plays set in exotic locations. In *Two Men in Morocco*, the sound of muezzins and market noises define the Casbah in Casablanca, setting the exotic scene for the play.[33] By contrast, for the 1936 film *Pépé le Moko*, set builders reconstructed the Casbah of Algiers, giving the actors a setting in which to play. Radio's architecture was created solely by those who worked behind the microphones.

This lack of a visual setting makes radio quite different from other kinds of broadcast media. With radio, the listener makes individual visual pictures inside his or her own head. The communications theorist Marshall McLuhan writes of radio as a "private world."[34] He argues that "radio affects most people intimately, person-to-person, offering a world of unspoken communication between writer-speaker and the listener. That is the immediate aspect of radio. A private experience. The subliminal depths of radio are charged with the resonating echoes of tribal horns and antique drums. This is inherent in the very nature of this medium, with its power to turn the psyche and society into a single echo chamber."[35] Because radio has only sound, the listener can center on one sense and imagine the rest. This absence of other senses gives a more immediate nature to the broadcast, as it is not dissipated by visual signs. The broadcast takes place as if inside the listener's head, to be reimagined personally, reinterpreted by each individual. McLuhan claims, "If we sit and talk in a dark room, words suddenly acquire new meanings and different textures."[36] Radio, then, could hold an essential and very personal place in listeners' lives.

Moreover, radio audiences often heard a play only once. It was not the individual play, then, that had great meaning, but rather the sum total of the works that radio offered. Fleeting sound images could and should be compiled into thematic groups that had much more impact than any individual play could ever have. Thus, in my book, I use specific plays to highlight certain larger thematic trends that French listeners heard on their radios.

I also rely on the texts and music of popular songs. Songs could have more impact than radio plays, as their repeated airing left a lasting cultural legacy. The French have had an interesting relationship to song for the entire modern period. As the numerous coffee table books on song and singing stars of the early half of the 1930s show,[37] many enjoy the history of song and share those histories with others.[38] Songs themselves have inspired their own historical revisions. Historians have even mapped the political and social trends of the Third, Fourth and Fifth Republics by looking only at music lyrics.[39] This work attempts to show that French people were quite interested and invested in lyrics' and songs' political and social meanings as much as, if not more than, in the music. They heard their own stories in song and paid attention to how those stories were sung. In French music, then, more than the chorus mattered.[40]

At a wedding in France in 1998, some of the guests asked me about my research topic. Surprised that an American woman would be studying French radio and songs of the 1930s, they started thinking about how their own parents and grandparents had introduced them to the music of the interwar period. Overhearing the conversation, the bride's grandmother and great-aunt called out their favorite songs from their teenage years: "Les Roses blanches!" "Quand on se promène au bord de l'eau!" "La Java bleue!" Others, the bride and groom's parents' friends, expressed their love of "retro" music and told me about their own compact disc collections of songs. They challenged me to recite and sing them the songs I knew. As the evening stretched on (and as more wine and champagne were drunk), the party turned into a sing-along of 1930s songs. The guests laughed over and performed the interwar singing stars' hits, from Ray Ventura to Maurice Chevalier, from Mireille to Tino Rossi. We sang together into the early morning hours.

That evening showed me that the relationship the French have with the stars of the 1930s is far from over. The songs of that period have entered into the cultural consciousness, allowing the children of the next generation to enjoy them as much as their parents did when they were young. Local stores and national chains sell the hits of the 1930s in their retro section. Today, any interested French shopper can find a collection featuring almost any singing star of the period.

While working with popular songs, I was struck by their connection to early radio. Most of the 1930s singing stars made few films; their concert tours, too, had limited audiences. Radio became the means by which these celebrities gained success and by which good songs became popular. Tino Rossi, Charles Trenet, Maurice Chevalier, Edith Piaf, Ray Ventura, and others relied on the radio to play their songs and to make them successful. All of them appeared frequently, some more than weekly, on the air to promote their work and sing their latest hits.[41] Robert Desnos, critic and poet, actually complained about the ways that stars used the radio in an editorial in a Parisian entertainment magazine. His remarks reveal just how frequently popular songs were played: "I never cease to be amazed at the listener requests that ask for certain records to be played nonstop, . . . When you like a record, you buy it. You don't impose it on thousands of listeners, annoying them to no end. For better or worse, artists should be interested in making sure that their audiences, or clients, don't tire of them and their recordings. A Tino Rossi, after benefiting from his extraordinary radio introduction, has ended up the victim of an excessively large audience."[42] Desnos's disparaging comments aside, Tino Rossi probably liked his "excessively large audience" and benefited greatly from his exposure on the radio. Radio audiences frequently requested their favorite popular songs and were happy to listen repeatedly to them. They turned the singers into celebrities.[43]

Radio, of course, fits into a larger context of mass media in the interwar years. Radio expanded the influence of vaudeville and film actors of the day, like Maurice Chevalier and Fernandel. Celebrity in film often translated into celebrity on the radio, with songs in film becoming hits on radio. Certainly Fernandel and Chevalier had stellar careers in both media. Radio relied on their celebrity to encourage more listeners. As we will see in chapter 2, it was Maurice Chevalier who introduced the country to a new radio station in 1937. Fernandel would star in numerous radio productions, including a series on Radio-Cité called *Fernandel and Company*. In December 1937, Fernandel starred in three radio plays on public radio about military life. This was, as he put it, "exceptional," as he had an exclusive contract with Radio-Cité.[44] He clearly saw radio as a means to further his career and took advantage of the opportunity to be heard over the air. Radio-Cité, too, saw the advantage of controlling the radio appearances of such a famous star who could act in skits and sing his hits for their audience. Radio did not operate in a media vacuum.

Yet radio did not function as a reflection of cinema or print media. Radio created its own auditory culture apart from other mass media. The airwaves had their own singing stars, most notably Tino Rossi and Edith Piaf, neither of whom had particularly successful film careers. The 1930s also introduced a new kind of voice personality. Male speakers and female *speakerines*, as the French feminine would have it, spoke to audiences daily over the air, creating their own catchphrases, like Saint-Granier's "*chers auditeurs*," and becoming successful in their own right. These speakers became celebrity endorsers for companies who advertised over the radio. Saint-Granier, for example, appeared in print advertisements for Lévitan furniture, a company that was a sponsor of programming on Radio-Cité.[45]

As much influence as film and print media had, by the end of the decade, radio was the dominant medium. It seemed that to know about and believe something, one did not simply have to see it, as those who study visual culture have shown; one also had to hear it. Political speeches, news stories, sports events, and *faits divers* all had their place on interwar radio. The sound of the event was immediate. Jean Renoir's 1939 film *La Règle du jeu* opens with a pilot's landing after a transatlantic flight. A radio reporter relays the news of the landing over the airwaves. The characters are brought together, as each listens to the broadcast in his or her home. The scene reflects a mass audience for the new medium both as a plot device and as a celebrity cameo. The reporter is played by Lise Elina, a celebrity news reporter and soap opera actress on Radio-Cité. The scene begins in the Radio-Cité recording booth on a truck and follows Lise Elina into the crowd, speaking on her Radio-Cité microphone, and it is given immediacy and a sense of reality by this radio report. Listeners, and filmgoers, knew the radio stars. If they did not recognize Lise Elina's face, they certainly knew her by her distinctive, high-pitched voice. She lent an air of actual celebrity to the film. By 1939, when French citizens wanted news or entertainment, they moved to their living rooms and turned on their radios.

Listeners and programmers had a complex relationship. Stations had to understand their audience and comply with its desires, but programmers had their own motivations as well. Private station owners, advertisers, and governments all had missions for the radio. In part I of my book, "Finding an Audience: Marketing to Families," I examine how these three groups viewed the French listening public and how they tried to combine political ideologies and market forces to produce a radio schedule and programs that that audience desired. In part II, "Family Values and French Identity on the Radio," I analyze the schedule and shows and the way their connection to a bourgeois ideal of the home and family shaped the overall message disseminated to listeners. Radio in the late 1930s created new markets from that audience and fashioned a new space for consumer culture. The result was a new synergy between mass media, mass politics, and mass consumption.

The first two chapters of the book explore the ascendancy of private radio in France. The first, titled, "The Publicis Antennas: Markets, Advertising, and the Rise of the Private Station," analyzes how early private station owners created new advertising markets and shaped their listening audiences. Marcel Bleustein-Blanchet, perhaps the most important French advertising magnate of the twentieth century, is the hero of this chapter. Bleustein-Blanchet found room for himself on French radio, created radio advertising in the early thirties, and bought his own private station in 1935. He understood the relationship between advertisers, programming, and the new medium of the interwar years, and he exploited it for his own gain. He created the "Publicis Antennas," an advertising service that worked for stations across France and changed the way radio could earn a profit. He was instrumental in taking radio out of the hands of the hobbyists and in placing it into the grasp of government and big business.

Chapter 2, "Opening up the Studio Doors: Fashioning Loyal Audiences from Markets," looks at the programming and propaganda that private stations shaped to and for their new French markets. Advertisers' goals combined with the stations' need for a loyal listening audience to create a private system that relied on the ideology of separate spheres and the notion of the patriarchal family as radio's central listening unit. Private companies wanted to sell their products throughout the day to mothers and wives during the daytime hours and to fathers and their families in the evenings. At the same time, commercial stations looked to foster listener loyalty through a sense of participation in the day-to-day functioning of the radio. They made their stations like part of the family, offering radio audiences the chance to participate in game shows and creating characters that reflected images, albeit ideal images, of the listeners themselves.

Chapter 3, "Family versus Liberty: Popular Front Programming and the Radio Elections of 1937," assesses the public stations and their place in the political landscape of Popular Front France. The Popular Front attempted to use radio as a means of mass education, setting up an elaborate cultural program for the radio in late 1936. The coalition ignored public radio's potential power as an intimate medium, instead focusing on the crowd as the receptacle of its message. By early 1937, the right had had enough of the explicitly left-wing radio program (and so had many listeners). With the radio elections of February 1937, the right, under the guise of an organization called Radio-Famille, used the rhetoric of family and nation to regain control of the public stations and to try to change state programming to reflect the moral notions of the Catholic patriarchal family. Their victory ensured that radio listeners would be seen by both public and private programmers to be part of traditional families. Further, to retain an audience, public radio would have to compete on the same rhetorical and cultural terms as private stations.[46]

My work, although connected with the Popular Front's ultimate failure in its efforts on state radio, is concerned with the culture that was only partly touched by the Popular Front. What is important is that the Popular Front's failure to galvanize support for its radio project pushed public radio into conservative hands. This created an on-air right-wing consensus on both public and private radio that espoused ideas about family, class, and empire that did not reflect left-wing, working-class, or Popular Front attitudes.

Chapter 4, "Around the Cradle: Family Portraits for the Family Audience," places these notions of family and consumption within the culture of the radio. In a way, the politics of the day, including pronatalism and the male politicians' rejection of feminism, reflected these same ideas of patriarchal family structures. This chapter examines how the ideology of separate spheres worked its way into women's programming, keeping it strictly limited to daytime hours. It also assesses images of men, women, and family in evening programming and demonstrates that while speaking to the family through the desires of the patriarchal father, radio shows reinvested meaning in bourgeois gender roles that limited women to the household and men to "codes of honor" that predated World War I.

Certainly, if the radio labeled the ideal French family as bourgeois and linked it to the ideology of separate spheres, many people fell outside of that definition. Chapter 5, "The Perils of the Single Life: Marginalized Working-Class Men and Women at Radio's Fictional Center," analyzes how single working-class men and women, marginalized by the notion of the bourgeois family, were then defined by radio culture. To be contented characters on the radio, single men and women had to aspire to marriage and bourgeois status. A myriad of radio plays and songs portrayed the working-class men who remained alone, without patriarchal control, as criminal, with no solid future. Radio's multitudes of working-class women, all victims of their untamed emotions, bounced from affair to affair, ending their lives as degraded and penniless prostitutes on the streets.

French radio defined the limits of behavior on a mass medium that had the home as its central listening point. Colonial spaces, then, needed special attention, as they remained outside of the safe sphere of household and metropolitan France. Chapter 6, "Boa Constrictors, Man-Eaters and *Le Cafard*: Colonial Landscapes on Metropolitan Radio," examines radio's ambivalent relationship to the colonial world featured in so many plays and songs. On the one hand, the radio was bound by national pride to celebrate France's "civilizing mission." On the other, the colonies were dangerous spaces, exotic landscapes filled with "less-than-French" people who were seen as a contrast to all that was good about the French patriarchal family and home. Radio had a double mission. The first was to bring the colonies to life in radio plays and songs, adding lavish sound decors to the non-French scenes portrayed. The second was to show the difference and danger inherent in the colonial enterprise. This maintained the alien nature of the colonial experience to the daily lives of French listeners, giving audiences a perilous, and untouchable, sound spectacle. Radio stations maintained this distance from the "real" exotic in another way, by bringing "half-tamed" stars regularly into their schedules. For example, Tino Rossi, the Corsican heartthrob, excited women with his exotic and wild love songs but remained a respectable love because, while not from the metropole proper, he came from Corsica, Napoleon's own birthplace.

Radio was a new and very powerful medium in the 1930s. The family fictions produced for radio and consumed by ever-growing numbers of French people became a fundamental part of entertainment and cultural politics in the 1930s. Because of its conservative view of the home, however, radio did not force open dialogue about the future of the nation, either abroad or at home. Both the songs and the plays fit into patterns that reproduced existing restrictive stereotypes of gender roles, sexual roles, class identity, xenophobia, and nationalism. These ideas were shaped by both consumer and political forces into a monolithic set of programs on the airwaves. By looking closely at radio in a turbulent, although peaceful, period in French history, I trace the perpetuation of the various gendered stereotypes of family and nation that challenged liberal notions of democracy in France and that ultimately forced a reevaluation of the impact of the interwar dual private-public radio system after the Liberation of France in 1944.

FINDING AN AUDIENCE
MARKETING TO FAMILIES

1 THE PUBLICIS ANTENNAS
Markets, Advertising, and the Rise of the Private Station

In 1937, a left-wing radio critic commented that "private radio is more lively, younger, more active, happier, more interesting than state radio." He expressed his dismay at this and condemned the private stations, linking them in his mind to the opposition to the Popular Front and state radio. He called them "fascist." Yet when he ranked all of the Parisian stations for listener enjoyment, he placed three private stations, Radio-Cité, Poste Parisien, and Radio-Luxembourg, at the top of the list, over even the largest and most well funded public station controlled by the Popular Front, Radio-Paris.[1] By the latter half of the 1930s, even for its severest critics—those who believed that the state should not tolerate a private system—private radio held a position of success and public influence. Private radio stations had superseded public stations in popularity and number of listeners, but left-wing critics still held that the private commercial mission was less than adequate to achieve socialist goals.[2]

Private radio gained its momentum in the mid-1930s, when commercial outfits gained sole use of ever-growing advertising revenue. Innovative young advertising executives brought the use of advertisements into the mainstream of radio programming, giving private stations large budgets that could be spent on popular radio personalities, new studios, great scriptwriters, and radio acting troupes. With money coming in from advertisements, these stations could offer listeners top-quality daily entertainment for free.[3] Public stations, by contrast, made do with smaller budgets and poor copies of the star power and songs of the original talent on private radio. Private stations also set up lucrative relationships with daily newspapers. Lifestyle reporters wrote supporting articles for radio programs and advertised the stations at no extra expense.

Advertisers, in turn, used their connections to radio programs in their own print advertisements in these same newspapers, thereby giving private radio shows more free publicity. This connection to newspapers brought articles about the radio into the home through a second and equally powerful mass medium, the printed press.

Radio's advertisers worked with the stations to create a product that satisfied both their economic interests and the desires of the home audience. Radio advertisements featured household items, medicines, foods, and wines that reached their market directly in the space in which those products would be used. The companies also linked their wares to popular programs and stars, associating merchandise with entertainment and family fun. Commercial stations, in their turn, as they expanded both their audience and advertising contracts, tried to construct programming that would satisfy their sponsors, bringing them the markets that their stations attracted. Theorist Erik Barnouw writes about a sophisticated late twentieth-century view that radio programmers in France in the 1930s were only beginning to understand: "Advertisers may 'construct' an audience in a more deliberate fashion than do film directors or authors; in commercial broadcasting, the material sent over the airwaves exists primarily to gather and retain an audience for the advertising."[4] As American radio historian Susan Smulyan notes, advertisers' goals to sell their wares limited the options for programmers.[5] Private stations created a radio community with shows that simulated audience influence and interplay between station and listener. Stations also chose entertainment over education because a friendly, familiar imagined radio community broadened the listening audience and thus sold more airtime and hopefully more advertised products. Programmers had little concern for the larger effects their radio might have on the populace, except for keeping the family at home in order to expand their market for advertising. Thus they often contributed to conservative notions of family and patriarchal authority in popular culture.

The new advertising market arose from a concerted government effort to create separate nationwide private and public radio systems. With the installation of the Ferrié Plan in 1933, the statute that proposed a full-fledged governmental scheme for the public airwaves, the Senate and Assembly decided to direct public radio from a government ministry, taking it out of the hands of amateurs. The Assembly placed it under the auspices of the Ministry of the Posts, Telephone, and Telegraph (PTT). The plan set up a radio tax to pay for this government service. Each radio owner paid a tax of fifty francs on his or her radio and a one-franc tax on every radio lamp used to run that radio. The law also called for a one-hundred-franc tax on radios in public spaces, such as those in cafés and local clubs, and a two-hundred-franc tax on all commercial radios with paid access—in movie theaters or private restaurants, for example.[6] For the first two years, this tax supplemented programming on government stations without depriving them of advertising income, giving them a much larger source of revenue than the existing thirteen private stations.[7]

In 1933, private station owners were mostly still local amateurs who now had government contracts for their broadcasts. They did not really have much to grumble about because advertising remained sporadic at best, was often absent altogether, and did not yet bring in much revenue. Rather, private radio operated on owners' personal incomes and served as a place to fulfill recreational desires to play music and speak on the air. Few advertisers yet thought of the radio as a real source of income. The public stations, on the other hand, benefited greatly from the new tax, as their budgets grew with the registration of each new radio. State radio could also take advantage of whatever advertising revenue it could muster.

The double revenue source for public stations would not last. In 1935, the center-conservative Bloc National appointed Georges Mandel as minister of the PTT. Mandel, a disciple of Georges Clemenceau after World War I, had proven himself both a bureaucratic wizard and a bit of an egomaniac. He had expected ministry appointments through the 1920s but was consistently turned down because his rivals saw him as self-centered and uncompromising in his opinions. By 1935, the government understood that, due to his seniority, it had to give Mandel a posting, but it wanted to keep him out of the central halls of power. Prime Minister Pierre-Etienne Flandin offered him control of the postal service, a small, inconspicuous ministry without much authority or status that seemingly ran on inertia. Surprisingly, Mandel was content with his posting. He saw much unrealized potential in the various branches of the post, including the radio, and wanted to have a noticeable effect on the running of his ministry, a display of control that might bring him more power later on. He wished to create an important ministry out of one of the largest and most inefficient sectors of the government.[8]

As part of his plan, Mandel desired "order and authority" for a public radio system strongly controlled by the state.[9] Two years after the installation of the Ferrié Plan, the ministry had yet to regulate the radio under its command. Mandel, now at the helm, pushed for an extension of the state network that included an expansion of the range of the major stations, which all operated at varying levels of power. Under his ministry, Radio-Paris began to emit at two hundred kilowatts, making it easily accessible all over Europe.[10] It became the principal station, representing the culture of France to the entire nation and to the world at large.

Mandel wanted state radio to run solely on its own tax money because he saw "his" radio as a public service that should have no private strings attached. He decided to push for sufficient radio tax revenue so that he could ban advertising on the state-run stations. He felt that if the taxes brought in enough money to support excellent programming, those who paid the tax deserved to hear their public radio without commercials. To achieve this goal, Mandel organized cooperation between the postal workers and the radio office in order to gain more tax money from radio registrations. Instead of demanding that all radio owners mail in their documentation or drop it off personally at the post office, Mandel had his postmen collect the registrations while on their routes. As an added incentive, he gave each mailman a two-franc bonus for every new radio registration he brought in. As a result, radio registrations jumped to over 1 million in the course of a few short months, and tax receipts climbed from 80 million to 150 million francs. By the end of his ministry in June 1936, the government taxed and registered over five hundred thousand more radios. By 1939, that number would reach over 5 million.[11] Public radio could now function on its own internal funds. As of January 1935, all state radio ran solely off the money from the radio tax.

With the new tax money, Mandel wanted to create programs with "quality, interest and diversity."[12] He sponsored ties between radio stations and national theaters, using the tax money to subsidize the theaters hurt by lower attendance during the economic crisis and then broadcasting live plays from the theaters. Mandel felt responsible to keep the theaters running if he could, seeing French drama, comedy, and music as integral parts of the *patrimoine*. Mandel did not have the vision to see radio broadcasts as part of this *patrimoine*. For him, the cultural heritage of France was in its high culture. Radio could serve as a vector for that culture, in broadcasts of live theater from the Comédie Française, the opera, and other established venues. He also thought that public radio could use the broadcasts to further its own cultural reputation. The stations gained easy and constant access to high culture and quality productions, even if the transmitted theater lacked the sound backgrounds necessary for easy audience comprehension of action. This use of tax money to support national theaters was attended by criticism from the radio press, who saw this as ultimately detrimental to public radio. State stations gave up most of their tax money to support national theaters and could no longer pay for innovations for the radio and programs specifically designed for a radio audience. According to Paul Reboux, radio critic at *Paris-Soir*, "It means that public radio's cash registers are dry, and the programs suffer."[13] In spite of protests, Mandel's ministry, and those that followed through the decade, encouraged the live broadcasts of over eighty plays from Paris theaters each year.[14]

The new tax and the abolition of advertising on public stations would have an unexpected effect on radio. As public stations began to rely solely on seemingly unlimited public funds, private stations in turn rapidly expanded their now-exclusive advertising income, in order to earn money for the shows they aired and compete for the growing radio audience. As Mandel's ministry began to run its public stations in earnest, with longer schedules and better programs, the distinctions between public and private stations became more extreme. The public stations became the voice of the state, while the private stations became bastions of fun and distraction for their listeners, ultimately gaining and keeping huge audiences. In a 1938 interview on programming, Radio-37's director, Fernand Pouey, demonstrated the growing gulf when he responded to a question about his private station's "educational" goals, "Don't use that word, I beg you! It is hostile and grating. To instruct is to amuse."[15] Because they relied on audiences for advertiser money, private stations did not want their programming and goals to be confused with the more uplifting public ones, programs that will receive further analysis in chapter 3.

To understand Mandel's full impact on the private radio system, the story must turn to another innovator. What Mandel brought to public radio, a young entrepreneur would give to the commercial stations. No one benefited from and exploited radio advertising more than Marcel Bleustein-Blanchet. From 1929 to 1939 he created a successful advertising company with a reputation based almost exclusively on radio ads. At the same time, in 1935, Bleustein-Blanchet launched the most popular Parisian private station, Radio-Cité. He proved to be an innovative programmer whose success came from a keen sense of radio listeners' tastes combined with excellent marketing strategies and an awareness of radio's potential to reach a new mass market of listeners.

Bleustein-Blanchet, a twenty-four-year-old son of immigrant Jewish furniture shopkeepers in Pigalle, began the advertising company Publicis on a shoestring budget in 1929. Looking for a way to make his mark, he saw an opportunity in radio advertising to get wealthy selling ads for his parents' and their friends' Parisian stores. At the beginning of the 1930s, when radio advertising was in its infancy, few stations and companies took advantage of the market created by the millions of new listeners. Bleustein-Blanchet wanted to persuade both advertisers and station owners to do otherwise. He began with Radio-Tour-Eiffel, the midsized public Parisian station, where he experimented with on-air advertising. When a single ad for a furrier in Pigalle brought four customers into a store that same afternoon, he understood the potential impact of radio advertising and that he could in turn demonstrate it to radio station owners and advertisers.[16]

Bleustein-Blanchet saw this untapped market as his chance to strike it rich if he could reach station owners and advertisers first. In 1933, before any other advertising firms, the young entrepreneur traveled all over France to make contracts with radio stations as their sole supplier of commercials. He wanted to organize and centralize his regional advertising in Paris, with standard commercials and sounds for all of his products. The studio, copywriters, actors, and musicians would all be in his office in Paris. Regional and national advertisers would reap the benefits of an efficient, centralized organization that could turn out new jingles and slogans within days, for both national and local campaigns.[17]

Both public and private stations became part of his network, including Radio-Lyon, Radio-Beziers, Radio-Toulouse, and Poste Parisien. He called his advertising network the "Publicis Antennas" and printed up glossy brochures to persuade others to join his group.[18] Bleustein-Blanchet connected his new advertising firm to the radio, giving his advertisers a broadcast network. The commercials would emanate from the Publicis studios like the radio waves coming from the local stations on contract with Bleustein-Blanchet. The Publicis office could have advertising running at all partner stations at once. It was a figurative national broadcaster, using each regional station as a hub. In his pamphlet, Marcel Bleustein-Blanchet looked at selling radio advertisements much like those in newspapers. He saw that radio stations had potential markets that could be geographically and socially defined. He knew that he had to demonstrate this to station owners and potential advertisers and convince them that he could market national products locally and local products directly to their prospective air audiences. The new company could sell national campaigns to local stations and perhaps persuade advertisers to run commercials outside their localities, giving their products national exposure and markets. He convinced the businesses he worked for in print advertisements to become regular radio advertisers, including André, the shoe company; Byrrh, the fortified-wine manufacturer; and Brunswick, the Parisian furrier.[19] Bleustein-Blanchet could also begin to offer national programs that could have single advertisers and be rebroadcast by many stations for local profit. A station that could not afford the highest-paid performers alone could band together with other stations and lure the best singers and actors.

To this end, Bleustein-Blanchet mapped out the broadcast area of each regional station and collected the maps into a large color volume. From his maps we can see a variety of both his marketing insights and larger issues about interwar radio.[20] The young executive understood that certain stations covered more area than others and were thus more valuable to advertisers. He showed each station's reach individually on maps of France and shaded departments for each antenna's broadcast area. These mapped regions translated into the fees and options for commercial airtime and program sponsorship at each station, printed on the opposite page. For example, comparison of fees and options for two stations with similar broadcast areas shows the differences between station markets. Radio-Nîmes and Radio-Côte d'Azur covered similar broadcast regions, and yet, because one was more powerful and located on the coast where more money could be spent, the fees and options differed greatly between them.

Radio-Nîmes, according to Bleustein-Blanchet's map, covered only four

TABLE 1.1. Advertisement Price Schedule for Radio-Nîmes

No. of Ads (forty words each)	Price per Ad (in francs)
1	90
10	85
30	80
60	75
90	70
150	65
250	60
365	55

Sponsored Concerts (all except Sunday) 250 f/program

departments: Lozère, Gard, Ardèche, and Vaucluse, and no major cities, unless Avignon and Nîmes, two small urban areas, were included. The station also had only two kilowatts of broadcast power. Bleustein-Blanchet offered advertisers prices between 90 francs for one forty-word commercial and 55 francs for 365 commercials. Program sponsorship, with three commercials in a half-hour show, ran for 250 francs at any time of day.[21] The whole yearly schedule looked like the one in table 1.1.

Radio-Côte d'Azur, more powerful and in a better location, had more and pricier advertising options. The station broadcast with twelve kilowatts of power and covered eleven departments, from the Alps in the north and east, the Mediterranean in the south, and past the Rhône in the west. They included: Isère, Savoie, Ardèche, Drôme, Hautes-Alpes, Basses-Alpes, Vaucluse, Gard, Bouches-du-Rhône, Var, and Alpes-Maritimes. The station covered

TABLE 1.2. Advertisement Price Schedule for Radio-Côte d'Azur

No. of Single Ads (forty words each)	Price per Ad (in francs)
1	150
10	140
20	120
30	110
50	100
100	95
150	90
200	85
300	80
365	75

No. of Sponsored Concerts (half-hour program)	Price per Program (in francs)	
	12h30-14h00	20-22h00
1	1,200	2,000
10	1,000	1,800
15	900	1,700
30	800	1,500

Nice, Marseilles, Valence, and Grenoble as major city markets. The station also broadcast to the wealthy vacationers on the Côte d'Azur. Its name alone signaled wealth, privilege, and fun. The commercials cost almost twice as much as those of Nîmes, from 150 francs for an individual advertisement to 75 francs for 365 or one for each day of the year.[22] Program sponsorship could run almost ten times as much, up to two thousand francs for a half-hour program between eight and ten in the evening (see table 1.2).

For a large station with relatively no market competition, advertising rates could be quite complicated and expensive. Radio-Normandie, which broadcast at sixteen kilowatts of power, had a regional market of nine departments: Manche, Calvados, Orne, Eure, Seine-Maritime, Somme, Oise, Pas-de-Calais, and Nord, with competition from regional stations only in Manche. The station had almost exclusive reach of the cities Le Havre, Rouen, and Lille. Publicis arranged commercial pricing by single ad, multi-sponsor programs, and single-sponsor programs. All of these were also broken down by time of day. The more radios on, the more families home, the more expensive the commercial. Evening hours, when families gathered around the dinner table or in living rooms, were the most expensive to sponsor.[23] Prices ranged from twenty francs for each individual daily advertisement for a block of 365, or one placement per day per year, to two thousand francs to fully sponsor an hour-long evening concert or program. (See table 1.3.)

Radio-Lyon proved an exception to the price and broadcast range. Because it was controlled by the powerful Pierre Laval, and because it was the private station in Lyon, a city of over five hundred thousand prospective listeners, the rates and options should have been very lucrative. Prices were lower than those of both Normandie and Côte-d'Azur because, as Marcel Bleustein-Blanchet noted, the populace, though large, was not wealthy and could not form a strong market for luxury goods. The audience could be loyal, however. Bleustein-Blanchet claimed that the "clientele [was] made up of mostly workers and petty bourgeois" but that these people "don't go out much and will voluntarily replace their newspapers with the wireless."[24] Individual advertisements ranged from one hundred francs for one to 65 francs each for 365. He sold hourlong sponsored shows for around a thousand francs apiece and half-hour programs for 550.

Bleustein-Blanchet had a clear notion of how to use the new revenue to create advertising on the modern mass medium. Understanding that radio ads had to sound appealing over the airwaves, he wrote catchy, alliterative,

TABLE 1.3. Advertisement Price Schedule for Radio-Normandie

No. of Ads	Price per Ad (in francs)		
	12-18h30	18h30-20h30	20h30-23h00
1	70	1001	50
5	60	90	140
10	55	85	135
30	50	80	130
60	45	70	120
90	40	65	115
150	35	60	110
200	30	55	105
250	25	50	100
365	20	45	95

Multi-Sponsor Concerts

No. of programs	Price per Program (in francs)		
	12-18h30	18h30-20h30	20h30-23h00
1	200	325	400
10	175	300	375
20	150	275	350
30	140	250	325
50 or more	130	225	300

Reserved (Single-Advertiser) Concerts

Program Length	Price per Program (in francs)	
	Daytime to 18h00	18h00-24h00
Half-hour	500	1,000
Hour	1,000	2,000

almost tongue-twisting, slogans such as "*Brunswick, le fourrier qui fait fureur* [Brunswick, the furrier who causes a furor]" and "*André, le chausseur qui sache chausser* [André, the shoemaker who knows how to shoe]." To control the sound of his company's commercials and to facilitate his production speed,

Marcel Bleustein-Blanchet installed a radio advertising section and studio in the office of his advertising firm, giving Publicis the capability to write, orchestrate, and record advertisements in-house and send them directly to radio stations around the country.[25] Bleustein-Blanchet also recruited young talent to write the jingles for his advertisements. He recognized early on Johnny Hess and Charles Trenet's potential as skillful and soon-to-be-famous musicians.[26] Together they wrote commercials for Thé des Familles, Volvic water, and Lévitan furniture, with jazz music backgrounds, subtle jokes, and clever rhymes like "*pas de santé sans ce thé* [no health without this tea]."[27] By bringing talent and money together, Bleustein-Blanchet turned radio advertising into a lucrative opportunity and helped private stations flourish during the 1930s.

The Publicis Antennas covered both public and private stations until Georges Mandel eliminated advertising on state radio in January 1935. This severely cut into Bleustein-Blanchet's advertising revenue. About half the stations Bleustein-Blanchet represented could no longer use Publicis's services. In response, Bleustein-Blanchet decided that he needed direct access to the radio industry. The expanding radio markets could bring in a double revenue stream for someone who owned both the programs and the advertisements. He started a new Parisian station that would feature his own commercials and his own ideas for shows. He arranged to buy the license from Radio-L.L., a minor Parisian station and then negotiated for a new frequency that would be easier to receive on radios within the congested city. To build an audience as quickly as possible, he gathered young programming talent around him, including an expert talent recruiter from Polydor records, Jacques Canetti, as his artistic director. In late 1935, Radio-Cité was born.[28]

Radio-Cité's almost immediate success would cause a lackluster group of private radio stations to become acutely aware of their audience and force them to compete to maintain it. Until 1935, most private stations were amateur affairs that paid little attention to programming and erratic airtime hours. For example, in October 1934, only Radio-Normandie broadcast continuously through the morning. Most private stations filled their airtime with programs that changed schedule each day and week instead of airing at regularly scheduled times that listeners could count on. Poste Parisien, the most powerful private station at sixty kilowatts (easily reaching all of France), played station-owned records for almost five hours every afternoon, simply filling in open airtime on the schedule with classical and popular music.[29]

Before 1935, Poste Parisien was, however, the most organized of the thirteen private stations, with a select number of regular evening and lunchtime weekly programs. Sponsored by the daily *Le Petit Parisien*, the station had support from the largest circulating paper in Paris. Almost every day the newspaper ran ads on the second page for the evening show on Poste Parisien. The station also supported major stars, including Mireille and Jean Nohain, the songwriting team that wrote the summer's hit song, "Asleep in the Hay," in 1933. Every week on *Mireille and Friends* the two songwriters shared the studio with celebrity guests who would discuss a topic and share songs on the theme.[30] The station also had a weekly program every Monday evening, sponsored by Cadum soap, with Max Regnier, a famous chansonnier, who sang and played comedy sketches for a half hour.[31] The station encouraged other stars to sing regularly on the air, including the famous singing duet of Pills and Tabet and hit-maker Lucienne Boyer.[32]

When Bleustein-Blanchet standardized advertising across his network, and as more radio stations began creating weekly programs, he offered new ways for companies to sponsor radio shows. By 1936, in a sign of his success, most popular programs cost fifty thousand francs per show, with frequent mentions of the product over the air during the course of the program, as well as a standard jingle played before and after the show came on the air. For example, the advertisement for O'Cap shampoo, played before and after the *Question Game* every Friday evening, sang with trumpet fanfare:

> With Lavender O'Cap
> We're feeling great
> With our beautiful hair.
> With Lavender O'Cap
> It will look marvelous.
> Sir, you just have to ask
> For this extraordinary product
> Because with Lavender O'Cap
> We add protein to our hair.
> Yes, with Lavender O'Cap
> We add protein to our hair![33]

During the program, audience members played a trivia game for small prizes, and the jingle was repeated with each contestant.

Monsavon soap sponsored the *Crochet Radiophonique*, a weekly program much like *The Gong Show*, using the music from "Quand Madelon" in its jingle. Yvonne Galli, cohost of the show and star of the Radio-Cité soap opera *The Duraton Family*, read seasonal copy about the soap at the top of the program:

> I want to say a few short words to our dear listeners and audience. You all know, without a doubt, that we're right in the middle of springtime. It is a magnificent season, but I know that among you there are many who don't really like spring much at all. Quite simply because spring brings the first rays of sunlight that are a bit too hot, that can lead to a sunburn. So, understandably, some ladies and gentlemen don't like that much. So, I just want to say to you: don't make the spring a sad season. Don't ruin the spring; it's such a beautiful season. It is so easy for you to find an admiration for it, just like everyone else. You just need to have a little Monsavon at home. Using just a little Monsavon each day will give you a marvelous skin tone. You won't fear getting sunburned—or getting those little springtime pimples.[34]

Then the jingle would follow, to the chorus of "Quand Madelon," which originally sang like this:

> Madelon isn't strict with us.
> When we take her by the waist or the chin
> She laughs, it's the worst thing she knows how to do.
> Madelon, Madelon, Madelon![35]

but was changed, for radio audiences, to this:

> If you want a toilet soap
> That is very soft, that suds and smells good
> The softest of all toilet soaps
> Monsavon, Monsavon, Monsavon![36]

The new lyric, written by Publicis copywriters, followed the recognizable tune, a song sung by the *poilus*, or foot soldiers, in the trenches of World War I. They thus connected the soap to France through the patrimonial heritage. If

"Madelon" was a national song, Monsavon was a national soap: good for the skin and patriotic, too! For fifty thousand francs a program, Monsavon became part of the national myth.

Companies also gained the right to use the show's name in advertising outside the radio. By sponsoring a show, advertisers could then use the show's popularity to sell their wares in newspaper advertising. For example, when Lustucru, a pasta maker, sponsored Ray Ventura's (and sometimes Fred Adison's) weekly show, *Lustucru Theatre*, on Poste Parisien, Radio-Toulouse, and Ile-de-France, they also advertised their connection with the show in their newspaper ads in *Le Petit Parisien* and other daily Parisian papers. The full-page ads featured Lustucru pasta prominently on the upper fold and gave space to the radio show on the bottom fold, giving readers information on which stars would be featured on that evening's program, with prominent photographs of the swing bands and the featured artists.[37] By connecting its pasta to a radio dance and variety show, Lustucru linked its prominent radio and newspaper commercials to experiences of entertainment, youthfulness, and dance. They also linked their pasta to the evening hours at home and a moment when families sat down together to listen to the broadcast.

Many of the newspaper product advertisements featured the artists of the shows they sponsored. For example, Lévitan, a furniture warehouse, had print advertisements featuring Georges Milton, a popular singing star, who appeared on the Lévitan variety show.[38] The company also used the radio speaker Jean Saint-Granier as a spokesperson while promoting his show. A front-page ad in *Paris-Soir* featured Saint-Granier at the Radio-Cité microphone giving his tag line, "Bonsoir mes chers auditeurs, bonsoir!" and promoting his daily radio show, *The Minute of Good Sense*, in its copy, which read, "The voice of good sense advised me to exchange my old 'wood' for a modern furniture set at Lévitan."[39] Audiences trusted Saint-Granier for his sense, and advertisers clamored to use him to promote the "sensible" purchase of their products.

Advertisers connected their shows to the hours of households. Banania, the company that sold a hot breakfast drink, hosted a morning show each day on Poste Parisien and Radio-Toulouse called *The Banania Wake-Up*. The variety show featured "Dr. Vitamin," the spokesperson for the drink, who emceed the morning concerts. Dr. Vitamin's character also appeared in the newspaper advertisements, crossing over to advertise both the drink and the radio program.[40] One ad campaign combined a show about marriage with a product that claimed to promote marital happiness. In it, Noël Noël—who played the clown and announcer Le Père Mathieu on Radio-Cité, Radio-Lyon, Radio-Toulouse, Radio-Normandie, and Radio-Luxembourg for the weekly couples game show *At Least Fifteen Years*—supported the Vin de Frileuse, the fortified wine that sponsored the show. While promoting the show, the advertisement claimed that by drinking its fortified wine couples would stay together, much like the contestant-couples on the weekly program. The copy concluded that "for five years the Vin-de-Frileuse has given joy to hundreds of thousands of people, by giving them physical health, moral equilibrium: HAPPINESS" (emphasis theirs).[41] Sels Kruschen, diet salts sold across France that claimed to be an "ideal slenderizer," sponsored Grandpa Kruschen, who doled out family advice and jokes every evening somewhere in France, between eight and ten o'clock. The show and dietary product were advertised in local papers, and this "family member" could be heard on Ile-de-France, Radio-Lyon, Radio-Toulouse, Radio-Agen, Radio-Bordeaux-Sud-Ouest, and Radio-Côte-d'Azur.[42]

An especially good example of the connection between products, radio, and family was a 1937 ad in *L'Intransigeant* for Cadum soap. The advertisement featured Max Regnier, a beloved radio comedian and chansonnier, promoting the facial cleanser. In the advertisement, Regnier saves a marriage by promoting the soap on his radio show. The soap makes the wife's face lovelier and makes her once again appealing to her once-bored and now-satisfied husband. She comes to the studio to thank Regnier for promoting the soap, and he replies, "Madame, you glow with freshness! Your joy is my best compensation."[43] Alongside the cartoon and copy, the advertisement gave a promotion for Regnier's Monday evening show. In turn, Cadum advertising would have been prominently featured on the air during the program. Cadum also featured the program in its regular advertising campaign, giving the show a promotion each time the company's ads appeared.[44] In a move that Cadum must have been happy with, Germaine Blondin, poet and radio critic at the weekly *Radio-Magazine*, wrote of Max Regnier: "I don't think there is a more popular star on the radio. His audience is every audience. The businessman, to relax after a difficult day, listens during his late dinner while his maid, frozen at the doorway, discreetly mixes her laugh with that of her boss. Married couples, if they are estranged for a moment by a misunderstanding which is often nothing but a small anxiety, are sure to find themselves agreeing when they hear him."[45] Blondin almost repeats the advertising message, furthering the notion of radio and family togetherness. Cadum, then, was able, through both its couple-oriented ad and its association with Max Regnier, to join its product to a popular show and the ideal of family harmony. And the show reached the entire nation, originating on Poste Parisien but rebroadcast on Radio-Toulouse, Radio-Normandie, Radio-Lyon, Radio-Luxembourg, Radio-Agen, Radio-Bordeaux-Sud-Ouest, and Radio-Côte-d'Azur.

Many other companies used successful stars and programs, drawing attention to their sponsored shows while advertising their products. This gave them connections to the ever more popular radio shows. Persil, a laundry soap, had a music-hall variety show on Ile-de-France, Radio-Mediterranée, Bordeaux-S.O., Radio-Agen, and Radio-Toulouse; Palmolive soap subsidized twice-weekly variety shows on Radio-Toulouse and Poste Parisien; and St. Raphaël Quinquina, a fortified wine, funded both the most popular soap opera, *La Famille Duraton,* on Radio-Cité and comedian Pierre-Dac's *Academy of Silliness* on Poste Parisien. Lesieur, a cooking oil company, advertised its weekly show called *The Lesieur Review* on Ile-de-France, Radio-Luxembourg, and Radio-Toulouse.[46]

Most of the products featured in radio advertising were household items that benefited from advertising directly into the home. Soaps and washing powders like Cadum and Persil and medicinal wines like St. Raphaël and Byrrh advertised directly to the housewives who used them for their families. Advertisers and programmers linked advertising directly with food products' appropriate meals, sponsoring programming during the breakfast, lunch, and dinner hours. For example, Banania, with its daily *Wake-Up,* used music and comedy in the morning hours to sell its hot breakfast drink. Why not drink its product while listening to its enjoyable show?

Critics' response to advertising varied. On the one hand, many disliked the intrusion that commercials made in the programs. On the other hand, some critics saw advertising as a necessary evil. Without commercials, private radio could not compete. Clément Vautel, of *Radio-Magazine,* wrote, "These commercials are not what we like best about the radio. . . . We have to understand that this 'tenth muse,' or the advertisement, feeds the budgets of private stations." He went on to claim that "courageous industry owners and businessmen" created radio altogether.[47] A Popular Front radio critic even wrote that public stations could benefit from commercials: "The fear of advertising could take us too far—far enough to turn French radio into boring radio."[48] Advertising brought money, star attractions, and valuable entertainment to the now-burgeoning private stations. It also helped to link these stations to ideal notions of the family and marriage through domestic consumption of advertised products and the happiness that radio claimed to give listening families.

By 1936, as private radio audiences and revenues grew, the lack of advertising had set public stations behind. Their funds became limited to what the government budgeted for them year to year. With direct ties to national theaters and orchestras, the public stations broadcast more classical selections played by studio orchestras (a necessity for every station) or transmitted live from state theaters. These performances were sponsored by the government and cost the stations nothing to play over the air. Some of the programming was not free, however, and the public stations had to be careful about how much they budgeted for non-state-sponsored groups. They established a regular pay scale for radio plays that kept the programs within budgetary limits. In 1938, an original one-act play cost the station 37F50, a two-act 75F, a three-act 112F50, and any more than three, 150F.[49] Acting troupes would then be paid a minimum fee to present them. Many of the studios contracted the best actors and playwrights, who wrote series for the public stations. Paul Clérouc contributed two sets of plays, one on Paris and its history and the other for children.[50] Jean Variot, a folklore expert, wrote numerous plays about Alsace-Lorraine. Jacques Cossin wrote and directed a crime drama series that appeared biweekly from late 1936 to 1939. All of these writers presented their own work with their own acting troupes paid for by the radio tax.[51]

With their budget limitations, public radio programmers could not afford to hire exclusively the best radio theater actors. The finest acting troupes performed for both public and private radio. This included the proficient radio actor and director Georges Colin and his group. Colin had a great talent for understanding the necessities of radio theater; he worked with sound engineers and excellent voice actors to bring his treatments to life. His troupe could command larger fees than any other acting groups. He also moved from public to private stations and treated each performance as an individual affair. Colin's group played in a much-touted miniseries, titled *France*, on public radio in January 1938.[52] He was also recruited by the popular private station Radio-Cité to star during the 1938–39 season in a weekly series called *True Stories*, which featured half-hour dramas about real-life French heroes and adventurers written by radio playwright Hugues Nonn.

Colin could maintain noncontract status because each time his troupe put on a play, its work was praised by radio critics. He directed and starred in productions one at a time. As early as 1935, Georges Colin and his troupe were credited with saving less-than-worthy radio plays.[53] Of Colin's ubiquitous presence on radio and great talent, radio critic René Gerly wrote in 1939: "Georges Colin, one of the first [radio actors], focuses solely on radio plays. He has played in over 1,000, I believe, and he understands completely what one must ask of radio theater. He knows that one should not abuse the sound décor, and that one must pull the most out of every written passage. Knowing the amount of sound necessary is an art, and those who know how to practice it are rare indeed."[54] Colin's popularity underscored the differences between stage and radio theater and reminded listeners that simple retransmission of live theater could not compare with a well-directed, well-acted, and sound-layered radio play. Public radio's live transmissions might have helped to keep Parisian theater alive through the subsidies companies received, but the plays would never attract the large audiences that studio-spun theater could.

Because they were in demand on both stage and radio, famous singing and stage stars could charge private and public stations tremendous fees for appearances.[55] Louis Merlin, who would head Radio-Luxembourg after World War II and worked for Radio-Cité and Poste Parisien in the late 1930s, wrote about the costs of bringing in celebrities. The more famous a star, the more each station paid for an appearance. Groups like the swing band Ray Ventura et Ses Collégiens could charge up to two thousand francs for an appearance, while even minor stars like Raymond Souplex, the comedian featured on Radio-Cité's weekly show *On a Bench,* and Jean Sablon, an older Belle Epoque singer, could fetch between three hundred and five hundred francs per performance, almost twice the price for a four-act play on public radio. The critics at the radio journal *Choisir* complained about the fees and the use of advertising that meant that public stations could not afford the best talent, "The abuse of advertising on private stations forces them to bring costly stars to their microphones. The price for them then rises with the disagreeable work they do. State radio cannot afford to pay the same salaries, and it is good programming that suffers for it."[56]

Advertising revenues brought substantial funds into each private station. Historian of advertising Marc Martin looked at revenues for all the private stations for the first five months of 1938 and showed that the two competing Parisian stations Radio-Cité and Poste Parisien made the most money from advertising revenues, at 11.8 million francs and 8.74 million francs respectively. Radio-Toulouse came in a distant third with 5.43 million francs.[57] With these kinds of budgets, the most profitable stations could afford to hire the

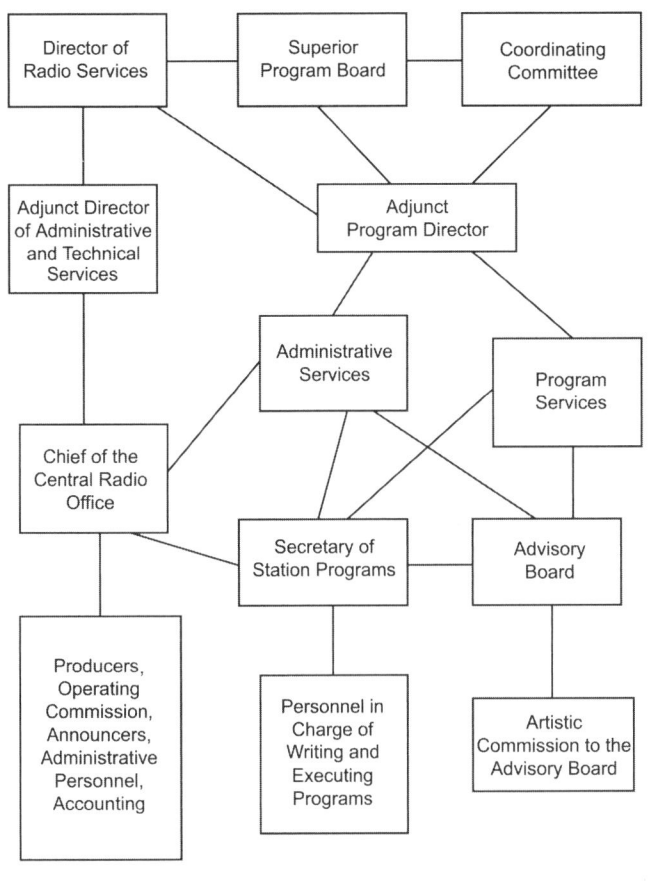

Management and Coordination of Programming for the Regional Public Stations, 1937

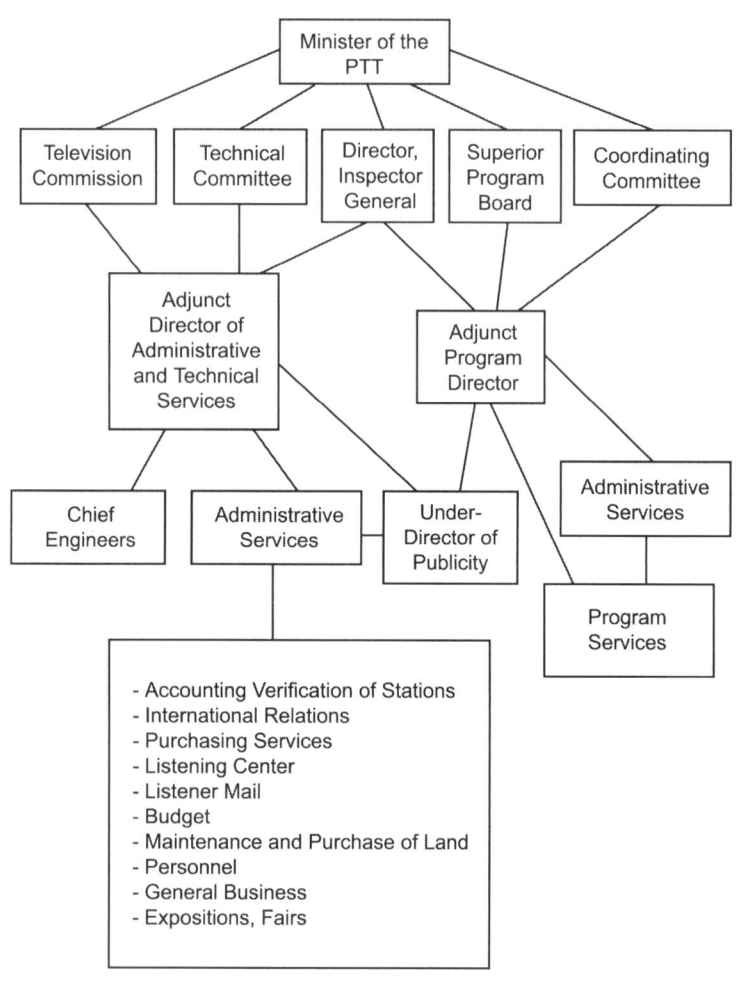

Management and Programming for All Public Radio at the
National Office of the PTT, 1937

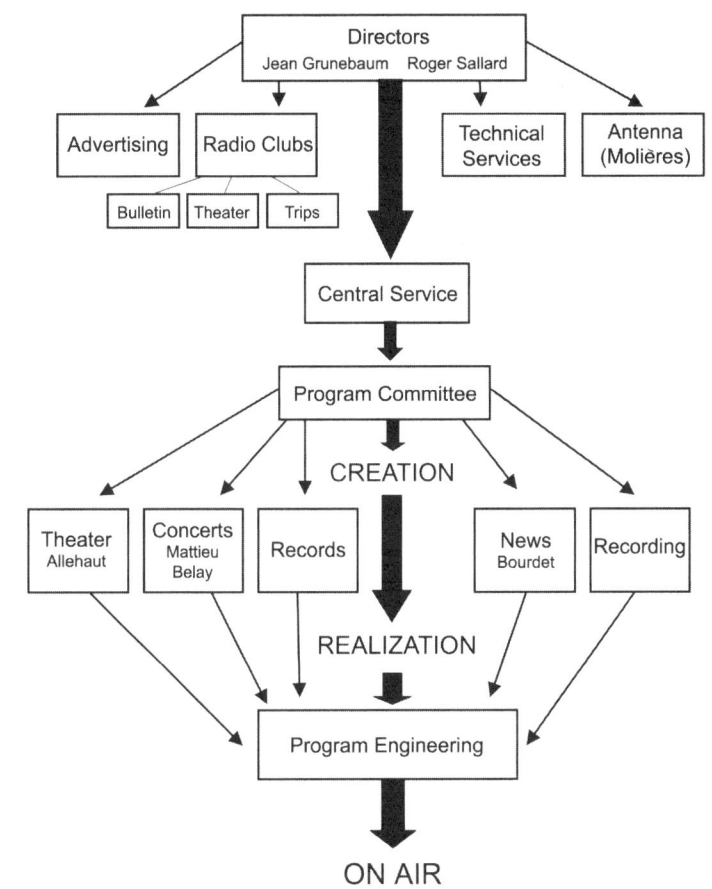

Private Station Poste Parisien Flow Chart, 1938

most popular stars, employ well-known scriptwriters, and adopt the most up-to-date technology in studios run by expert engineers. To compare to public stations at the same moment, 180 million francs was split among the thirteen stations, including payment for theater subsidies and support for the massive bureaucracy, leaving state radio little extra money for expensive singers and comedians after expenditures on new technology (with more powerful antennae) series scriptwriters, orchestras, and actors.[58]

Comparing the administration of the public and private stations shows the differences in budgets of public and private stations. Private Poste Parisien employed seven men in top administrative positions, while each public station employed multiple committees to make every decision. (See figs. 1, 2, and 3.)[59]

Marcel Bleustein-Blanchet's Radio-Cité employed only one man to head each department, making programming changes and decisions easy to implement. While Bleustein-Blanchet owned the station, he relied only on Jean Guignebert as program director, Jean Antoine as news director, and Jacques Canetti as artistic director. Public stations, by contrast, were ungainly, relying on too many voices, with an enormous bureaucracy that needed exorbitant funding and could not react quickly to new developments in radio.[60] It was a wonder that anything ever got onto state radio at all.

It is clear that by 1936, private radio had coalesced into a viable and popular network of stations. Marcel Bleustein-Blanchet, with Publicis and radio advertisement, had convinced private companies that the listening publics could be seen as ideal markets for their wares. Now it remained to define those markets. Stations had to keep listeners loyal through programming that both fit and shaped their daily lives. The next chapter will look at the ways in which private radio stations defined their listeners, programmed their stations, and sold their product over the air.

2 OPENING UP THE STUDIO DOORS
Fashioning Loyal Audiences from Markets

As radio grew into a mass medium in the mid-1930s, private stations competed among themselves for the lucrative funding of advertisers and the listenership to support their programming. They had to forge loyal audiences with emotional and brand ties to their stations, stars, programs, and products. If they could prove their worth as companies and stations with individual identities and national importance, they could continue to grow in revenue and audience and make a lot of money for their owners. In order to gain fame through abundant free publicity, many radio stations relied heavily on the partnerships they formed with local and national newspapers, as well as on the many radio journals that served as guides to weekly programming. These papers printed stories on the stations, noting their programming and engineering marvels. They also offered free advertising for the stations, letting readers know what would be on the air each evening. Those programs often included new swing bands that sang and played songs that embraced radio audiences by reflecting in the lyrics their feelings and experiences as individuals and citizens.

Parisian stations needed newspaper sponsorship most of all. The city's radio airwaves were the most competitive, with four stations vying for large listening audiences. Each had to fashion a unique identity with help from a newspaper that would feature it prominently in its pages. Each looked to create a loyal listener base by appealing to different tastes. Poste Parisien made its reputation as a fun-filled comedy station; Radio-Cité became the youth-oriented, "democratic" station, with most of its programming featuring audience participation; and Ile-de-France boasted a homey, village-dance ambiance. Late in the game Radio-37, founded in early fall 1937, struggled to find a spot within the already saturated airwaves with the help of its parent newspaper, *Paris-Soir*, the fastest growing Parisian daily.

The link between stations and their well-known partner newspapers gave necessary support to unknown radio stations during their launching. Two major Parisian stations that competed with Marcel Bleustein-Blanchet's Radio-Cité proved this point well. Poste Parisien, the first truly mass-audience private station in the mid-1930s, recognized early on that Radio-Cité would offer real competition. In response to this threat, Poste Parisien used its partner newspaper, *Le Petit Parisien*, for far-reaching and continual promotion. Radio-37, which began programming in September 1937 at the International Exposition in Paris, understood from Poste Parisien's example that frequent mentions in parent-newspaper *Paris-Soir*'s pages were necessary if the station was to create its own listenership in the competitive Parisian market.

A particularly fruitful newspaper partnership produced a series of articles about Poste Parisien in late 1937 in *Le Petit Parisien*. At that time, Radio-Cité was gaining a wide audience with its increasingly innovative programming. As the new season geared up, Poste Parisien used the articles to advertise the station along with the new shows it featured in the 1937–38 season. These stories outlined the nature of running a radio station. Called "Domestic Universe: The Secrets, the Life, the Marvels of the Radio," the series appeared in the paper every three or four days from mid-October through mid-November. The newspaper articles became a vehicle by which the station could gain publicity without outright advertisements, shaping the reports as human interest news, even though the articles clearly benefited the media company that owned both newspaper and radio station.

While describing the inner workings of Poste Parisien, the series' author, Louis Léon-Martin, also emphasized Poste Parisien's place within the private sphere. He made sure to underscore that the station's programming was suitable for the entire family. The series introduced the radio studios, stars, and schedule to listeners in an attempt to make them feel comfortable with the station. Acquaintance with a new medium that must have seemed strange, almost magical, as well as voices that were alien to audiences at first would allow listeners to rest easy with the idea that the station's programs could enter into their homes at any time during the day. Radio programs needed an aura of familiarity to adapt to the intimate space of the listeners' homes. Even the title "Domestic Universe" suggested the familial relationship that Poste Parisien was trying to cultivate with its listeners, the family programming that the station offered, and the space at the hearth where radio could be heard every day.

The newspaper *Le Petit Parisien* emphatically supported its daughter station by printing these articles on the front page. Each radio feature began on page 1 of the paper with a photograph and short copy and continued on one of the inside pages in greater detail. The first article of the series, "One Evening, at Seven O'clock at Poste Parisien," introduced the author, Léon-Martin, who toured the engineering control station with the reader, showing how transmissions made their way from the studio to the radios at home.[1] While traveling through the offices and studios of Poste Parisien, he introduced the major stars of the station, as well as the program directors, Jean Grunebaum and Roger Saillard, and the artistic director, M. Mathieu. He thus gave listeners a sense of the scope of activity at the station and the most important people in it, making them feel as though they, too, played a part as a cherished guest of the owner. He ended his first tour with an idealized mission statement that encouraged listenership of Poste Parisien on quasi-patriotic grounds: "We descend through the fever of the hallways, an ordered fever, without improvisation and without end. Aside from the artists and the musicians, one hundred and twenty men and young women . . . working here every day with one heart and coordinating their efforts so that France and every reachable listener, by the hundreds of thousands, listen in the best possible conditions to a little bit of Paris, feel our climate, our culture, our tastes. . . . The goal is beautiful and justifies the discipline." He also gave a metaphor for the station—a radio ship that had to run as smoothly as the navy—and introduced the various components of the "ship" and the articles to come.[2]

In the series, Léon-Martin described almost every part of the Poste Parisien, including the electronics, the offices, the news service, and the performers. He gave readers an intimate knowledge of the station they listened to by including detailed tours of the back rooms and studios and explaining how sound engineers, editors, producers, and performers put programs together.[3] He included stories about celebrities who made their careers working in radio (and thus with Poste Parisien). Actress Marguerite Moreno, crooners Jean Sablon and Tino Rossi, and singer-songwriter Mireille all owed careers to the magic of the radio microphone.[4] And all appeared regularly on Poste Parisien. Léon-Martin cleverly used the article to let listeners know which stars could be heard on *Le Petit Parisien*'s partner station.

Léon-Martin understood that newspaper readers and would-be listeners saw the radio as a home appliance, and one that had an intimate sound and character. He pursued his domestic theme more directly in an article called "Radio and Life: Around a Wireless," where he described radio as a family medium that addressed listeners as individuals, not as a mass audience that listened together.[5] Léon-Martin gave reasons for listening to the radio from the standpoint of various individuals: an intellectual, a businessman, a neighbor, a child, and a single woman. He professed the belief that the radio was the perfect company for anybody: "Dilettantes, writers, intellectuals, businessmen, each follows his temperament and finds what he wants, but radio is above all a friend." This friendship, or imagined companionship, of the radio helped to bring in its audience by filling the loneliness of the home and by giving listeners a new group of people to listen to. By listening to the radio at home, one joined the family of the studio, the stable, comforting family that Léon-Martin described in his articles, and when people listened to Poste Parisien "they were among family. Certainly the family had grown." Yet he let them know that in spite of increasing numbers, the intimacy of audience and family would not diminish: "The atmosphere never changed, however."[6] Poste Parisien offered listeners an extended family.

Léon-Martin saw radio as specifically household oriented and created for families: "I cannot consider today's radio as anywhere but with the family at home." He thought that the radio could fulfill the needs of every household: "It is not strange at all that radio, which addresses itself to everyone, reaches each person particularly, in the intimacy of his lodgings, in his preferences, in his habits, and that might be the secret to its persuasive power." For journalist Léon-Martin, the radio, and specifically Poste Parisien, could appeal to the family because it spoke to every individual in the home at the same time and could fulfill the diverse needs of every household in the nation. *Le Petit Parisien* gained listeners for its partner station by convincing them that its radio station's daily programming performed an invaluable service for the entire family, both specific and general.

Another of the articles pointed to the family nature of the radio by looking closely at the children's programming on the station. In "The Children's Hour," Léon-Martin introduced his readers to Jaboune (singer-songwriter Jean Nohain's character), whom he classifies as a "big brother" to the young listeners of his show, *The Little Friends' Club*. Léon-Martin encouraged prospective young listeners to make the show a regular part of their weekly schedule and Jaboune a part of the family: "He really is your big brother and even in the future, far in the future, when he has silver hair at his temples or no hair at all—it happens—he'll never stop being your big brother."[7] Léon-Martin also reminded parents that Jaboune taught children moral lessons and that Poste Parisien could act *in loco parentis* during the workday:

> Radio, once again, reveals itself in its good works. It is useful because it is so loved and all the children are faithful listeners. . . . Radio in school is a current issue. All of the teachers asked, or most, seem to want it. The only place they disagree is in the method. They should come here. Far from theories and principles, they'll see that, in practice, it's what Jaboune already does. They tell me that he pleases the kids as much as he teaches them. . . . I propose that we nominate Jean Nohain as academy inspector of scholarly radio!

Radio, or Poste Parisien, deserved, according to Léon-Martin, to become a lifelong partner, teacher, and family member who would help to bring up children and accompany them through their productive lives. The radio was not simply a source of entertainment. Rather, it was a service organization that reached out to children and families. This came, Léon-Martin would argue, not from a capitalist urge but ostensibly from a sense of responsibility to the needs of the listening public. *Le Petit Parisien* used the articles to convince readers that by listening to their radio station they could increase their happiness by both increasing the size of their family and inviting the now-intimate Poste Parisien to become their primary daily entertainment.

This association with the image of family combined with a partnership with a newspaper was seen by radio owners as crucial in founding a radio station. The popular daily *Paris-Soir* created its own Parisian station, Radio-37. Radio-37 represented its inauguration to the public as a baptism, complete with Maurice Chevalier as godfather at the christening. Paris's fourth private station, after Poste Parisien (1924), Ile-de-France (1926), and Radio-Cité (1935), was the idea of Jean Prouvost, who, according to Marcel Bleustein-Blanchet, wanted to cash in on the revenues generated by private stations, many of which also featured the dailies in their own programming. He also wanted to tie his daily newspaper to a radio station that could potentially increase the readership of *Paris-Soir*.[8] Prouvost put his paper behind the new station, giving it a prime opening day, including the first broadcast at the end of that summer's International Exposition in Paris.[9]

As part of the advertising for the new station, *Paris-Soir* featured a two-column advertisement for its opening broadcast two days before its inauguration. The broadcast itself would be hosted by Max Hymans, the undersecretary of state in charge of the Exposition. The location was the Hall of Radio at the Exposition, in an obvious attempt to make Radio-37 seem like one of the nationally sponsored exhibits and thus not simply a new station but a triumph of French ingenuity and technology. To bring extra panache and publicity, Maurice Chevalier would "baptize" the microphone, while Sacha Guitry would present a "toast" to it and continue the event by emceeing the first variety program, called *The Bar of the Stars*.[10] On the day before the first broadcast, *Paris-Soir* ran a front-page photograph of the station's new recording room with the headline "Allô! Allô! Ici RADIO-37 . . ." Pierre-Jean Lespeyres's article that followed described the new station and its prospective programming, letting readers know that, unlike other stations at their debuts, the days would be filled with Radio-37's programming from its very first broadcast. Every morning would begin with the family in mind with "'Advice for the Market,' with which, from what looked fresh at Les Halles [the central market in Paris], we will let listeners know what to buy that day. Afterward, and based on that information, Aunt Marcelle will give advice, a daily menu, and recipes." Daily shows would also include film reviews, interviews, and sports news.[11] Radio-37 wanted to become a part of Parisians' daily regimen, offering the city dwellers another choice in what they heard in their homes and giving them more stars they could hear and begin to see as family members because they could listen to their casual conversation every day. From Aunt Marcelle's friendly kitchen advice to the gossip around the *Bar of the Stars*, Radio-37 wanted to share a convivial voice with its new listeners. Lespeyres pronounced that Radio-37 "will be another voice that you will want to hear each day." "Radio-37's Baptism" was also celebrated that day in the radio program guide, with a short article and a large-print, detailed program schedule that dwarfed the material about other stations.[12]

This idea of a baptism of Radio-37 served a dual purpose. First, it showed the programmers' recognition that Radio-37 was the newest of the seven stations in Paris, the "baby" in the market, and celebrated that status. Second, the baptism placed Radio-37 squarely into the family of Paris listeners. Paris, and hopefully listeners, welcomed the station as a new child, with Maurice Chevalier as its godfather. The station symbolically became a part of the Catholic family of France, complete with a pseudoreligious ceremony.

The coverage of the inaugural day included a front-page article that featured two photographs, one of Max Hymans making his short speech and one of Maurice Chevalier kissing and anthropomorphizing the microphone for his "baptism." The photo caption featured a quote from Chevalier's speech, "My little microphone, I won't break a champagne bottle over you because I don't want to cause you pain. I'd rather just give you a big kiss." By personifying the microphone, Maurice Chevalier seemed to give it (and Radio-37) life. He was also chosen to serve as "godfather" (*parrain*) to the station, as the new radio was brought into the family of Paris and officially joined the community. The article also pointed to how special this moment was to Chevalier, as he made time in a very busy touring schedule for the event. At the microphone, he had "only a half hour before his departure for London." Surely Chevalier found the new station's baptism important enough to work into his celebrity-touring lifestyle. He admirably fulfilled the role of "godfather," inducting the station with a kiss and a song of joy: Charles Trenet's hit of the season, written for Chevalier in early 1937, "*Y'a de la joie.*"[13] The song, a joyful, surrealist hymn to Paris, linked the station to popular music and jazz, as well as to its mother city and urban audience. Chevalier sang that day of the sights of the capital familiar to its citizens:

> There's a small miracle at the Javel station.
> We see the metro come out of its tunnel,
> Blowing its smoke of songs and flowers into the blue sky,
> It runs to the wood; it runs as fast as it can!
> There is joy!
> The Eiffel Tower goes for a stroll.
> Like a crazy woman, she leaps over the Seine!
> Then she says, "Sorry if I seem insane to you,
> But I was tired of being alone in my corner!"[14]

Chevalier's role as station godfather and entertainer also hinted at his further and future connection to the station, making the new radio shine with the possibility of celebrity and star power.

Paul Reboux, author, painter, and radio critic for *Paris-Soir* who also hosted the *Jeu des Questions* on Radio-Cité, repeated the connections made by the Radio-37 inauguration. He wrote two weeks later of that debut, personifying the station as a child, much as Chevalier did at the "baptism." He stated, "It is always moving to watch the birth and see how a new being adapts to life, betters his means of existence, progresses, grows up, tends to his success and succeeds."[15] The station owners used the newspaper publicity of the inaugural celebrations to convince listeners that they could accept the new radio, repeatedly giving them the image of their city of Paris adopting the new station as a child of its own.

Jean Prouvost continued to use his parent daily to promote his station in the weeks that followed in order to ensure Radio-37's success. *Paris-Soir* featured short articles on the station's most popular program, the *Bar of the Stars*, which, through the use of heavy advertising and the quality of its panoply of invited guests, was already a success. Advising listeners to keep current with the best in radio, a *Paris-Soir* journalist wrote, "For a short while, everyone's been talking about that recently opened and already famous, fabulous bar. I'm only telling you what you need to know to be with it. Do you want to go?"[16] This short piece continued, reminding listeners that the stars could be part of their own seemingly elite club—but with easy access, right inside their own homes: "My God, I'd give you the address, but for what purpose? This unique bar will come to you, at your home, whenever you want, and it will come with its elite clientele, all of our great stars who have begun and will continue to parade through." The *Bar of the Stars*, with its intimate chats led by René Lefèvre, could bring celebrities into his neighborhood bar, taking them to meet the family and neighbors (and radio listeners), including shows that featured such combinations of guests as playwright Sacha Guitry, boxing champion Al Brown, and music-hall star Lyne Clevers. These surprising mixtures accentuated the idea of the eclectic neighborhood, where a local bar might bring all kinds of people together. And listeners never knew who or what they might hear. With such a diverse crowd at the *zinc*, conversations could focus on just about anything.

Pointing to the homey nature of the shared conversations, another write-up continued, "They talk about a little bit of everything, Parisian life, theater, cinema, they sing, they make music, they tell stories in the bar where René Lefèvre delicately leads the conversation."[17] Stars in Lefèvre's bar became more ordinary because they spoke about banal subjects, not just about their careers and success. They could have easily fit into the neighborhood bar or neighborhood home of Radio-37's listeners. Within three weeks of its debut, Radio-37 sponsored a weekly contest in which the winner would win a lottery ticket and "an invitation from René Lefèvre to have a cocktail with his friends at

'The Bar of the Stars.'"[18] This contest allowed listeners direct contact with the station and its roster of celebrities. Those who did not win could live vicariously through the "ordinary listener" in the studio (or at the fictional bar). The winner was no celebrity and needed no famous exploits to gain access; he (or she) was one of their own fraternizing with the stars. And perhaps the listeners would win the contest themselves one day, and have the chance to join the fun, becoming a part of the show they heard and becoming a member of the neighborhood family of the station, if only for a moment.[19]

Paul Reboux went even further to claim family ties for the new station. Emulating Léon-Martin's claims for Poste Parisien, he assured listeners that the familial and youthful spirit of Radio-37 had the ability to mend family relationships and simultaneously please everyone in the household. He also reassured listeners that, while often youthful in tone, Radio-37 had an old-timey feel that appealed across generations: "The young people [who program the station] know that they have the resources of the past to guide them. Every Thursday evening, 'Radio-37' resuscitates the old café-concert. Sons will say, 'So that's how they had fun!' And their fathers will say, 'Those were some great times.' They'll listen together. And 'Radio-37' will have friends in the two camps of generations so often in disagreement."[20] Radio-37, through its own newspaper's radio critic, thus portrayed itself as family entertainment that could stabilize and ameliorate home life in France.[21]

While Poste Parisien and Radio-37 used newspapers to their advantage, Radio-Cité's relationship with its partner newspaper, the conservative, republican *L'Intransigeant*, was less productive. The daily newspaper did not promote Bleustein-Blanchet's station in its pages as expected and did not see the partnership as a useful means to gain a larger readership. By 1937, *L'Intransigeant* and Radio-Cité had broken off all ties. Radio-Cité, in response to its partner newspaper's lackluster participation, began its own weekly fan newspaper, for, as with his station, Marcel Bleustein-Blanchet created for himself what he could not find elsewhere. Available at newsstands and by subscription, the paper was called *Ici . . . Radio-Cité*, the oft-repeated catchphrase for the station while on air. The paper, published from January 1938 to September 1939, advertised the station on newsstands and on home coffee, dining, and kitchen tables while presuming to offer a service to its readers by giving them vital and entertaining information about Radio-Cité and its programs. The paper included interviews with radio personalities, letters from listeners, short fiction, games, and a section on the activities of the Radio-Cité fan club. The club, which any listener could join, enjoyed trips, tours, and regular meetings.[22] Because the club occupied a prominent place in the station's literature and could meet to comment about the direction the station took, members and subscribers could entertain the notion of being participants in the running of their favorite station.

Radio-Cité directors Jean Guignebert and Jacques Canetti, along with owner Bleustein-Blanchet, placed listener participation at the center of their station's programming agenda. In an article on programming at the station for the 1938–39 season, André Sevry of the weekly radio guide *Mon Programme* concluded that "the principle of 'collaboration' with the public is so real at Radio-Cité that anyone who wants to, whenever he wants to, can join in conversation with [artistic director] Mr. Canetti at the studio on Boulevard Haussmann. The director's door is almost on the sidewalk, and even has a picture window; before entering, you can see Mr. Canetti at his desk and he'll greet you the moment you enter."[23] Surely an exaggeration, if not a total fabrication, this semblance of an open-door policy with the management offered listeners a sense of belonging to a democratic community and a sense of being heard by those in power.

In an effort to include audiences in the programs on the station, the directors created two kinds of live shows, open free to the public, that relied on active crowds and theater studios. The first was a series of weekly open-microphone forums and the second a weekly evening lineup of "public programs" that centered around a huge studio audience's participation. Both of these series encouraged listeners at home to feel as though they, too, were vital to the day-to-day functioning of the station. In an interview with Pierre Domène of the weekly program guide *Radio-Magazine*, Jean Guignebert tried to explain the impact that public shows had on radio audiences: "You have no idea how moving, how profitable contact with listeners is. It's because of this that we understand that radio needs to be simple, practical, familiar, how much it needs innovation. If one of our announcers coughs into the microphone? The next day he receives ten boxes of lozenges. We have to respond to this attentive kindness in our audience. Our most important shows get their inspiration from this daily support.... Under the constraints of success, we have decided to open widely our studio doors to our listeners."[24] Guignebert informed his listeners and the readers of *Radio-Magazine* that Radio-Cité heard and responded to its audience and felt obligated to let them join in the programming of the station, becoming part of its family. The station would take care of them with the same solicitude that their listeners took with sick announcers. He understood that listeners needed to feel comfortable with the voices that emanated from their favorite home appliance and to feel a vital part of the family of the radio. The "profitable" relationship with the audience was both emotional (as Guignebert readily admits) and monetary. The more the listeners felt heard and loved, the more they listened. The more they listened, the larger the market was for advertisements and advertiser and station profits.

The forum series, like similar programs in the United States such as *The American Town Hall* of the 1930s, which brought Americans together in New England–style town meetings in front of the radio microphone, gathered listeners into open-mike theaters where they could discuss and debate weekly topics.[25] The series split into four shows: a women's forum, a youth forum, a cinema forum, and a radio forum. The first two featured weekly themes about social issues and politics with only women and teenagers allowed at the microphone, while the third focused on that week's film releases, with an audience open to anyone who wished to comment. The final forum show, airing every Sunday evening, allowed Radio-Cité listeners to come to the studio to comment on the station's programming, offering criticism, praise, and suggestions. Whether or not the station's program directors, Jacques Canetti and Jean Guignebert, would ever actually implement listeners' suggestions, those who spoke over the microphone and those who listened regularly to the programs could feel as though they formed part of the management—and working family—of their own station. At Radio-Cité, the idea was that the audience and its opinions *were* the station. As such, it may have been more likely to make Radio-Cité's programs a part of a daily schedule.

As opposed to the small theater-studios for the midday forum programs and debates, Radio-Cité broadcast its evening shows live from a packed two-thousand-seat theater, the Salle Pleyel near the Place des Ternes in the seventeenth arrondissement in Paris. These shows also included audience participation as their central and vital marketing tool. The week included three game shows, two in which listeners chose their favorite married couple (*Les Plus de Quinze Ans*) and fiancés (*Les Fiancés de Bhyrr*) and a quiz show (*Le Jeu des Questions*). The other evenings featured a showcase of young, unknown talent (*Le Music-Hall des Jeunes*) and a "gong show"(*Le Crochet Radiophonique*) in which the audience voted on which contestants should stay to finish their numbers and which should be "hooked" off the stage.

On face value, these shows appealed to mass audiences, as listeners could feel part of the cheering (and sometimes jeering) crowd. Public programs may also have spoken directly to listeners as individuals who could participate in the show at home along with the contestants. Home listeners may have seen the oft-appearing star hosts (like Noël-Noël and Saint-Granier) as part of their family circle, entertaining them in their living rooms every weekday evening. The shows also gave listeners a real connection to Radio-Cité and a sense that they could control the programming they heard by becoming part of a participatory audience that voted on contestants, spoke out in debates, and answered trivia questions. Their radio was flexible, easy to argue with, and seemingly responsive—more of a friend than a simple entertainment product.

Many Parisians who listened regularly would even have the chance to become studio audience members themselves, increasing their sense of control. Each week over twenty-five thousand Parisians became part of the studio audiences in the huge theaters that Radio-Cité employed.[26] The tickets and entertainment (pre-, peri-, and postprogram) were free, which, during the economic crisis of the decade, must have been a wonderful (and cheap) evening out for many struggling young Parisians. Bleustein-Blanchet wrote of the sold-out shows in his memoirs: "In less than three days, the seating for the next ten weeks was already taken. The Salle Pleyel had never held so many people: its 3,000 seats were all filled; the halls, the staircases, the aisles were full to bursting. The people who showed up without tickets each night—and who had to be turned away—could have filled up half the theater."[27] He even claimed that the cabarets and music halls of Paris, after trying to stop the public programs altogether, had to postpone their curtains to nine in the evening in order to guarantee audiences for their performances. Audience members could even see their own stars rise on the radio. In each public show, the contestants came straight from the streets of Paris. *Le Music-Hall des Jeunes* continually looked for new talent to perform, introducing the voices of up-and-coming major stars such as Charles Trenet, Edith Piaf, and Jean Tranchant, all of whom might also perform off the air on other nights.[28] Any young singer or comedian could hope to audition and become a star him or herself one day, even though, in reality, the talent was scouted by Jacques Canetti long before the programs aired. Trenet, as noted in chapter 1, already had a job in the Publicis studios writing advertising jingles and was already penning songs for singers like Maurice Chevalier, and Piaf and Tranchant came to Radio-Cité at the urging of talent scouts and agents that Canetti already knew. The contestants for *Le*

Crochet Radiophonique also came from auditions where people were chosen both for talent and for lack of talent. Even (and especially) the most tone-deaf singers could have their moment of stardom before they were pulled off the air. Many had possibly auditioned on purpose for just that reason. Answering even one question correctly for the trivia show *Jeu des Questions* won players anywhere from twenty to one hundred francs, and winning the fiancé and married couple competitions could mean a fully furnished house.[29] Everyone, it seemed, stood to gain if they had the chance to play. Furthermore, studio audiences played a role on each of these shows, supplying the trivia buffs, voting for favorite performers on stage, booing and jeering the worst singers, and adding the background of live applause, laughter, and the general noise of a full theater. Radio-Cité offered audiences the chance to win stardom or money as contestants or become the radio programmers themselves as the audience-judges and, either way, to join the family of the station by letting the station into their own families and homes.

Marcel Bleustein-Blanchet went to great lengths to create a community, or a larger family, of the radio audience in these programs open to the public. The contestants and listeners were not only given a sense of a voice in the shows; they were also enjoined to participate in and see the station as a form of charity. The shows about couples, *Les Plus de Quinze Ans* and *Les Fiancés de Bhyrr*, which will be further explored in chapter 4, rewarded deserving couples with the lives of their dreams. They seemed more than simple game shows. Instead, like *Queen for a Day* on 1950s American radio and *Extreme Home Makeover* on television today, they claimed a higher purpose for commercial radio. Radio-Cité did not just entertain; it gave back. The station functioned as church and conscience. At the same time, advertisers, in this case two fortified wines (Bhyrr and Quincana) and a furniture company (Lévitan), associated themselves with good works.

Bleustein-Blanchet did not stop there. Not only did he use the public programs in an idea of charity; he also engaged his listeners in philanthropic campaigns. In 1939 he began a campaign to purchase an "iron lung" for children in Paris who suffered from polio and could survive only with the machine's assistance. With repeated appeals over the air, he called for his listeners to donate what they could. Listeners lined up at the station by the thousands to contribute their spare change. Bleustein-Blanchet described the crowd as "those who give without show, without recognition, without publicity, the humble, the modest, the simple, the workers, the store clerks . . . the man of the street, the true people of Paris."[30] After the eight-day radio campaign, the station raised over 1 million francs, or enough money for five iron lungs, more than five times what was expected. Most of the money came in small amounts from individual listeners who felt compelled to donate money to the cause. After the announcement of Radio-Cité's success, thousands gathered around the station offices to celebrate, a station's audience coming together as a community linked by conscience and by sound. Radio became, for Radio-Cité and Bleustein-Blanchet, a locus for the public trust, for functions usually left to the state or religious institutions. Radio-Cité, through the campaign for the iron lung, solidified its audience and its place in Parisian hearts.

By overtly and successfully supporting a charitable cause, Bleustein-Blanchet took his corporate enterprise out of the realm of big business and into the sphere of the greater good. By doing so, he cemented the belief that listeners had in his station as more than an outlet for mindless entertainment and rather a pillar of the larger community of Paris and of France itself. To listen to Radio-Cité could, for some, be explained as a result of social and moral obligation rather than as selfish desire. Radio-Cité's place seemed firmly ensconced in the life of the city and nation, less a frivolous money-making enterprise and more a necessity to the successful running of the community. Even more, the listeners understood that they themselves constituted a family or community that could assemble in times of need. Radio-Cité's listeners were there for the station and for each other. Bleustein-Blanchet worked to convince his audience that Radio-Cité and its listeners could, together, make a difference.

Visual culture, too, had a role to play in defining and creating a radio audience. When creating audiences for the new medium, the programmers, advertisers, and station owners imagined their audience. This fictive audience appeared often in images and representations of radios in print, film, and radio broadcasts. This audience was, with a few exceptions, represented inside the home, listening to the radio in family groups. These images served to sell radios and radio programming to a new audience, a public perhaps wary of the new mass medium. Over the course of the 1930s, radio turned from a hobbyist's obsession to a controlled mass medium broadcasted to millions of individuals and families, and those millions may have needed to be convinced of the need to buy the newfangled appliance.

Radio manufacturers sold radios with frequent advertisements in the national and regional press. In the majority of these ads, radios are pictured with their prices, usually with a method for payment by installment. Regional, national, and international radio manufacturers used these kinds of advertisements, most frequently in the mid-1930s when radios were first becoming a necessity in the home. Radiola, Radio-Pathé, Philips, and Ducretet-Thomson advertised in both regional and national daily newspapers, including *Le Figaro, L'Intransigeant, Paris-Soir,* and *Le Petit Parisien*. Regional manufacturers advertised in their local papers; for example, Le Matérial Téléphonique, a company with agencies in Nantes and Erquy, ran weekly ads in the daily paper out of Rennes, *L'Ouest-Eclair*.[31] The radios range in price from five hundred to three or four thousand francs, depending upon the model or furniture casing. Even though the most expensive were well out of the price range of the average French household, installment plans on the lower-cost radios began as low as fifty francs a month, well within the budget of a working or petty-bourgeois family. The radios pictured in these advertisements looked like furniture, ready for installment in a dining or living room. In one of its shop-window advertisements, Radio-Pathé pictures its radios in various rooms of the house, the kitchen, the salon, and the dining room, all with a couple listening together.[32]

This image of the family as the radio audience was sometimes repeated in the newspaper advertisements. When people appear as listeners in these ads, they always appear at home. One Radiola ad shows a woman in an armchair with a radio on the side table next to her. Behind her is an image of a theater audience with a silhouette in the front row where she would otherwise be. The copy reads, "In whatever room, whatever the concert might be, with your Radiola, you are always in the best seat in the house."[33] The radio is in the home, giving the listener the public concert inside her private space. Another ad, for Ducretet-Thomson, shows the delivery truck bringing the radio directly to a traditional-looking home, complete with smoke billowing out of a chimney.[34] Another advertisement, for Inovat, with the copy "The wireless for all, the joy at home!" depicts a couple dancing with their son and puppy jumping up around them.[35] A 1937 advertisement for Radio-Nain in *L'Intransigeant* shows a father, mother, and son listening to radio through three pairs of headphones. Using obsolete technology, the company can sell a complete radio for the whole family for only thirty-nine francs.[36] The old technology, which required the use of headphones, could appeal to the desire to listen as a family simply by allowing up to ten ear sets to listeners at once. Radios, for those selling them, were a new kind of home furniture, marketed to private owners and families, not for use in public spaces.

Another set of images of radio audiences appeared in print between 1933 and 1935. This was a series of six woodblock prints by the illustrators and artists André Dignimont, Dagoussia, Hermine David, and Pierre Dubreuil. Dignimont, in particular, was a celebrated illustrator; he worked for the *Comédie Française* and Paris Opera. Hermine David, winner of the Legion of Honor, was a celebrated illustrator of her day. The images were shown on the cover of *Radio-Magazine*, a radio guide that ran to over two hundred thousand copies. The six prints ran repeatedly in cycles for over two years.

These images focus on family and community. Three show families of different classes, the peasantry, the middle-class, and the aristocracy. The images show families in stereotypical homes, in stereotypical roles. In the first, a peasant family listens to the radio in simple surroundings. The image recalls paintings by the seventeenth-century artist Louis Le Nain, with a premodern family in a cottage, complete with rustic wooden furniture, a large fireplace, timeless clothing and clogs.[37] The only technology that speaks to the 1930s is a wall clock and a radio. Radio functions in this room as a symbol of harmony. It adds color to the peasants' lives, giving the family entertainment to occupy the air in an otherwise dull and ordinary evening. These are good French peasants, holding on to customs from the past but embracing the modern in their radio and their literacy. The family father reads *Radio-Magazine*, while his daughter or daughter-in-law breastfeeds his grandchild at the table, her breast exposed but her hair, at least, modestly covered. Her husband or brother, standing in front of the fire, drinks coffee from a bowl, and her sister fiddles with the radio dial on the buffet in the background. Peasants here are timeless, continuing the rituals of their ancestors, incorporating the radio into their otherwise static lives.

The middle-class family, by contrast, is fully modernized, and the radio plays a more active role in the household.[38] Here, too, is an ideal family, with a living room with a modern fireplace and furniture and electric light—in a large lamp on a sofa table. Instead of a scene in a simple cottage, this living room, with the requisite radio over the fireplace, has wood paneling on the walls and heavy drapery. The radio here serves to bring generations together, much as the one illustrating the peasant cottage, but this family looks to the future. While the mother sits at a table knitting a sweater, a cat at her feet, the grandfather looks on as his two young grandchildren (a brother watching over his younger sister) play in front of the fire. The young girl reaches her hands up to the radio as if embracing the emanating sound. In the background two stylish young couples dance together, waltzing or fox-trotting to the radio music. The radio plays both a passive and an active role here, as entertainment for daily tasks (for the mother) and as dance music for the young adults in the room. The radio serves as a vector for family harmony, present and future, as well as a control over active middle-class youth, whose energy is placed into creating new middle-class families.

The third household image is that of the aristocracy or high bourgeoisie. In this case an expensive radio, encased in a large, modern wooden cabinet, sits in the foreground.[39] The household is no longer limited to the family and perhaps a few friends. Instead it is the location of a large party where the music from the radio plays the role that a hired band would have filled. Couples and singles chat on plush sofas and in small standing groups, and the aristocracy plays its role in the game of high fashion and style, in long gowns and tuxedoes. The home is grand and richly furnished, with a full bar in the corner, columns on the window and door openings, and frescoes on the walls. The house sits on an estate, as through the large draped window in the background appears a garden with large trees. The style is distinctly art deco and highly stylized, putting an emphasis on modern fashion and taste, the true milieu of the lingering haute bourgeoisie and aristocracy. Taken together, the three woodblocks attempt to show radio's ideal role for each class. The object and programming transcend class because they work for all classes and at the same time for each class's particular function. Conspicuously missing from these depictions is the working-class home, images of which did not fit into the conservative image that the editors of *Radio-Magazine* had of and for the nation.

Three other woodblock images appeared on the covers of the weekly journal depicting the radio in more public settings. One shows a radio as the music for a village *bal musette*, where happy couples share food and dance in the town square.[40] The scene could be one of a harvest festival, as wine and food cover the tables. Foregrounded in the image is a family, the mother holding a baby and the father relaxing next to his daughter. While the setting, then, is public, the people still listen in family groups, and the radio still serves as a support to family harmony and the future generations in the village.

Another of these images depicts a group of young adults listening to the radio while on a day off from work along the banks of a river.[41] This image shows a fantasy, as bringing a radio into the public air would have been uncommon in the 1930s. The object itself was much too valuable to serve as outdoor entertainment, driven to a picnic in a car. But this image works for a larger purpose. Reminiscent of the subject of images from Argenteuil by the Impressionists, it depicts the leisure time of French youth. The trains and steam that would have appeared in an image by Monet are replaced by an automobile crossing the bridge under a cloud in the sky. The female figure in the foreground, who looks strikingly like the *Odalisque* by Ingres and who would have been unclothed in that neoclassical painting, is, in this case, garbed in modern leisure dress, with a sleeveless top and knee-length skirt, her head obscured by a summery wide-brimmed hat. A copy of *Radio-Magazine* is spread on the grass at her feet. Her friends gather around the radio pouring and drinking wine. Two swimmers, a man and a woman, sit on a pier behind them. Radio, through this fantastical image, is placed into the larger frame of national art. Like paintings by Monet and Ingres, radio would join and support the modern *patrimoine*.

The last image of the series takes the radio out of metropolitan France and places it in the colonies.[42] The radio sits in the foreground, a "civilized" emblem of the colonizer in between the wood-carved "primitive" icons of Tahiti and Africa, one a waist-high totem, the other an enlarged mask. A male colonist, complete with pith helmet, lounges under his hut, surrounded by two naked women, one Polynesian in flowers and a flowered skirt, the other an African, completely unclothed. The two women gaze at the colonist as he lies in his chair and casually smokes his pipe. A (his?) ship sails off into the distance—perhaps back to France—on the sea in the background. Radio serves here as a patriarchal symbol of the domination of the metropole over its colonies, as the iconic male served by colonial subjects symbolized by exotic, unclothed women. This is the only image in the series that is, at face value, an imagined space. The colony represented here is an "everyFrench colony," as the women depicted in the frame would have been separated by oceans. It is unclear from this image whether radio served only the metropolitan French who lived in the colonies or was part of the *mission civilizatrice* that they brought with them, although it appears that the radio is under the colonist's domain, as much as the totem and the mask are under the control of the colonized women. One of the ironies of this image, as we shall see in chapter 6, is that colonial women's voices never broadcasted from metropolitan radios. They were entirely absent from the airwaves. They are seen only in images and here are exoticized and eroticized for readers of the weekly radio guide.

Images like these envisioned radio audiences as largely family groups who listened together at home and sometimes in public. Radio, through visual culture, was depicted as a medium that could promote community and, especially, family harmony. Households could benefit from listening to the radio. Much like the articles by Léon-Martin, these images reassured the populace about the emerging mass medium. More than simply a passive feature in the house, radio was a modern necessity, helping to keep families stable and happy.

But as much as charitable works, visual culture, and community-minded programming brought the audience together, music had a much more important role to play in giving a sense of belonging to listening audiences. Private radio also exploited the use of the swing band and songs with jokes in each verse that quickly became hits across the nation. Swing bands, including Fred Adison and His Orchestra, Ray Ventura and His Collegians, and Jo Bouillon, played weekly concerts on most of the private stations, featuring upbeat music that included instrument and vocal solos from almost every member of the band in turn. The vocal soloists played individual characters that parodied every conceivable French citizen. From peasant to worker, servant to aristocrat, young to old, country bumpkin to Parisian, priest to Jew, and wife to cad, all voices sang verses of the songs. Radio audiences heard themselves and everyone they knew represented in the swing numbers. The most popular of these songs gave the band the opportunity to play the family of France in three minutes flat.

The most successful swing band of the 1930s, Ray Ventura et Ses Collégiens, had at its helm a half-Alsatian, half-Turkish Jewish man who understood the impact that swing and jazz could have on the French, who embraced the American musical form wholeheartedly.[43] Ventura teamed up with friends to form a band that would create its own repertoire of songs and also translate American and British jazz music and lyrics for French audiences. The whole band participated in the writing and adaptation of songs. Paul Misraki (changed from the too-Jewish Misrachi) played piano, sang, and wrote music and lyrics for a number of songs. André Hornez, Coco Aslan (Grégoire Arslanian), and Max Blot all wrote, played brass, and sang for the band, while Loulou Gasté played guitar, Noël Chiboust played violin, and Pierre Mingaud sang and contributed comedy sketches. Others took their turn with the band and then went on to other popular groups.[44]

The swing bands had their great success in live concerts and on the radio. Ray Ventura and his band had a weekly show sponsored by Lustucru pasta called *Lustucru Theater* on Radio-Cité in the 1936–37 season and on Ile-de-France, Radio-Luxembourg, and Radio-Toulouse from 1937 to 1939. Like the public programs on Radio-Cité, this show, too, aired from the stage of the Salle Pleyel. These shows were not quite free, however. Parisian audiences could get tickets only by mailing in proofs of purchase from boxes of Lustucru pasta.[45] Each two-hour show featured a celebrity guest singing artist backed up by the swing band, singing his or her standards. In addition, Ventura's band would play its own music, debuting songs weekly and singing old favorites to keep its audience happy. The show forced the band to constantly write new arrangements and keep abreast of the most popular swing music from France, America, and Great Britain.[46]

Many songs used the band as a group that sang verses as individuals and the choruses together. "Cleopatra's Nose" uses small incidents from the past to explain why life is so hard today, with each band member coming up with sillier facts. In "Knock, Knock Everywhere," Ray Ventura plays the straight man to a series of knock-knock jokes told by members of the band. In "It's Too Bad I Can't Show It to You," band members relate silly and sexual situations that would be too risqué to show. "The Archduchess's Shirts" uses a common tongue-twister to give band members the chance to play for laughs characters with speech idiosyncrasies and impediments; lisping, stuttering and the lockjawed Auvergnat accent all became the butt of jokes as each soloist sang (or attempted to sing), "Les chemises de l'archiduchesse sont elles sèches, archi-sèches."[47]

"Everything's Fine, Madame la Marquise," arguably the most popular song of the 1930s, demonstrates how Ray Ventura and his band played characterizations of various French people in their songs. The hit tells the story of an aristocrat who, while on vacation, calls home to find that her gray mare has died. She speaks in turn to her various household servants and soon finds that in addition to the death of her horse, all of her wealth is gone, her property destroyed by fire, and her husband dead from suicide. Ray Ventura himself plays the marquise, phoning home, more agitated with each call, to find out more bad news which in the last verse gets placed into its correct chronological sequence with members of the band singing each line in turn:

> Well, here it is, Madame la Marquise:
> After learning that he was ruined,
> Barely over his surprise, the Marquis committed suicide.
> And it was kicking over the bucket that he knocked over some candles
> That put a flame to the chateau, which consumed it from top to bottom.
> The wind that blew on the fire, took it to the stables
> And that's how in a moment we saw your gray mare die.[48]

Each servant has a distinct sounding voice—one a high nasal tenor, one a bass, one a crooner, and one a baritone, each easily representing a recognizable character to radio listeners. At the finish, the servants bond together, practically rejoicing in their mistress's fall from grace. The song ends with a rousing brass flourish, celebrating in the demise of aristocratic power.

The song played into the idea of the average Frenchman, who could be any male listener, laughing at the foibles of the upper class. Audiences could also relate to the politics of the song; they lived in a period in which the Popular Front was rising and here in song, the working class has its collective laugh. Even the bourgeoisie could understand the power of the song in the midst of the economic crisis, and after all, the beleaguered marquise was an aristocrat, not a *bourgeoise*. Conservative music critic René Bizet, writing for *Radio-Magazine*, praised the song: "You only need to listen to the celebrated '*Tout va très bien, Madame la Marquise*,' a song that has rapidly taken on, thanks to the irony of its lyrics, the allure of a national hymn in these difficult times, to understand that if this catastrophic story wasn't played by the artists Ray Ventura *et* Ses Collégiens, it wouldn't have the bite or the liveliness that we love in this tune."[49] Bizet picked up on the swing band as the ideal medium for the song. It is the lively nature of a group that shares the chorus which made the song rollicking fun and participatory. For who could not see themselves (and their daily worries) reflected in the characters who sang a verse and then joined in the ironic refrain, "Tout va très bien, tout va très bien!"

Ray Ventura often picked up on national feeling in his swing numbers. Playing into the excitement around the rise of the Popular Front and the massive ensuing strikes, his band created a song called "The Orchestra's Strike."[50] In the lyric, the band goes on strike not for money (Ventura offers them each a thousand-franc raise), not for vacation time (he proposes a full year's paid leave), but because "it's fashionable" and they "want to annoy the boss." The band's demands reflect the actual calls of the Popular Front—for large raises and paid vacations—while joyfully poking fun at the excesses of the strikes and the happiness of the strikers. The song cleverly played to both the strikers and their bosses. Bourgeois listeners could enjoy the lyrics for the way they joked about striker demands, while the working class could laugh in solidarity with the band. Ray Ventura's success depended on a close connection with a wide audience and an acute sense of national sentiment.

"Comme tout le monde," another Ventura hit, played into the idea of togetherness in the face of difficulty.[51] The title itself spoke to notions of national identity, neighborliness, and shared traits. After all, to be "comme tout le monde," or just like the "everybody" repeated over and over in the chorus, meant that listeners were on the inside and included in the game. The song used every trick—sexual innuendo, political and economic jokes, silly wordplay—to make its point that despite differences, all French people were fundamentally the same and essentially in the same mess together. So the song, which deserves a close reading because it is so symptomatic of the intent of the swing band, begins with the most basic thing that human share—biology:

> We all look the same
> A nose, two eyes and two ears.
> In spite of our small differences
> Down deep we're all the same.
> We have our beating hearts. . . . Like everyone.

And then, in the middle of the first chorus, the band turns to its joke and looks to the biological response to love that every citizen may have shared, around which so many popular songs were sung:

> We sometimes softly sigh. . . . Like everyone.
> When we are bitten by the lovebug. . . . Like everyone.

But in typical swing band comedic fashion the idea gets turned on its head:

> Then one day we get cheated on. . . . Like everyone.

From the biological and emotional, the song moves outward on the body, to clothing, mores and fashion, inside and out:

> We have the same customs
> The same desires, the same tastes.
> We put on the same suits
> And even the same underwear.
> One has a decent pair of pajamas. . . . Like everyone,
> Woolly long underwear. . . . Like everyone.
> We have cute little blouses. . . . Like everyone.

And then to the reality of fashion in hard economic times, something the audience in 1938 would surely understand:

And of course holes in our socks. . . . Like everyone.

In the next verse, economic hardship is dealt with more closely, but here the "everyone" has a populist slant; it is a renter who struggles to pay the bills, pay for food, and pay for taxes:

> We pay our landlord. . . . Like everyone.
> We pay the gas and water bills. . . . Like everyone.
> We pay cash for the casserole. . . . Like everyone.
> It's only the taxes we avoid when we can. . . . Like everyone.

The band added or subtracted as necessary, given different audiences, recordings, or performance times, most having to do with love affairs, changing diets, manners, or getting the flu in the winter. The last verse always turned to politics, the one thing that seemed to rip French people apart. Here Ray Ventura and His Collegians tried to stem the tide of hatred without being too political themselves, a sentiment that many in their audience may have shared:

> Because we're all identical
> We should have the same ideas.
> Yet when it comes to politics
> We can never seem to agree.
> We have our own principles. . . . Like everyone.
> We talk about current event. . . . Like everyone.
> We call each other: sellout! . . . crook! . . . Like everyone.

And here the band refuses to get into the fray altogether, preferring to make contentious political aims seems like nothing, once again bringing together all French people, no matter what their politics, finishing the song with one more joke and a dance:

> But underneath it all we don't give a hoot. . . . Like everyone!

France, in spite of enormous differences, is brought together in song, one radio audience hanging through tough times as one. All political dissent and feeling is masked under the guise of an evening's shared love of swing.

Another huge hit that shows how the band seemed to represent every member of the nation-family, making light of economic difficulty and making fun of those who didn't quite fit in, was "It's Better Than Catching Scarlet Fever," which gave a series of seemingly horrible occurrences and sang the events from the point of view of some who might not mind them.[52] Each verse was sung by a different character, each with a distinctive vocal tone, while the chorus was sung by the group as a whole. Many of the verses focused on various strange practices and sexual fears and desires of various French (or not so French) people. For example, an average Joe sings of his experience on the metro:

> In the crowded metro no one knows where to hold on
> And while the train is going we just shake around.
> The other day someone exclaimed, "Hey you've grabbed my breasts!"
> And I replied, "Ma'am, there's no reason to be so mad!"

This passage relates fears about changing sexuality and fears of women in public but also jokes about what was a probable occurrence on the subway every day—a startling sexual result of the problem of a crowded public transportation system. Every commuter in Paris, Marseille and Lyon could relate to the incident.

Other characters make fun of sexuality and display the fears the audience had of sex as well—an old woman will not pass up a rape, and two Jews relate the benefits of circumcision. In an especially telling verse, homophobia mixes with a fear of the colonies as a gay voice sings:

> They were speaking about torture at a popular *salon*
> When a man mentioned that on the island of Mauritius they impaled people.
> Everyone said, "That's so bloodthirsty!" But a young man, excited, said,
> "My goodness! If you want my opinion . . .
> It's better than catching scarlet fever
> It's better than swallowing rat poison
> It's better than sucking down mothballs
> It's better than drowning slowly in the Seine!"

Jews, colonial subjects, and gays, although funny narrators with funny voices, could not have the same sentiments as average radio listeners. While their point might be taken, their strange practices left them outside of the normal definitions of "French." The band's listeners could laugh along with the band and feel all the more comfortable (if not Jewish or gay) with their own accepted status.[53] These verses clearly defined the limits of the nation-family.

The swing bands even used the joke-versed songs to turn the tables on themselves, their audience, and the private stations that supported them. Ray Ventura and his bandmates and songwriters André Hornez and Paul Mizraki were quite aware of their place in creating commercially viable radio markets with wider listening audiences. After all, if listeners could come to swing performances by bringing in pasta box tops, and if performers were paid based on their popularity, and if those swing bands wrote songs about everyday events, why not combine all of this into a hit song? "It Was a Commercial," a song written by Rudolf Révil and Georgius for Ray Ventura in 1938, made fun of the way that the electronic media, and especially advertising, had become a part of life, accepted willingly by audiences even under the most ridiculous and unmarketable circumstances.[54] By using absurd situations, like nudists protesting purity, politicians playing children's games in the Senate chamber, and two authors fighting a duel in a city park, the song shows an understanding of the media's fascination with and overreliance on advertisements and catchy slogans. As each event occurs, a crowd gathers, including "the newspapers and the radio," to witness the strange events. The events themselves are staged by advertisers, who, once they have gathered an audience, sing their slogans to the crowd. The nudists sing of "Bosex Pills that keep you looking like you're twenty," the politicians praise "Krochnouillans Salts, that turn old folks young again," and the authors tell the crowd of their own theater, "with reduced-price tickets for youth and soldiers."

The song ends with a morbid comedy, with a verse about how there are "Advertisements to implant in your head / You can go anywhere, they'll haunt you." It finishes with a shootout, and "while the whole crowd bled to death twelve gangsters interrupted":

> It was, it was, another commercial
> It's true, just because it was.
> And dancing they began to sing,
> "Demand the Kiratpa browning revolver. . . .
> Only three hundred francs
> You can kill your friends and family,
> Without pain and with a smile!"
> It was, it was, an ad and a slogan!

With the crowd dying on the street, and audiences (hopefully) dying of laughter from self-recognition, the song could poke fun at the new radio culture. The combination of joke verses in "It Was a Commercial" lay open notions of Frenchness while poking fun at the ubiquity of the radio advertisement and its acceptance by audiences—the swing band's own sources of revenue.

With the pervasive programming of groups like those of Ray Ventura and Fred Adison, private radio continued to exploit its knowledge that the rhetoric of family and neighborhood appealed to listeners who made the public medium of radio a daily part of their private lives. These audiences wanted to play a role in their own entertainment. The new stations offered them that chance. By the end of the 1930s, private radio and advertisers also made commercials a primary part of the auditory landscape. Private station owners like Jean Grunebaum of Poste Parisien, Marcel Bleustein-Blanchet of Radio-Cité, and Jean Prouvost of Radio-37 exploited the idea that advertisers could sell household products over the radio directly into the homes they supplied. Advertisers gained access to an ever-growing market for their goods—ready-made and delivered to them by radio owners—a loyal listening public. The now-necessary connection between home and radio both gave listeners a new family to welcome into their lives and offered companies a new, compliant market for their wares. Private stations succeeded in creating a new mass market that would benefit their coffers as much as their advertisers', and they made the dubious claim of benefiting the audience as well.

Yet in order for private radio's star to rise during the late 1930s, public radio had to lose its lion's share of the audience. The state would learn too late that there was power in commercialization and a new rhetoric of a radio family that seemed to care about its listeners. In 1936 and 1937, when the Popular Front wanted to create a public radio with a left-wing political and cultural message, the group would find it difficult to reach radio listeners. It would compete with the rhetoric of family with a language of the masses and would come up against a public that already understood (and wanted to know) the radio on intimate and entertaining terms.

3 FAMILY VERSUS LIBERTY
Popular Front Programming and the Radio Elections of 1937

Until 1933, French governments had a laissez-faire relationship with the radio. It was only with the Ferrié Plan and the implementation of the radio tax that politicians began to take a close look at the development of radio and the way radio was being used by the people who programmed and listened to it. When Georges Mandel eliminated advertising on state radio in 1935, a new, successful commercial radio network developed. Innovative schedules and vibrant shows connected the young stations to their audience and made their programming ever more popular. But what the French would do with their other radio system, their public radio stations, and how the stations that made up that system could compete with the flourishing private companies became a serious question both for those in government and for those who listened.

In the early 1930s, radio programs, even those on public stations, had not had an overtly political aim or message.[1] That changed when the Popular Front left-wing coalition between the communists, socialists, and radical-socialists won national elections in May 1936. The Popular Front was the first government that understood the enormous power of the radio as a tool for propaganda. The new coalition wanted to use the radio to help implement sweeping cultural and social changes that they proposed for France. The Popular Front saw state radio as an ideal mass medium for transmitting its left-wing beliefs through control of the public stations and influence on news reports, educational programming, and entertainment. The administration viewed listeners as a mass audience and tried to implement changes that would affect masses of listeners as a body. But, as we shall see, the Popular Front's inability to recognize families as radio's central listening bodies impeded its ability to get its message across effectively.

The new government saw radio as a useful propaganda tool in reaction to two contemporary currents in European and French radio. First, it had examples of government-sponsored radio in Germany, Italy, Great Britain, and the Soviet Union. The British and Germans, for example, had the two most successful, if very dissimilar, public radio systems. The British saw radio as a public service, to offer citizens education, entertainment, and high culture without an overt political party message. Radio was a democratic medium that served the state in its neutrality and openness.[2] German public radio, on the other hand, led by the Nazis and Minister of Culture Joseph Goebbels, served a purely political function, to promote fascist ideology and spread Nazi propaganda across Germany.[3] The Popular Front would make an effort to combine these two approaches into a radio that both served the public and spread the left-wing message of a socialist state concerned mostly with its workers.

Second, the radio took longer to develop in France than in other parts of western Europe and the United States and thus became a true mass medium only by 1936.[4] The French, then, as inheritors of the other nations' experience could look to their examples and apply or ignore them as desired. Earlier governments had little reason to exploit the radio for their purposes because they did not see radio as a mass medium that reached enough ears. In their 1938 history of French radio, conservative radio critics Benjamin Huc and François Robin listed the number of radios in the world in 1937. The United States far outstripped European countries with over 26 million machines, Germany and Great Britain followed with 8,412,848 and 8,347,000 respectively, while France trailed behind with only 4,018,000.[5] If one looked at radios in proportion to population, Huc and Robin found that France fell to a dismal thirteenth in Europe, behind not only Great Britain and Germany but also Denmark, Sweden, the Netherlands, and Switzerland.[6] The two men thought that France fell behind because, unlike Germany, in which the Nazis subsidized radio purchases, the French Republic gave no monetary incentives for its citizens to buy radios.[7] Instead the government taxed them for the privilege. Still, 1936 marked a great shift in radio; with over 10 million listeners, it had finally moved from a hobby for radio and engineering enthusiasts to a mass medium that reached every corner of France.[8]

The Popular Front also had public limitations on its broadcasting schemes because state radio was legally tied directly to its audience, which limited the freedom with which any democratic government could dominate the airwaves. In a proposal unique in Europe, all registered radio owners could vote for candidates to control radio programming boards in radio elections in 1937.[9] The radio tax not only kept public radio free of advertising; it also gave each radio taxpayer a say in how that radio should sound. Thus the Popular Front had to sell its cultural product to the enfranchised listening audience. The elections offered a forum for those who disliked the Popular Front to criticize its cultural mission by campaigning for the elections. The radio elections of 1937 would pit the right- and left-wing parties against one another in a rhetorical battle over two opposing ideas of French culture. With the votes counted before new governmental elections, the results of the radio election would show whether the Popular Front's cultural project was a success or a failure to the listeners who would soon become a large faction of national voters.

The notion of radio elections first took form in the Ferrié Plan of 1933. To give radio listeners the chance to direct how their tax money would be used, the Ferrié Plan created Conseils de Gérance, or Advisory Boards; they would program at least one-quarter of the radio hours each week on their local public stations. It divided France into eleven regions, each with its own public station and radio organizations' candidate slates. Each region would vote for its own Advisory Board from the slates that would afterward control those stations' broadcasts. This would make elections manageable for local election boards from the post office and give listeners a voice on the public station they could easily pick up in their homes. For example, listeners living in Lille voted for the Advisory Board that ran Radio-PTT-Nord, the radio that covered the northeastern part of France; the residents of Nice or Cannes voted for the board for PTT-Nice-Côte d'Azur; and those living in Nantes, for Radio-PTT-Rennes. The Parisian regional board would control one of three local stations, Paris-PTT.[10]

The boards were composed of thirty members, fifteen appointed by the sitting government and fifteen elected by radio owners who paid the yearly fifty-franc tax. The groups would control some of the programming of the station, not including news and much of the daytime hours. The appointed members would come from both political and artistic backgrounds. Both appointed and elected members would serve for two-year terms, meeting frequently to discuss and propose programs for the local stations.

Some radio critics were very skeptical of the Advisory Boards, assuming that they would be indifferent in their work and would offer no real balance against the government bodies that already controlled state radio. The editor of *Radio-Magazine* insisted that no one on the committees would have much interest in steady participation, especially the high-ranking ministers like André Tardieu or Léon Blum and famous artists and authors like Paul Valéry, all of whom would have much more pressing obligations elsewhere.[11] Clément Vautel wrote before the first elections in 1935:

> I don't want to be seen as a "fascist," but I must admit that these parliaments don't do much for me. . . . Every new trend will be represented, and there will be more speeches than action. In the beginning, all the delegates will be passionate: they'll have so many contradictory ideas, will want to reform everything, and pull everything apart. . . . Then members will become disinterested, with skepticism and justifiable absences at meetings. In the end, the meetings will be attended by only a few zealots who will do all the work. That's how things are in the Chambre [des Deputés], the Senate, in all the elected assemblies, in every committee. . . . I even know some important overseas missions where in practice everything rests on the shoulders of a simple secretary! I would prefer one authority and personal responsibility in each region.[12]

Vautel, who had ties to the monarchist, protofascist Action Française and the weekly, rabidly antisemitic newspaper *Je Suis Partout*, used his editorial forum to attack both the Ferrié Plan and the Republic, blurring the lines between radio elections and general elections and condemning the centrist and parliamentary government and its plan for the radio. Soon these lines would be crossed by many other critics of both the Third Republic and the Popular Front's political right to use the radio.

The first radio elections were held in 1935, the same year that public radio discontinued all advertising. Georges Mandel, Minister of the PTT and head of state radio, wanted to finish the installation of the Ferrié Plan. Elections were planned through the first quarter of 1935 and finally held in late May. Little publicity surrounded them. Regional boards put up local constituents and the elections occurred without much news coverage, even in the radio press. Only the weekly guide *Le Petit Radio* made an extra mention of the election, printing an example of the request to be included as a candidate for an Advisory Board on its front cover.[13] The vast majority of radio's listeners did not expect great change to come from the Advisory Boards. Only 14 percent of the tax-paying public voted. No discernible changes in radio programming occurred.[14] State programming was not yet overtly political in tone or very interesting to many listeners, and neither were the first radio elections. In fact, 1936 was the first national assembly election in which the candidates used the radio at all.[15] No previous government had thought of the radio as a necessary propaganda tool, relying instead on rallies and newspapers as the major forums for political propaganda.

In spring 1936, as the Popular Front consolidated its power and the French awaited the new government, strikes broke out across the country, shutting down major industries. National leftist parties led some actions; others were locally or individually led, all in solidarity with the incoming left-wing administration. Among the businesses affected were newspaper offices and distributors. Radio workers, however, were under strong right-wing state control. Directly supervised by Georges Mandel, the ever-efficient minister of the PTT, they could put up scant resistance. Mandel's history of strikebreaking made clear to postal and radio workers that if they called for a walkout, they would be fired. Radio was thus the only mass medium to remain in uninterrupted operation.[16]

The radio became a stable and useful source for political news and opinions during the national elections, and the Popular Front took advantage of this change. After the strikes had ended in June, and it had taken over the reins of government and thus control of radio programming, it continued to broadcast political speeches and discussions.[17] Yet, in contrast to those in the German, Italian, and Soviet dictatorships, the microphone in France was never closed to political dissidents and the studio rooms were open to debates on many topics. Prime Minister Léon Blum himself was acutely aware of the unfair advantage his party had over others by controlling state radio and, with a sense of the importance of the freedoms of intellectual exchange that a Republic demanded, tried to give his opponents some room for their ideas on the air by giving them time to participate in debates and political speeches.[18]

While democratic in outlook, and willing to parse out some airtime to opponents, the Popular Front came into power with a strong sense, derived from the German and British radio projects and the success of their political speeches during the 1936 election campaign, that state radio could and should be used as an aid in implementing the sweeping cultural changes that the left wing proposed for France. In this vein, they offered hours of left-leaning theatrical and educational programming to the listeners. While there is little room for extensive analysis of Popular Front programming, a look at the programming guides from the 1930s shows a huge reliance on university lectures, retransmissions from theaters, and educational programs. One, plainly titled "Economic and Social Programming," instructed listeners in civic and social responsibility and gave economic lessons to the working classes. The Popular Front went as far as to create radio acting troupes like "Art and Work" and "May 36" to produce the plays of such authors as Jean Cocteau and Maxim Gorki. These often featured background scores written by left-leaning composers including communist Arthur Honegger.[19] These programs were attempts at propaganda, but whether they could truly entertain or win audience approval was not yet clear.

The Popular Front had an ambitious cultural project when it came to power in June 1936. Along with the social program legislation that it passed through the government that summer, including two-week paid vacations, the forty-hour work week, and the beginnings of a social welfare system, it wanted to implement comprehensive cultural change. As historian Pascal Ory shows, the government had an ambitious plan to bring high culture to the masses, educating the culturally illiterate while placing left-wing ideals into the center of cultural life. The Popular Front used every medium in its power, including film, music, painting, and sculpture.[20]

Expanded theater and radio programming would help achieve these goals. New theater groups performed in open-air arenas, offering free entertainment to people throughout France. The party claimed it would "uplift the souls of the crowd."[21] Many of these performances were rebroadcast on regional and national public radio stations. The Popular Front's first and most important theater group, called the Théâtre du Peuple, qualified for subsidies from the radio tax. The radio tax continued to keep many other national theaters, like the Comédie Française and the Odéon, afloat during the economic crisis of the decade.[22] Here, although continuing in its standard practice of retransmitting standard theater, implemented under Georges Mandel, public radio now aired plays with a specifically left-wing agenda and left-wing authors, like Maxim Gorki's *Mother*.[23] Unlike the Odéon or the Comédie Française, the People's Theater was directly affiliated only with the Popular Front and thus owed its allegiance not to France, but to the Popular Front's cultural and social ideological goals.

The government formed two other acting troupes for radio productions, "Art and Work [Art et Travail]" and "May 36 [Mai 36]," both of which performed in regional theaters and on the state radio. *Vendredi*, the weekly Popular Front paper, claimed that these two troupes were especially necessary for the radio because "stupid Boulevard slapstick and obvious moral tales of virtuous behavior may be all that can be found in the literary baggage of certain elected Advisory Board members for public stations. A radio worth its cultural mission shouldn't stoop to satisfy them. Radio should be at the forefront, looking for the newest trends, leaving banality behind. 'May 36' and 'Art and Work' are moving in this direction."[24] The two theater groups used the airwaves to perform in new radio productions of classics and new theater from many traditions, plays, and novels. They rewrote scripts specifically for radio theater, including sound effects and voice-overs in their digests of the various stories.[25]

This rewriting of the classics had become a regular feature of radio—*Salammbo* had been recast by Gabriel Germinet, the first author of French radio plays and the definer of the medium for later generations, in 1925—but this was the first time that a political group overtly sponsored the strategy and asked that the writers and musicians in the Popular Front participate. In 1936, left-wing author Carlos Larronde wrote *The Invisible Theater*, a book that described what radio writers could do when scripting plays for radio audiences. In the work he included two plays as examples of radio writing. Both were explicitly socialist in tone. *The Twelfth Gong of Midnight* focused on the importance of work as part of the realization of happiness. While the actors cried out in chorus about the merits of their labor, a score by modern composer and communist Arthur Honegger filled the background.[26] In this way, the best of French musical composers put his work into a play that represented the fight for the leftist cause.

The Song of the Spheres shed light on the conflict between the Catholic Church and the early modern scientists in the life story of the scientist-philosopher Giordano Bruno. Although Larronde alleged in his preface to this work that it "does not oppose the church and science, today reconciled," it is clear that his play proposed that the medieval scientific thinker Bruno won a moral battle against religion and superstition in the name of modern thought. It also seemed to reflect the contemporary struggle that the left fought against the right-wing Catholic Leagues.[27]

The Laboratory of the Theater of Art and Action, one of the predecessors to the troupes of the Popular Front, performed both plays in 1934.[28] Art and Work and May 36 continued this tradition, performing pieces from canonical writers like Sophocles and Edgar Allan Poe, as well as newer French playwrights such as Jean Cocteau, J.-R. Bloch, and Paul Nivoix.[29] Many of the pieces they chose for the radio had specifically leftist leanings, like Aristophanes' *Peace* and Girardoux's *Siegfried*, which both spoke directly to the conflict in Spain, hoping for its peaceful end in the victory of the republicans.[30]

The government also sponsored in 1936 an evening variety show and political rally that celebrated its progress and victory. On October 18 of that year, the Popular Front gathered some of the biggest stars of the day at Luna Park in Paris, including the crooner Tino Rossi, who thrilled the crowd by singing his hit "Marinella." Popular comedian Pierre-Dac performed sketches for the crowd. Along with the music and comedy, the party mixed in political speeches by the socialist president Leon Blum and communist Paul Rivet, nationally broadcasting a huge celebration of the elections and calling it "May 1936."[31]

If political speeches were mixed into musical celebrations, public addresses also became a regular radio feature at all hours of the day. Léon Blum, Jean Zay (the minister of education), and others spoke regularly on the radio, using the airwaves as a bully pulpit for their social programs, educational projects, and political views.[32] In an earnest left-wing effort to educate the populace, radical socialist Jean Zay tried to use the radio to educate both the children and adults who made up the daytime listening public. Every day on state radio, time was set aside for educational programming, which received its own space in the daily radio guides. *Vendredi* wrote appreciatively of the project: "When we think of the teachers in small villages who don't have enough supplies for their lessons, when we think of the foreign language teachers who have trouble teaching English and German accents to their students, we begin to understand the enormous service that these programs could give to provincial, and even large city, educators."[33] With their radios, people could take English and Spanish lessons, learn about new steps in agricultural studies, and even tune in to beginning accounting courses. In one sample week, over twenty-two hours were devoted to original educational programs (see appendix A). Many of these shows were also rebroadcast by other stations in different regions of the country so that all citizens could benefit from them.[34]

Public radio also featured vast numbers of colloquia on almost every topic, offered to foster learning on all levels for every listener. One sample week of lectures shows a great variety of programming in the hours of lectures for the radio listeners. Women at home got lessons from other women on shopping and keeping house, as well as some comparative education about the lives of foreign women. Doctors taught them about childhood diseases that could affect their own children. On a more scholarly level, men and women at home could learn from university professors and teachers about literature, economic policy, and international politics. For example, in the week of March 7, 1937, lectures came on a wide variety of topics, including moral themes such as "The Seven Commandments of the Happy Man," and "The Eyes, Mirror of the Soul" and literary themes such as "The Poet Jean Lebrau" and "The History of Lyrical Theater in France from the Revolution to 1900: Edouard Lalo." After listening to the "Lecture for Housewives," women at home could learn about "How to Make Up a Menu," with the ingredients from "The Fresh Produce of Lent," while every citizen with a radio could learn how the socialists benefited their lives with lectures on "The Legal Mechanisms behind Collective Organizations" and "Family Allocations in Agriculture" (see appendix B).[35]

These lectures may have covered every topic, but they also gained the reputation of boring their listeners, especially in comparison to the programming on private stations. For example, on Radio-Paris, Wednesday, March 15, 1937, at 5:00 p.m., a lecture titled "The Geology and Geochemistry of Helium" was offered. On another public station, Bordeaux-Lafayette, listeners could tune in to a literary lecture titled "Ramond de Carbonnières and the Conquest of Mont Perdu" by a university professor. By contrast, private radio offered at the same hour a recorded broadcast from the Parisian cabaret "Le Boeuf sur le Toit," featuring music and comedy sketches on Poste Parisien, and dance music on Radio-Toulouse. Admittedly, public radio lectures may have had educational merit, but they were less likely to please the mass audience.[36]

This reliance on lectures continued some of the practices that had been in place by the early 1930s, where regular lectures filled out the schedule between concerts and plays. For example, a few months before the election of the Popular Front, during the week of January 12–18, 1936, public stations had aired just over fifteen hours of lectures, while the Popular Front programmed over twenty hours in the week of March 7, 1937. The program guides also left many of the lectures untitled in the early 1936 schedule. Hours were simply marked as lectures so that they could be filled in as needed with any available speaker. By 1937, lectures were specifically planned into the radio schedule early enough to send the appropriate materials to the weekly radio journals. And up through 1936, no lectures were featured on the weekends at all during high radio-listening hours when families had leisure time together at home.

The Popular Front programmers, on the other hand, saw weekends and evenings as an ideal time to offer educational programming to citizens who would otherwise have been at work (See appendix B).[37] The programmers before the Popular Front had no educative plan; rather, they filled the time with untitled lectures that could be either replaced or filled as needed. The new government, on the other hand, planned each lecture in advance as part of a concerted government project to educate the masses through their use of the radio.

The Popular Front also produced a daily fifteen-minute evening program, plainly titled *Economic and Social Programming*, that gave economic and civic lessons to radio listeners and instructed them how to understand the major changes that the party planned for France. *Vendredi* wrote that one of the Popular Front's goals for this show was to produce a series on different citizens at work, celebrating the working class and its ideals.[38] The shows originated in Paris and were relayed to the provincial stations. This seemed like an excellent way to spread the politics of socialism to every corner of France. The Popular Front's minister of the PTT, Robert Jardillier, even wanted to place radio receivers in every small-town kiosk, ensuring that state radio would reach every French ear, even in the poorest, remotest locations.[39]

Even though the regional Advisory Boards had little power, the Popular Front still needed the support of the tax-paying public to achieve their proposed cultural changes. So in spite of Herculean programming efforts, the Popular Front's accomplishment of their political goals was not a foregone conclusion. The government believed in the power of radio as a tool of democratization and wanted vocal public endorsement of its programming. The 1937 radio elections would show the Popular Front the public's true opinion, and whether their mission had failed or succeeded.

The listening public was unprepared for state-run radio with a political mission. And as the radio stations broadcast into the private homes of listeners, radio voters rejected the politicization of the private sphere. Before the elections of 1936 it had had no experience with a government that recognized the importance of radio. Never had a political group saturated the airwaves with brazenly partisan programming that expounded its ideals in political speeches, songs, and plays. Right-wing groups in France were not likely to listen to the imposition of a left-wing radio program without responding politically themselves.

The radio elections of 1937 became a testing ground for the public reaction to new radio programs and the effect of the right wing's attack on the state of public radio and the state of the government in general. This time not 14 percent but over 40 percent of radio's taxpayers participated.[40] A large and vocal public fought over the politics of programming the radio. The people had a say in what their radio would sound like, and what political leanings, if any, it should have. And this election, whether from encouragement from the government or from personal interest, the people would vote.

The changes on radio forced listeners to confront politics on the weekends and on weekly programs that became a fundamental part of radio airplay. The political and cultural changes also ran afoul of the majority of the owners of the radio press, most of whom belonged to right-wing parties. Those publishers were unhappy with the direction the Popular Front had taken the radio. As the 1937 radio elections approached, the height of power of the Popular Front passed and political instability seemed once again imminent. The government's radio programs now began to be censured by the radio press.

Much like today's TV guides, the French radio press printed the weekly schedules of programs on all the stations in France, as well as the major European stations and worldwide shortwave-radio broadcasts. Daily city and regional newspapers also printed schedules for their locality, featuring local programming. But because many listeners could tune in broadcasts from farther away (especially at night or on cloudier days), the audience bought the weekly guides in order to know what would play all day on all the stations within reach of their antennae.

Most radio press editors had begun as hobbyists who published news about the latest radio technology, how to make better radios, how to tune in as many stations as possible, and what to listen to on the various amateur-run stations of the late 1920s and early 1930s. By 1934, however, the most successful magazines had evolved into full-scale publications with reviews, interviews, and pages of coverage of the radio programs. Magazine staffs printed weekly editorials and commentary on both public and private radio stations.

None of these radio guides leaned politically leftward, and only one or two could be counted as moderate. Most were vehemently right-wing. *Radio-Magazine*, the most popular of the group, had weekly music and film columns by Lucien Rebatet, who also wrote film reviews and antisemitic articles for *Je Suis Partout*, one of the extreme-right weeklies in France.[41] The radio guide also received advertising money from the paper, which ran weekly subscription calls in *Radio-Magazine*'s pages. *La Semaine Radiophonique* and *Le Petit Radio* published editorials that bashed the Popular Front and state radio almost every week. *Choisir*, the Catholic weekly guide to radio and movies, followed suit. The only two that did not belong to the extreme right were *Mon Programme* and *Haut-Parleur*.[42] The former also complained regularly, if coolly, about the boring programming of state radio, and the latter retained a readership of amateur radio builders, as it rarely included more than a program listing and a montage of diagrams of new radio products, teaching hobbyists how to maintain their homemade equipment and avoid static.[43]

By the beginning of 1937, the guides' commentary had become quite critical of the state. Radio elections rapidly approached, and all opinions on the course of public radio took center stage. This time the elections were central to the radio guides and listeners, as the Popular Front's mixture of politics and programming came up for public review. All those who wrote about the radio on the left and the right wanted to see a larger voter turnout. The Popular Front wanted to see more participation in the vote to get confirmation of listener confidence in the programming it had begun. The right wing, on the other hand, hoped for a condemnation of all the changes made to the radio in the course of late 1936 and early 1937.

Because the participation in radio elections of 1935 had come from a small minority of radio listeners, the government felt obligated to change the voting system in order to encourage more people to vote. Instead of mail-in ballots, in 1937 the ballots would be collected in all post offices for a full week and counted in regional centers. Voters would attach a valid tax receipt to their ballots in order to certify their participation. They would have easy access to voting materials in their local post offices and plenty of time and places in which to vote. The elections were open to anyone who paid the radio tax. For the first time, women could vote, either as representatives for their family radios or as singles with their own machines.[44]

Other election rules more directly affected the limits of influence of the radio elections on government decisions about public stations. The Advisory Boards would now consist of twenty government-appointed members, including ten from government and ten from the arts and sciences. Instead of the fifteen members elected in 1935, voters would be able to choose only ten members of each Board, now giving voters only one-third representation on the committees as opposed to the earlier one-half.

If the voters saw the election as a chance to make their voices heard, the radio press viewed it as a chance both to change the programming of the radio, taking it out of the hands of the Popular Front, and to send a loud message that left-wing politics had no firm place in the French culture and patrimony. As we shall see, the right wing also understood that elections were about much more than radio culture. They were about the politics of culture in France as a whole and the politics of the household and family in particular.

By early 1937 the Popular Front ran into trouble. Having already passed their big reform bills, the coalition that had formed started to come apart. In 1937, with the problems of pleasing both the centrist radicals and the communists, strikes paralyzed the work projects the Popular Front wanted to continue, especially the construction sites for the planned Exposition of 1937, a world's fair that was to point to the glory of the nation and its socialist government.[45] At the same time, the radicals grew frustrated with the continued demands of the striking communists and threatened to leave the coalition.

When the radio elections approached, the fragile Popular Front turned to its own radio organization to front candidates for the Advisory Boards who would continue its cultural mission. Founded in 1936 and called Radio-Liberté (Radio-Liberty), the group began to publish a monthly magazine devoted to left-wing expression about the radio. This was not a radio guide like the others but a simple magazine. It appeared less frequently and offered no broadcasting schedules for readers. Also unlike the other journals, this one had a strictly left-wing turn that, at least at its beginning and while the Popular Front maintained power, steadily supported the government control of radio. This radio organization was organized around the 1937 elections, and it put forward Popular Front candidates for the Conseils de Gérance.

Left-wing intellectuals and politicians concerned with the place state radio took in politics of the mid-1930s created Radio-Liberté. They saw hands-off policies as a serious problem. They believed that the government, in spite of its efforts, underestimated the power of the airwaves for cultural propaganda, and they wanted the Popular Front to exploit the radio for left-wing political and social goals. Like the Popular Front, Radio-Liberté had members from across the spectrum of the left. Among the ranks of those affiliated were politicians Edouard Daladier, the radical socialist and near-centrist leader, and Paul Vaillant-Couturier, a committed communist. Literary figures included Pierre Cot, Jean Piot, and Paul Compargue, editors of left-wing daily newspapers, the communist *Humanité* and *L'Oeuvre* and the socialist *Le Populaire*, respectively.

In its magazine Radio-Liberté outlined a mission statement that reflected its Popular Front connections with a resounding approval of the changes that had been made on the radio by 1937:

Radio-Liberté believes that radio must have a triple goal: news, recreation, education.
Radio-Liberté wants objective, impartial reporting, disengaged from

any political, philosophical or mercantile entanglements.

Radio-Liberté wants the recreative side of radio to be informed by the choices of the laboring masses, and to produce artistic programs that respond to every listener's tastes.

Radio-Liberté wants the people's intellectual, artistic and moral education to be served with thought and nuance, making the programs useful for everyone.

Radio-Liberté wants a free radio. Barring a bad quality of presentation, the group will not exclude any idea or any group from the use of the microphone.[46]

The group claimed the wish to elevate the French polity by giving it "what we would never search for ourselves, and what [the radio] will offer, sometimes against our own wishes, a personal perfecting to which all who can call themselves men must aspire."[47] Writers for *Radio-Liberté* advised that radio should not try to distract its audience but rather to instruct. To this end, all the journal's recommendations of upcoming programming featured traditional, canonical (albeit socialist in character) plays and classical music.

Radio-Liberté worried that a minority of business owners controlled private stations and unregulated public radio and used radio to "dominate and lower" those who listened.[48] The journal also believed it shared the republican views of the French masses. The logo on the cover of its monthly magazine featured a globe superimposed by the cockade, symbols that would bring to mind the far-reaching power of the airwaves, the global nature of the communist movement, and the republican national character of France. With its mission for the radio, *Radio-Liberté* fought another French revolution against foreign right-wing governments, local fascist parties, and private interests.

The group consistently pushed a left-wing, yet somewhat patriotic, view of their public. For example, the cover of the June 1937 issue of *Radio-Liberté* showed a view of the International Exposition in Paris. The shot overlooked the new Palais de Chaillot with the Eiffel Tower enormous in the background casting a shadow over the Soviet pavilion in the left (!) foreground. Conspicuously excluded by the photo frame was the Nazi pavilion, which directly faced the Soviet building across the square.[49] The right wing and fascism were cut out from *Radio-Liberté*'s message altogether. With this shot, the editors of the magazine reminded their readers that national interest remained primary to them and that their link with the communists and Stalin was subordinate, though firm. This showed the inherent contradictions in the Popular Front coalition. The communists, tied with the Soviets, had to acknowledge the authority of a national state in order to create a left-wing government with the socialists and radical socialists.

In 1937, the right wing had many factions that united around the radio elections and against the cultural projects of the Popular Front. The republican right, or Bloc National, viewed the Popular Front as usurpers of its political power. While still believing in a democratic France, the Bloc feared a Marxist revolution inspired by Popular Front ideals. The antirepublican right, including the fascist and quickly growing Croix de Feu, the Catholic Leagues, and the royalist Action Française, among others, hated the Popular Front because it was both left-wing and republican. And even center-left radical socialists expressed fear of the Popular Front's agenda with a Nazi salute at a party conference in late 1936. As historian Robert Soucy elegantly puts it, "If only for a moment and if only symbolically, the majority of the delegates at the congress in Biarritz had allowed their anti-communism to submerge their anti-fascism, to the point of visually associating themselves with fascism."[50] Pascal Ory finds three fronts of right-wing assault on the cultural mission of the Popular Front: from the political republican right, the extreme right, and the Catholics.[51]

These three groups also worked together more specifically under the guise of one radio organization to bring an end to what they saw as a left-wing-controlled radio system. With the 1937 radio elections on the horizon, the various factions of the right wing felt a need to respond directly to the Popular Front's creation of Radio-Liberté. Playing off French dislike of the new melding of politics and radio, Catholic groups, in turn, created Radio-Famille (Radio-Family), an organization that would front its own candidates for the radio elections. Most right-wing groups joined them in order to unite as a front against Radio-Liberté. The right would use associations with family and morality and an understanding of the position of the radio squarely inside the home as tools to win the radio back.

Radio-Famille's mission statement accused the Popular Front of collaboration with the Soviets and focused on making state radio fun, morally upright, and suitable for family consumption:

> This list was constituted in a large part from the desire to represent all radio listeners who want a radio to be:
> National, which means representative of all French people, not of

one party, one opinion, one faith, for forwarding a foreign political idea, not that of France;

Free, which means delivered from the dictatorship that weighs on the radio and wants to Bolshevize its programs;

Artistic, which means concerned with making good programs, fun, happy, instructive, acted and written by competent artists and not by ignorant and depressing party members;

Moral, which means appropriate to enter into every household and worry about the safety of all listeners, no matter of what faith and of what opinion.[52]

Radio-Famille was strongly supported by the Catholic Leagues, and their entertainment guide, *Choisir*, became its central organ of propaganda. The group proved savvier than its left-wing counterpart, however, by keeping its political leanings in the background. The group openly espoused a total separation of politics and radio, with a professed moral stance that they claimed had no basis in politics.

The leaders of Radio-Famille imagined listeners in their homes, listening in intimate spaces with their families. They spoke, not to a mass of people, but to individuals, asking them to vote for personal and moral reasons. The group understood the intimate nature of the radio and how it spoke to families who listened together and not to masses, as did the cinema or political speeches. Radio was different and reached masses but as individuals and families, not as large groups. Radio-Famille used the connection that radio had to the living room, and thus to the family unit, to its advantage. In 1938, the center-right daily *Le Figaro* would state this connection explicitly, praising Jean Nohain's ability to enthrall his audience on Poste Parisien: "Radio needs intimacy. M. Jean Nohain, who understands everything about radio, has understood this well, and has taken public speeches (which punish the listener) into intimate dimensions."[53] They understood the Popular Front's programming to have no real connection to the people who listened to the radio every day. Lectures and rallies spoke to masses but did not translate to the families and small groups listening at home.

Radio-Famille's idea of family was a political one, extremely fearful of the ideas of the working class and the left. It expected that radios were found in patriarchal, bourgeois households in which fathers would cast the family vote. In Radio-Famille's assessment, singles and unmarried groups did not own radios and thus did not fit into the campaign rhetoric. Radio-Famille perfectly summed up its idea of family in the inducements to listeners to vote: "Listeners, fathers and mothers of families, become aware of your responsibility. If, one day, radio becomes an evil thing, it will be due to the negligence of family-minded listeners—who are the majority—rather than the actions of their enemies. If, afterwards, that radio contributed to the failure of France's civilizing mission, it would again be due to that negligence."[54] Radio-Famille called "for a *free* [emphasis theirs], happy, family-oriented, artistic radio, which really means for our families, for our children, for France."[55]

Radio-Famille members rallied around the issue of a conservative patriarchal morality. *Radio-Magazine*, although alleging no political bent and thus smartly claiming to be above the fray, still included only a list of all the national candidates for Radio-Famille. They compared them with those for Radio-Liberté, saying, "There are generally two slates present: Radio-Famille's, which will encourage a national radio while keeping safe our patrimonial spiritual and moral values, and *Radio-Liberté*'s, patronized by all the organizations of the Popular Front."[56] G. Nicolai, of *Le Petit Radio*, looking to a father's right to control his household, professed that the first mission of the radio "must be moral: the programmers must constantly remember that not only adult ears are listening. The French canon is rich and varied enough to never sink into trivial rudeness; fathers must be able to leave their children in front of the wireless at any moment with no worry whatsoever."[57]

Choisir, as the Catholic radio review, wrote most widely about the moral message of Radio-Famille. Calling Radio-Famille the progenitor of "a radio of peace and general good works," *Choisir* claimed that the group would "defend family and moral interests."[58] Speaking against the Popular Front's educational projects, Henri David, one of the leaders of Radio-Famille, wrote to the paper of the "familial responsibility" of each voter because radio was in "every home" and "fathers of families are particularly interested in what the radio represents in order not to reverse their efforts at educating their children."[59] The Catholic groups wanted radio to be "MORAL [emphasis theirs], which means able to be heard in every home, and concerned with not hurting any listener, no matter what their beliefs or opinions."[60]

Radio-Famille urgently desired to remove what it saw as the now-intrusive leftist politics from the radio. Concerned about the left-wing control of the state, the group did not want to listen to the Popular Front's politics on the radio in speeches, educational programming, or dramatic productions. To arouse the public against Radio-Liberté, Radio-Famille continuously accused the Popular Front of being a communist organization that would make France the pawn of the Soviet Union. In his weekly column, Henri Hennon of *T.S.F.-Revue* commented that listeners needed a group to oppose the aims of Radio-Liberté. He hoped it would include "those who have solidly come down against the Bolshevism of the French airwaves."[61] The *Figaro* sponsored a large campaign for Radio-Famille, urging all of its readers to vote for the list against "the worst, if Radio-Liberté triumphs." To them, Radio-Famille opposed "this group which is inspired by communists."[62] Later they advised their readership, "You have the job to avoid the takeover of the French airwaves by communists like the Vaillant-Couturiers, the Langevins and the Ducloses. *Vote for and get others to vote for the national list. Only that will bar the path of Radio-Liberté* [emphasis theirs]."[63] *Choisir* also alerted its readers to "Vote Radio-Famille" to rescue radio from "the DICTATORSHIP [emphasis theirs] that weighs on the Radio, put in place by those who wish to Bolshevize its programs."[64] Editorialist Jean Morienval warned his readers that the radio was already a tool of the left, "because don't we already see on the Radio a staff from the left and extreme left?"[65] The journal reminded readers that only one list would oppose that of the "communists," Radio-Famille.[66]

Confusing the leader of Radio-Liberté with the entire body of members, C.-M. Savarit of *T.S.F.-Revue* wrote, "Alas! its head, Mr. Radi, is communist; he has created his Association and his body as an arm for the communist takeover. And the Radio, as it exists right now, with its political propaganda, its fantastic view of economics, its false reports on Spain and elsewhere, is a large part of his work."[67] Radi might have headed Radio-Liberté, but he had not been its creator, nor was he in total control of its policy decisions. Radio-Liberté was a politically minded organization, but it included membership from all factions of the Popular Front.

Although strictly antileft, Radio-Famille and its supporters alleged that they wanted a radio free of all partisanship. G. Nicolai, an editorialist from the weekly *Le Petit Radio*, listed his desires for the future of radio, asking for a "neutral," "popular," and "free" state-run radio.[68] In the weeks following, he continuously exhorted his readers to vote for Radio-Famille, which to him meant, "Radio for all." During the election week he again reminded readers that "the neutrality of the radio is indispensable."[69]

Choisir, too, continued the rhetoric of Radio-Famille's political neutrality. In pushing its organization, it stated, "Listeners have the right to choose who they want, but the fight shouldn't be between one political party and another: it is for a good free radio for everyone, or for a radio with a restrained propagandist role."[70] In his wish list for 1937, Clément Vautel, editor of *Radio-Magazine*, wanted "politics to no longer trouble the airwaves."[71] By denying their own political leanings, which would be clear to any close reader, the right wing hoped to gain voters who would react, not for right-wing causes, but for a radio that had none of the political speeches and programs that disturbed the political and patriarchal order that *Choisir* wanted. They hoped to convince all voters that Radio-Famille would choose no sides once it controlled public radio.

The Radio-Famille supporters linked its "nonpolitical" goal to the idea of the radio tax. They thought that the people who paid the tax, and not the elected government, should have the power to determine the content of radio programming. C.-M. Savarit wrote, "It's a question of good faith and honesty. Everyone pays for the state microphone, so it should not be in the service of some against others who pay."[72] Jean Reibel, of *T.S.F., Phono, Ciné*, had this to say: "All honest listeners pay the tax. . . . They don't pay to hear sad political speeches that are always contrary to most listeners' opinions." He continued in another article, "Instigating hatred in homes, creating divisions between French people, even though our union is indispensable . . . this is the purpose that radio serves."[73]

While the right-wing coalition fought against Radio-Liberté, it worried about its appearance as extremist. To defend its anticommunist position, *Le Petit Radio* laid out its goals for the radio while denouncing those who called them fascist. It asked if it could truly be considered fascist if it wanted "a neutral radio, disengaged from all political influence, only concerned with the double role it must fill: to distract and to educate." It claimed that its editors had always been against politics and radio, long before the rise of the Popular Front, and that those editors would protest against both right- and left-wing programs on the radio.[74] It neglected to mention that the Popular Front was the first political party to try to use the radio and that the mission of Radio-Famille to eliminate this voice by labeling it Bolshevik and unfair was itself a political one.

Radio-Famille also tried to assert its political neutrality by professing to have the allegiance of all religious groups. *Choisir* declared, "Radio-Famille is not religious because it has Protestant and Jewish members, along with the Catholics."[75] In *T.S.F.-Revue*, C.-M. Savarit maintained that Radio-Famille was neither political nor tied to the Catholic groups. Yet it did have a moral message: Radio-Famille, "without any distinction, groups together all the Associations concerned with the respect of the family home, of morality and of religion."[76] By trying to impress voters with their diversity, Radio-Famille's proponents only underlined their Catholic underpinnings. Never did they include any data that would give voters a chance to see how that religious breakdown looked among the candidates they presented, and it is clear from the rhetoric that the group used that there probably were not many members of other faiths, nor many nonreligious adherents. Once again, they hoped that by claiming a religious tolerance they would get more votes.

This moral and political message represented a strict control over the content of all programs of the radio. By looking at the commentaries on various programs given by the Radio-Famille collection of newspapers, one can see the values that the group espoused. The papers hated anything popular or slightly vulgar, calling for the end of "all the café-concerts."[77] One article listed the kinds of shows Radio-Famille wished to banish from the air, including police dramas, scary plays, and "noise with no purpose."[78] The publications also complained about any play or song with sexual suggestion, once even writing to a female performer on Paris-PTT when she sang a collection of prewar songs, "Aren't you ashamed of singing that in front of a man?"[79] The papers sometimes even demanded responses from the stations that aired the "immoral" material, exhorting them to publish the apology and make the retractions public.[80] Here, morality was political. Radio-Famille would not only remove left-wing rhetoric from the radio; it would also take away all but the most banal and Christian programming on the air. Yet during the campaign the group avoided mentioning what this moral message meant in practice, focusing mainly on the amoral, antifamily nature of leftist politics.

The Popular Front's lists were politically based, as the right wing claimed, but not primarily communist. They represented all of the parties of the Popular Front, including socialists and radicals. Cecile Méadel's 1994 study of the composition of the lists shows that only 19 percent of the candidates came from the left-wing socialist and communist parties. Almost 13 percent came from the centrist radical-socialist party. In profession, by far the largest number of members were teachers (37 percent), with many claiming allegiance to the League for the Rights of Man and the Committee for the Vigilance of Anti-Fascist Intellectuals.

Unlike those of Radio-Liberté, Radio-Famille candidates did not give political party information in their lists, which makes it impossible to know which political groups they represented. What is clear, however, is that the professions of the candidates show them to lean to the right. The Radio-Famille lists are filled with business owners, as 37 percent of the nominees, and businessmen and professionals together as another 25 percent of the list members.[81] Bourgeois, conservative men filled the ranks of the Radio-Famille lists, a group that generally supported the center and right in their politics.

The right-wing Catholics, monarchists, and fascists that informed much of Radio-Famille's rhetoric never really trusted electoral government and certainly not the fairness of left-wing politicians. They worried that if the Popular Front held the radio elections, election fraud would occur so that the left wing would get its own candidates elected. *Choisir* encouraged its readers to vote in strong numbers to combat the problem of false vote counts. They believed that Jardillier, the minister of the PTT, would be incapable of running an orderly election.[82] Reporter L. Jude agreed and compared the disorganized voting procedure to the Soviet elections, "General interest insists that the elections take place calmly, in a well thought out, just manner, with no hurry and no Soviet dictatorship: we all know how, over there, they vote!"[83] Later the paper continued, "When we look at the whole system, we must conclude that it gives no great guarantee of impartiality to the proceedings."[84] They worried that public apathy would lead to close results that could be faked. They believed that in order to "fight against the administration that controlled the 'urns' and that would do its utmost to be partial, we must have the pressure of a large majority of radio listeners."[85]

Other right-wing papers also fretted about election fraud in the hands of the left. *Le Figaro* claimed that Jardillier wanted to rush the election, "to ease the election of the *Radio-Liberté* candidates." The newspaper called for all of its readers to vote for the other national list, Radio-Famille.[86] During the election week they reported that the government wanted to report false results by making it very difficult for their opponents to vote. They reported on the voters' dissatisfaction with the process as well.[87] Later in the week, *Le Figaro* claimed that it would not support the outcome of the election.[88] The newspaper sent a reporter to the vote count, and he found that it was in "an obvious disorder." He wrote of no checks on stealing ballots, papers everywhere, and only Radio-Liberté present as ballot counters. He was left unimpressed by the method and worried about false results even though he reported that Radio-Famille was already ahead by a wide margin.[89]

In the weeks leading up to the election, the radio journals, especially those of the right, prepared their subscribers for the election. Since it was the PTT that controlled the polling places, this was no ordinary election controlled by an election board. Voters would have to vote at home and bring their ballots to their local post office. There they would be sent to the regions and counted.

Choisir and *Le Figaro* printed the voting rules, but they included only the lists that opposed Radio-Liberté in their articles. *Choisir* included the professions of the Radio-Famille candidates to impress upon its readers that the lists contained no professional politicians. It also repeated the instructions three times, so that none of its readers could vote incorrectly.[90] *Le Figaro* printed an article that explained "how to vote against the list inspired by communists." It included all of the addresses of the right-wing radio groups so that readers could send away for the appropriate lists of candidates for their region.[91]

The relatively moderate *Mon Programme* and *Paris-Soir*, a daily Parisian newspaper, simply explained the method and made no mention of who to vote for. They explained which departments made up each regional station to help their readers know for which candidates they would vote. Each ballot could contain the ten names of the candidates they voted for. They could choose individuals or vote for an entire list presented by Radio-Liberté or Radio-Famille. They would place the lists inside prepared envelopes they could pick up at the post office. With the lists, the voters had to staple an official label that identified them as having paid the radio tax.[92]

The fears of fraud proved unfounded; during the week of February 22–28, the elections transpired with few problems. When the ballots were counted, Radio-Famille won in ten out of the eleven regions, losing only in Toulouse. About 4 percent of the ballots had to be discounted because the proper receipts were not included. Of those, 80 to 90 percent voted for the Radio-Liberté. Because of their repeated access to information of the voting rules, Radio-Famille voters had less trouble with the rules.[93] Altogether, Radio-Famille's large and focused campaign paid off. (See table 3.1.)[94]

Most of the radio journals celebrated the victory of Radio-Famille and hoped for change in the future.[95] *Le Figaro* decided to poll its conservative readership to find out what changes they wanted to see on the radio. They asked readers to send in letters listing both "what and who they don't want to hear anymore on their radios." They gave their readers two weeks to respond by mail and printed the results the following month.[96] Not surprisingly, most readers wanted to get rid of all political programs, "no matter who the speaker and what the opinion." One response said that listeners "above all wish for peace in the family home." Second came cabinet speeches, and then "questionable news," including bulletins about the Spanish Civil War, and "theatrical productions with no value, dangerous to our youth because they deride religion and authority." Those who answered seem to think that any news also had a left-wing slant and needed to be changed or removed. The conservative readership also asked that realist songs be taken off the air as "the vulgar side is only exaggerated by radio" and "young ears are listening."[97]

The largest national papers seemed unimpressed by the propaganda from both sides. *Paris-Soir*'s daily radio editorialist Paul Reboux had only one column about the radio elections. He wrote against politics from either side, asking for more music instead. He satirized the missions of both sides: "But music itself could also become political. One day we'll discover that Beethoven was for the Popular Front while Mozart was a fascist."[98] Reboux understood that both radio lists had political leanings. If the listeners voted, they had to choose sides between the left and the right wing. The largest newspaper, *Le Petit Parisien*, ignored the elections almost completely. They printed nothing but a cartoon in which a woman complains because she cannot vote for popular crooner-heartthrob Tino Rossi.[99] Largely, the centrist papers left the elections to the partisan groups concerned about the results.[100]

There are many possible reasons why Radio-Famille beat Radio-Liberté in all but one region. First, the appeal for nonpolitical programming seemed to play to French audiences. While Radio-Liberté's agenda was explicitly left wing, with a candidate list that featured national political players, Radio-Famille placed no professional politicians on its lists. This gave credence to Radio-Famille's claims of political neutrality. The party was also able to couch its opposition as a communist organization that would turn France into a satellite of the USSR. Second, Radio-Famille had great support in daily and weekly journals and was able to get the word out about its programs and candidate lists. Radio-Liberté's program appeared only infrequently in left-leaning papers such as the socialist weekly *Vendredi* and only monthly in its own magazine. Third, it is possible that women voters affected the outcome. If, as was commonly believed and perhaps proved in postwar national election votes, women voted more conservatively, their votes here may have tipped the balance.[101] Fourth, the vote may have been a rejection of programming the public deemed uninteresting. After all, the lectures, classical music, and political speeches on public radio might not have received an enthusiastic response from audiences at home.

Most important, Radio-Famille recognized that most radios were found squarely in French households and that the heads of those households would

TABLE 3.1. Results of the 1937 Radio Elections

Station	Radio-Famille		Radio-Liberté	
	No. of Votes	%	No. of Votes	%
Paris-PTT	286,171	53	250,176	47
Rennes-Bretagne	54,800	64	30,800	36
Montpellier-Languedoc	14,00	95	511,574	45
Strasbourg-PTT	82,100	71	33,698	29
Lyon-PTT	91,350	59	64,400	41
Bordeaux-Lafayette	30,609	57	23,029	43
Limoges-PTT	20,778	56	16,100	44
Radio-PTT-Nord	183,400	58	131,300	42
Marseille	29,492	54	24,893	46
Toulouse-Pyrénées	20,450	44	26,500	56
Nice-Côte d'Azur	16,050	60	10,500	40
Alpes-Grenoble	14,000	100	abstention	0
Totals	843,209	58	622,910	42

decide the result of the elections. The party appealed to people and families that individually owned radios as opposed to Radio-Liberté's appeal to the masses as a unified whole. Radio-Famille's more-frequent rhetoric touched on the emotions of fathers, asking them to protect their children from communist incursion on their lives and calling on them to create a safe and sane French radio. It spoke directly about the kinds of changes it wanted for the radio and gave voters a solid program for change. It wanted a radio that would distract, not bore or incite, listeners. It would preserve the home as a haven away from politics and the animosity of the public sphere. In its view, a conservative, Catholic radio would be a moral and emotional break from daily life. And although the Popular Front wanted to air an educational program of high culture and intellectual discussion, the masses did not necessarily embrace that idea.[102]

The editors of *Radio-Magazine* were cynical about the results, understanding that the elections were now for only one-third of the members of every radio council. Clément Vautel wrote about the candidates, "They will either be opportunists, and won't bother the rest of the administrators, who will be at the government's orders, or they will be overruled, crushed by the power of the official dictatorship."[103] *Le Figaro* agreed, at first rejoicing in the victory but later understanding that the advisory groups would have only a one-third membership from Radio-Famille. The newspaper blamed Jardillier and the Popular Front, angry that the councils would have had half the group as elected officials before Jardillier changed the rules. After these changes, Philippe Roland assumed that "the command levers are still in the hands of the government."[104]

Some chalked up the win to the boredom of the French listener, as did J.-G. Poincignon of *Mon Programme*: "In fact, we don't think that those who voted against *Radio-Liberté* are all hostile to the Popular Front. For many, the vote was a protest, not a profession of political faith. We know, as a fact, that many 'left wing' radio listeners voted against Radio-Liberté in fear that, if it won, they would see politics take a larger role in radio programs than at present. And these listeners keep proclaiming that want distraction, not indoctrination, from their radios."[105] Even right-wing George Nicolai, from *Le Petit Radio*, admitted in his summation of the election that "all the listeners are fully saturated with massive doses of lecture programs; they are unanimously hostile to debates on the air at mealtime."[106]

Standard radio journals often complained about boring radio programs. These journals claimed that private radio had the most interesting programming since it included variety and fun. Public radio, with its lectures, classical music, and canonical dramas could hardly compete with the constantly changing list of singing stars and comedians who performed on private radio. It is also clear from the election results that most listeners wanted a change. At the ballot box, the Popular Front's cultural radio project was a failure.

The Popular Front also began to seek ways to amuse its audiences as well as to educate them. After the election results were posted, *Radio-Liberté* changed its position about educating the public, trying to win back the support it had lost: "To defend the listeners means to concern oneself with programming that satisfies all tastes; that means getting listeners quality shows that are youthful, lively, diverse and distracting, because radio, above all, must distract."[107] As a result, the public stations began to add more light fare, which was interspersed into the regular programming.

This light fare consisted of a new emphasis on crime drama, with more plays by radio author and actor Jacques Cossin, whose show, *Half Hour of Crime Drama and Adventure*, was a great success with listeners.[108] The stations also increased the hours of variety shows, featuring new jazz orchestras who could play the latest swing hits from French and American songwriters. Jo Bouillon and his orchestra, a group comparable to, although less expensive than, Ray Ventura or Fred Adison, were featured often—up to four or five times a week—playing hits and dance music. Public stations began airing hit records, including American songs like Gershwin's "I Can't Get Started" and Cole Porter's "Easy to Love." Radio-PTT-Nord even spent an early evening playing Tino Rossi's hit music. Comedy acts like Bilboquet the clown and Jean, Jac, and Jo, who also acted on Radio-Cité, were now heard often on the state airwaves.[109]

Not everyone in the Popular Front agreed with this reprogramming, including the radio columnist at *Vendredi*. Almost every week radio critic Jacques Amaire commented on the stupidity of the new shows and acts that state radio broadcast.[110] Almost one year after the election he complained, "How many crimes (little ones—"criminiscules" we could say) must we commit in the name of competition with the private stations?"[111] The elections forced the Popular Front to make programming changes that moved its educational mission into the background.

All in all, the elections sent a clear message to the government that French citizens were dissatisfied with much of state radio.[112] The Popular Front failed to convince radio listeners of their cultural goals and radio project. They did continue with most of the programming they began in 1936, productions such as those by Art and Work and May 36. Much of it even outlasted the Popular Front altogether. But private radio had become much more important in the meantime, and public stations had to play catch-up to increase their popularity and placate their listenership, including much more light fare in their program hours. In spite of the hassle of commercials, private radio was much more capable of capturing the listening ear of France. Only the most banal public programming could compete—all the Boulevard theater and song that the Popular Front wanted so badly to do away with. After the elections even *Vendredi* had to admit, "Lately, as in the past, we have forgotten that the listeners want entertainment and liveliness. If we want to instruct and convince the public, we have to first avoid boring them instead. The private stations understand this."[113]

FAMILY VALUES AND FRENCH IDENTITY ON THE RADIO

4 AROUND THE CRADLE
Family Portraits for the Family Audience

As we can see, visions of the family dominated the perspective of private radio advertisers and programmers as they sold household products on a mass medium that gathered an audience by incorporating listeners into the new "family" or community of the individual stations. At the same time, the Catholic radio party Radio-Famille appealed to public radio listeners in the elections of 1937 with policies that called for a conservative moral framework for radio programs attached to patriarchal supervision of the family. Radio owners could not have but realized that the idealized bourgeois family had a primary relationship to radio culture and to their own listening practices. They voted Radio-Famille candidates into advisory positions on their own public stations, giving them an average of 67 percent of the tally across France. They also participated in huge numbers in the public broadcasts of their private stations and made those stations successful.

Both private radio advertisers and owners and public radio Advisory Board members and programmers had vested interests in keeping listeners at home and celebrating traditional gender roles and patriarchal order within stable families. Only with women home during the day could radio stations have a large enough audience for their programs and markets for their advertisements. The home even provided an ideal sphere for listening, as advertisers could plug household products while women used them or performed the daily tasks that required them. Radio station owners could sell daytime advertising time because companies were assured of an audience for their commercials. With this in mind, programmers treated women as a separate group, gearing distinct programming toward them at times when they were supposed to be listening alone. Radio critics, too, saw women's time at home as central to the creation of daytime shows. Daytime programming addressed women on the topics of housekeeping, cooking, gossip, and fashion and beauty advice. Yet although daytime programs were geared to women, radio programmers on both public and private radio saw men as the general radio listeners and programmed all family hours with them in mind. Evenings and weekends played for men first and women and children second.

Evening radio programmers reflected notions of a traditional patriarchal family, expanding shows' themes to fit male listeners into the schedule, especially in their depiction of bourgeois families and characters in radio plays, songs, and game shows. In a throwback to the nineteenth century, radio shows illustrated and celebrated the notion of separate spheres, with little regard to social and cultural changes that had come for women and men after World War I. Programmers, songwriters, and playwrights placed male characters in public spaces and female characters in the home, reasserting the power (and comfort) of the patriarchal, "traditional" family in a changing modern world. Radio's fictional men led heroic lives, while its women worried about their husbands, households, and children. The strong patriarch led the ideal fictional family with the tacit support of his motherly wife. Radio plays, songs, lectures, and variety programs focused on the stable family, with father working, mother at home, and children obeying patriarchal authority. Children were often only implicitly present in radio's fictional families, and their own voices were rarely heard over the air.[1]

This vision of family was especially ironic because many of radio's employees were the very women who day in and day out wrote and played traditional women characters. From Catholic women playwrights to soap opera mothers, from entertainment reporters to recipe givers, from songwriters to great singers with their own variety shows, women appeared prominently on the very programs that seemed to relegate them to daily work inside their own homes. Constantly working in the public on a mass medium, radio's women rarely challenged traditional assumptions about family and the private sphere in their roles on the radio. In fact, they often reinvested meaning into stereotypes, with playwrights making successful careers out of demanding maternal roles for their female listeners and actresses reminding listeners in interviews that their real-life first love was for their families, not for their burgeoning radio careers or stardom.

This traditional outlook had the tacit support of almost all the political groups in France on both the right and the left. In its 1937 radio-election rhetoric, Radio-Famille had articulated the opinions of many politicians concerning family policy and the ideology of separate spheres. By 1936 even the communists had given up their earlier call for gender equality within the proletarian revolution and had returned to an emphasis on "traditional" activities and single-sex organizations for women that taught housewifely arts in order to gain support for the party within the structure of the Popular Front.[2] Radio-Famille's rhetorical strategies of religious morality might not have appealed to the more secular left, but its ideas about home and family did not contradict socialist and radical policy.[3] Socialists had made feminists' and women's inclusion in their party quite difficult at the turn of the century, giving women little credit for the work they put into the creation of a new, viable, socialist party.[4] Though Léon Blum appointed three women ministers to his cabinet in 1936, he attempted only to assuage feminist interests and never made the appointment of women ministers a necessary part of government. Still hesitating to call for any changes in women's status in France, the socialists refused to place a suffrage statute in front of the Chambre des Députés or Senate.[5] The Radical Party was also central in denying women suffrage throughout the early twentieth century. During the interwar period, the radicals, afraid that women would vote conservatively and thus remove them from power, blocked all efforts for women's suffrage.[6] (It was ironic, then, that it was in the radio elections that women had the opportunity for suffrage.) In 1939, when the radicals reclaimed power in France without the Popular Front, they instituted the Code de la Famille, a set of laws that created a national, centralized family policy. The Code put family size before monetary need when creating French welfare, giving allocations for each child rather than focusing on whether the family had sufficient income for any children at all. The Code also imposed real punishments for abortionists and women seeking abortions. This decision fit into government policies about the fears of the declining birthrate in France.[7]

The tacit agreement of the left with the 1937 victory of Radio-Famille, combined with the strong desire of advertisers to sell household products directly into the home, allowed very little flexibility about and for families in programming on the radio. Radio programmers and critics assumed (incorrectly?) that fathers voted for their families in the radio elections and represented strong heads of household in political matters, and fathers were portrayed similarly over the air. Radio critics spoke about men and fathers as the radio listeners when they talked in general about radio programs. For example, when *Paris-*

Soir's radio critic Paul Reboux complimented Radio 37 on its program *The Bar of the Stars*, he thought about fathers and sons who listened together and benefited from the radio, not about mothers and daughters.[8] Germaine Blondin, too, wrote about the male listener and his female domestic servant behind the door when commenting favorably on Max Regnier's radio program. So although, as we shall see below, Blondin was particularly interested in women as listeners, she imagined the general listener as male.[9]

Housewives and women were of great specific concern to radio critics and programmers because of their assumed daytime role within the home. As we saw in the first two chapters, they were an obvious market to be targeted during the day, especially as (or if) they used the advertised household products as they listened. Also concerned about the real changes in gender roles in society, conservative male and female radio critics also wrote in the weekly radio guides about women and their more specific relationship to radio. Many felt that the radio could serve a special purpose for women, entertaining them during their time alone in the house and averting feminist attempts to destabilize the patriarchal family by encouraging women's equality and work outside the home. Most of the articles fell into typical stereotypes about women's sentimentality and lack of judgment. Often these editorials used the same stereotypes but contradicted each other. Each critic and writer purported to understand the behaviors of bourgeois women, yet each came to different conclusions about women's desires for radio and the ways that radio could address women's needs. Some saw the female listener as too difficult to understand; others saw her as the ideal radio listener; while still others thought she needed more support from radio programmers in order to satisfy her need for daily entertainment. None of the conservative critics saw radio as a useful medium for women who worked or for the "new women": the independent women who gained sexual and social freedom before and during World War I and thrived (at least in the public imagination) during the 1920s.[10] They envisioned women listeners ensconced in the household and wanted to keep them there.

Radio critic François Jardy, writing on the "psychology of the listener" in the radio guide *Le Petit Radio*, defined women as a listening public too complex for male programmers to truly fathom. He proved his own vision rather limited, however, by his use of stereotypical images that linked all women listeners to their male partners: "In this feminine public, there are different elements. The married woman, the happy woman, the unhappy woman, the woman in love, the discarded woman, the young maid, the old maid, the family mother."[11] To Jardy, men, on the other hand, were simple to understand because they "resembled each other more" since they were defined by their personal accomplishments and were not tied to their wives and mothers or defined by their varying sexual/contractual relationships and emotional states.

He remarked on woman's fickleness with the radio dial because "she [did] not belong to herself" but rather was controlled by her passions. For Jardy, "feelings dominate, but all-variable feeling, and music, like theater, like speeches, never fits [her emotions] exactly." Mysterious, ever-changing passions dominated women's choices of programming. Jardy saw the solution in "variety, imagination and a solid psychology from the men who create the programs." He envisioned a male-run and -programmed radio that could only attempt to reply to the sentimental and mysterious qualities of female listeners by varying programs and compensating for their short attention spans. This would thus create a loyal female audience.

Germaine Blondin, who contributed regularly to *Radio-Magazine* and lectured on and read French literature on public radio, saw women listeners quite differently from Jardy. She felt that male programmers had both the responsibility and the ability to program more effectively for women listeners. She wrote in *Le Petit Radio* that women needed radio more than men as women were in the home during the day, and thus programming had to focus more specifically on them. She knew that many bourgeois women were dissatisfied with their roles as housewives and mothers. She wanted to expand programming for women, but Blondin was no feminist. She did not want to encourage women to work or enter the public sphere. Instead, she wanted a radio that would appeal to "modern women" so that "women have no more desire to look outside the home for their happiness." She saw the radio as a model solution for boredom in the house and the dreams of leaving the domestic sphere behind: "Men believe that women's lot is enviable. They think that way because they are men. And most women might believe that too if there weren't all of those hazy, hollow and empty hours in their lives. And if, in those hours that were neither hazy nor empty, because they have to clean, sew, arrange, stay at home, the spirit did not wander, dream and get lost. And a woman who dreams is most often the woman who is bored, who is sad."[12] Blondin wanted radio to fill those hours with imagination and saw tremendous possibility for women to enjoy their domestic lives. "Radio can be a distraction and a lesson, a class and a party. The programs must be without banality, whether they are news, tours, plays or (why not?) lessons in morals and philosophy, guides to happiness, professors of optimism, judicious counsel." She looked for radio to work in opposition to feminists' demands for equality by keeping wives and mothers happily at home. Ironically, although she herself had a successful career in writing and broadcasting and must have spent most of her days in the public sphere, she believed in radio's possibilities for maintaining the traditional familial order in France.[13]

In 1938, Isabelle d'Urdes wrote a new (and short-lived) column for women listeners in *Radio-Magazine* to point them to programs of interest.[14] Like Blondin, Urdes saw traditional bourgeois domesticity as the reason that radio was so much more important to women than to men. In contrast to Jardy, she claimed that women were less likely to change the dial than men, as they were "more patient." Men, on the other hand, listened as "fugitive butterflies, perched on twenty different footholds, never actually landing anywhere." She called women more "faithful, assiduous, and persevering," thus more adapted to the radio and its programs.[15] Women would be willing listeners who could gain from the radio if only they knew when and how to listen.

Urdes viewed radio as a useful medium to dispense knowledge to the women at home during the day. But she did not see women as intelligent or serious enough to understand much of what the radio offered. She asked that knowledge not come in lectures, which she believed would be "too difficult" for women listeners, but in "amusing and lively anecdotes." She also wanted women to learn "information on the elegance of dress and beauty, the beauty and ease of conversation, making the places she moves in lovelier, and finding the solutions to one of the thousands of domestic problems that are posed each day to a busy housewife." Urdes knew that all of this information was already programmed into radio hours and so created her column to inform women listeners of exactly when they could tune in and learn. She saw her column as a place where women could also share their ideas about domestic and beauty matters, contributing to the ideal of bourgeois domesticity.

Paul Reboux, a centrist radio critic at *Paris-Soir*, understood the radio in gendered terms as well. While complimenting women at Radio-Paris on their programming talents, he explained that each type of programming had a certain hour at which the listeners would most appreciate it:

> Every Thursday morning, [*The Half Hour about the Home*] gives an analysis of the markets. I know very well that this news is also given in

the evening, at dinner time, when a parade of numbers about the price of livestock bores us exactly when we could do well without any news. That's why *The Half Hour about the Home* is on at exactly the right time. It indicates that the women who program the show have some understanding. Their program comes on at an hour when we feel like hearing news, and not at a time when we want to relax and have fun.[16]

For Reboux, radio needed stricter schedules that programmed specific time for women listeners, when information vital to their needs, like prices in the local markets, would play. He believed that radio programmers should have left general airtime in the evenings to entertainment only, when work-weary men listened. He also saw women's role as housewives as essential to the broadcast schedule.

Thus programming itself participated in the articulation of separate spheres, by scheduling women's shows solely during daytime hours, between nine in the morning and seven in the evening, when radio programmers assumed women to be at home alone doing housework. Their husbands, uninterested in women's programming, would be out of the house at work. For example, Radio-Lyon-PTT offered an hour of women's shows on Tuesday afternoons during the 1938–39 season. The slot began at 5:45 p.m. with the *Women's Program*, which featured songs and poems, followed by the *Feminine News* at 6:06. Afterward, two apparently useful lectures on womanly topics of interest aired. On November 8, for example, lectures played on "Fabric in the House" and "Taking Care of Your Hairdo." Thursday, in the late afternoon, Radio-Paris had its own *Women's News* at 5:45, with a lecture called "Women Travel Writers."[17]

As radio columnist Isabelle d'Urdes claimed, programmers geared a range of programming specifically toward women on the radio. These shows gave the household tips and beauty counsels that Urdes asked for in her radio column. In the 1937–38 season, for example, Radio-37 offered daily recipes from "Aunt Marcelle" at 7:00 p.m., at the moment when housewives would be cooking their own family dinners. They also had a Thursday evening program that combined radio personalities with the in-house women's magazine *Marie-Claire*, which premiered in 1937.[18] Radio-Cité offered a *Minute of Beauty* each evening that gave beauty tips to its listeners. Afterward they could tune in to the *Minute for the Perfect Housewife* for household tips. This "minute" was a gendered reflection of the *Minute of Good Sense* presented every evening by station host Saint-Granier. Saint-Granier's "good sense" appealed to a general audience and thus was accorded an 8:00 p.m. time slot, as opposed to the early evening spot for womanly advice about creating a "perfect" household. Other lectures from the week of February 13, 1937, included "Advice for Farmers' Wives," "The Baby," "What Shoes Are the Stars Wearing?" "Softening and Thinning the Waistline," from a physical education series, and the ever-useful "Plastic Surgery: The Responsibility It Can Bring."[19]

This kind of domestic- and beauty-oriented programming did have its critics. Left-wing feminists wanted a better selection of programs for women that did not make stereotypical assumptions about their interests and needs. Although disparaging the standard programming fare, these critics never challenged the notion that daytime radio served women who stayed home during the day or the idea that women had the responsibility to remain at home each day. To claim individualist feminist sensibilities could have repercussions. Left-wing feminists often had to choose between socialism and feminism. Women who challenged socialism's lack of enthusiasm for suffrage and feminist goals were often disparaged by the party as turning toward bourgeois and right-wing ideals, giving up the ultimate goals of socialism which had to come first.[20] And most French feminists understood themselves as essentially female and different, or "relational," as historian Karen Offen has noted, tied to their families and status as mothers and wives.[21] Part of feminist radio critics' inability to problematize the status of the family on and off the radio also may have come from their attempt to gain suffrage and equal rights on the basis of sexual difference. As historian Joan Wallach Scott points out, while giving them a reason to participate, a focus on women's inherent difference paradoxically hurt feminists' campaigns. How, as a different kind of citizenry, as domestic wives and mothers first, could women ever truly be equal to men?[22]

In *Radio-Liberté,* the radio journal for the Popular Front, Suzanne Cilly expressed the frustration of many women when she targeted women's programming directly:

> No more expensive, impracticable kitchen recipes that are almost impossible to transcribe, unless one is a practiced stenographer. No more beauty advice that the majority of listeners cannot use (like reasons for plastic surgery that in even the smallest case costs thousands of francs)! No more heavy and conformist lectures about Saint Jeanne of Chantal or Madame de Maintenon! No more interviews with screen, sports or theater stars, which reveal their incredible lack of knowledge and

large egos! No more mundane speeches in which the speaker's vanity is only equal to her pretension, like that lecture by Madame Fernandez, on Paris-PTT, on the importance of optimism and serenity in the conservation of beauty. No more Maurice de Waleffe, born Kertoffel, foreign-born, as her name indicates, with French taste and beauty marks, speaking endlessly about her memories of Buenos-Aires.[23]

Here Cilly lambasts all of the basic forms of women's programming from the cooking and beauty shows to Catholic plays to gossip columns. Unlike Germaine Blondin, she did not hear on the radio a solution available to women. She did not expect that radio could or would change on its own. Cilly called her readers to action: "It is up to [women radio listeners] to fight so that women's shows lose their superficial, stupid and vain character that they have in the majority of cases, and, without losing listenership, gain interest and meaning." Cilly, although disgusted with radio's bland and useless offerings, did not picture radio as a site to change French women's lives. She only wanted programming as intelligent as the women who listened. She knew that women performed housework at home during the day and thus needed programming adapted to educated people who led nonpublic lives. She expected more nonconformity and intelligence from female listeners and an equal response from radio programmers. For Cilly, the audience was there. Programmers simply needed to recognize it.

In spite of this continued rhetoric, standard gendered programming rules did not always apply. Radio-Paris offered a weekly fifteen-minute wrap-up of the "feminine press" that featured articles from feminist newspapers. And public radio offered some lectures on women's political issues, although usually quite short and sandwiched by more standard programming. For example, Lyon-PTT offered a weekly *Women's Hour* at 12:15 on Thursdays that featured lectures such as "A Businesswoman's Rights," talks that explained more serious issues that working women confronted. But the lesson in economics was placed between a lecture called *The Facial Feature of the Week* and one titled *Hygiene and Beauty*, both of which downplayed the former's social and political significance. Although the *Women's Hour* sometimes featured feminist and political issues, the show never guaranteed time for serious lectures and never placed serious issues at its center. Sometimes women gave longer talks, perhaps on Tour Eiffel, the public education station, which offered an afternoon lecture on "Understanding Feminism." Most stations furnished little time, however, for women's political groups to have their say. Lille-PTT-Nord programmed time for the Union for Women Suffrage but gave the group only ten minutes of early evening programming, a period of time that did not come close to matching the amount given to other groups and lectures, which often filled whole half-hour and hourlong blocks. No feminist or politically significant lectures appeared on any regular schedule, and none at all were programmed into private radio hours.

While lectures and educational programs were given short shrift, the extremely popular and controversial *The Women's Forum*, a weekly open-mic show on Radio-Cité, proved the only consistent exception to this rule. In the 1937 and 1938 seasons, *The Women's Forum* and Radio-Cité invited all women to come and speak on the radio. For thirty minutes every week, women freely voiced their opinions about cultural, political, and social subjects ranging from current cinema, to the question of women's right to vote, to the positive and negative impacts of working outside the home. The show was the most polemical part of a new and larger public programming strategy for Radio-Cité, which featured three weekly forums that would give voice to those commonly left out of on-air radio commentary.[24] These programs, as we saw in chapter 2, came from the open-door strategy to encourage wider listenership. The first of these open-mic shows, *The Radio-Cité Forum*, aired each Sunday evening. It featured the weekly mailbag and open microphone for all Radio-Cité listeners who could comment about any programming choices the station made. The second show of the triumvirate, *The Youth Forum*, aired on Thursday afternoons, the weekday that children had off from school, and allowed its teenage listeners to discuss topics that they chose. The third public debate show was *The Women's Forum*.

Each week *The Women's Forum* featured a different issue for debate, always in a full studio theater. Any adult woman could participate in the program, although in its second season, after a scheduling change, the participants would be practically limited to bourgeois women. Although in its first season the show was broadcast live on Saturday afternoons, in its second season it was switched to Tuesday afternoons at 2:30, so only bourgeois women with no work or child-care obligations could come to the tapings. While working-class women were likely to have been too busy working either at home or at their jobs to arrive for midweek broadcasts, bourgeois women often had in-home help to take of children and most did not work outside the home. Those who could come to the studio would line up on the sides of the stage to take their turns at the microphone. The only man present in the studio was the director of the show, but he did not often get involved, leaving the debates up to the women. After they made their points, all of the speakers would join the audience in listening to the comments and debate. At the end of each show, a vote would be taken to see where the audience stood on the issue of the day.

The show sometimes focused on nonpolitical topics like opinions about current cinema and novels, but most of the debates centered on serious political and economic issues that affected bourgeois women and their families. The debaters sometimes talked about more traditionally male-centered topics like national defense, as in the 1930s France faced a double threat of fascism and communism, but generally they debated family and women's issues. Many of the debates concentrated on three major issues: whether work or education outside of the home was expected for married women and mothers; how raising children affected their responsibilities as mothers to their families and the state; and lastly, whether women should have the right to vote (which they did not until 1945). The women participants asked and answered each other's questions about welfare and family allocations given to families by the government. They questioned the social responsibility of the government to families and children. They debated whether women should not have children in a time of economic crisis or whether they should continue pronatalist behavior, birthing the next generation of citizens. All of the debates raged on both sides of every issue, with loud and frank discussions from the ordinary women who took turns at the microphone. These average women displayed an eagerness to be part of public life and debate, to express their opinions, and to discuss topics outside of the traditional and expected realm of female conversation.

Sometimes famous feminists would make appearances on the show to lend their weight to the debates. Yvonne Netter, a feminist lawyer famous for her cases about women's issues, came to the show at the end of its first season. Featured prominently in the French press, Netter argued for women's suffrage and legal changes in the status of women and, especially, wives.[25] On *The Women's Forum,* she argued that all women had an obligation, not a choice, to work in the public sphere, because women who stayed at home lost touch with the political, social, and cultural realities of their nation. Without the contact with the full social and political world, she claimed, women could not properly run households and raise the next generation of citizens.[26] For Netter, women had a responsibility, not a right, to work outside of the home and to become fully functional denizens of France. Needless to say, her comments sparked serious discussion on both sides of the issue, especially as, unlike Yvonne Netter, the great majority of women who participated in the debates did not work outside of the home.

In a sense, all of the debates on *The Women's Forum* were about bourgeois women's role in society. All of the economic and social issues the women touched on led back to their responsibilities and obligations as bourgeois wives and mothers. Women debated topics as gendered quasi-citizens, without the vote, but with sincere interest in affecting the debates about and the realities of their own lives as French citizens. Whether pro or con, no matter what their political position, women vigorously debated the issues that were close to them, showing how concerned they were with topics that most radio programmers assumed were out of their depth and interest. Women, in their forum, joined the public sphere and influenced, or believed they could influence, the men that made the political decisions about their lives.

Reaction to this show, both pro and con, was strong, with many letters to the station carping on how women had no right to discuss these kinds of topics on the air as they had no innate intelligence, only innate feeling, and others commending women for their outspoken opinions. In 1939, an angry journalist, political scientist, and teacher at the Lycée le Grand, Hubert Bourgin, wrote a column in the radio station Radio-Cité's guide. Bourgin, as a man, wanted, and felt he had a right, to give his own public opinion of the show and its participants. But he could only have his say in print, because there was no room for him on the all-women format of the show. In describing the program's participants, he had this to say: "In general inept at forming ideas, at convincing and pleasing in argument, woman says nothing about what she thinks but only about how she feels or measures her feelings. Her opinions are nothing but the reflections of those feelings, and all of her emotional and passionate personality shows itself . . . to the depth of her tastes, her desires, her instincts, her temperament. . . . Is it not true that the distinctive disposition of women brings nothing to these debates but ignorance?"[27] Bourgin was angry about the quality of debates he heard on the show, and he used stereotypical images of women (as François Jardy did) to debunk them. *The Women's Forum* clearly hit a nerve with him because he felt that bourgeois women had no right to be on the air or in the public sphere at all. And Radio-Cité's management willingly placed his opinion in its own fan newspaper, as it came from an intellectual source, a professor who had written numerous works on politics and democracy.[28] Perhaps the editors and programmers silently agreed in part, or perhaps they understood that the controversy surrounding the show only made it, and in turn the station, more popular.

Many other listeners wrote letters to the station saying that women's voices sounded awful over the microphone, especially when raised in angry debate. (Public radio had no women announcers at all because the debate over the ugliness of women's voices on the microphone raged on throughout the 1930s.)[29] Letter writers probably used this complaint to express an intrinsic dislike of women in the public sphere, in political debates on the radio. Between 1938 and 1939, out of the fifteen or so letters that the station published in its weekly guide, *Ici . . . Radio-Cité,* an average of ten a week dealt with *The Women's Forum.* The extraordinary response to the show in print showed the anxiety that many citizens had in a culture of changing gender roles. Whether feminist or antifeminist, women and men listened to the show regularly and wanted to join in the debates. Thus *The Women's Forum* was an amazing exception to the standard rule—this program was a place where women's voices were heard first, without moderation, and without strong male control.[30]

It is important to understand that the medium of radio was essentially controlled by men, and on radio male journalists, politicians, and critics constantly talked about political issues in which women had almost no say. The fact that so many women participated (the studio theater was always full), and the fact that so many people responded to the show by letter, showed that Radio-Cité had hit a chord by giving women a rare moment to speak out freely over the air. It also showed that standard women's radio programming, focusing on bourgeois domesticity, often missed the mark, or at least did not reflect the scope of women's desires for programs. These shows left out issues and ideas in which women listeners wanted more information and more participation.

Though a significant counterweight to the standard women's programming, *The Women's Forum* never truly challenged notions of a patriarchal mastery of women's voices. With the show, Radio-Cité's programmers relegated women's free-flowing speech to a specific half hour each week. Producers assumed that all the other hours of broadcasting not specifically set aside for women spoke to men. This was why women needed a special half hour of programming to be heard at all. Programmers did not invite their political, public voices into the radio as a whole, either in news segments or in other "serious" programming. The only other forum (and public program) closed to men was *The Youth Forum,* in which children debated issues that concerned them. In this way then, *The Women's Forum* placed women's views in the same realm as those of their children, outside of the framework of standard radio fare and evening hours. Bourgeois women's speech, like that of children, had to be regulated in a defined space on the air, ultimately subject to patriarchal control, and ultimately not heard by many men (or women) who worked during the day.

Evening hours, unlike daytime airplay, operated under a different notion of what constituted the radio public. Programmers assumed that fathers listened, men who wanted entertainment after a long day's work, as Paul Reboux reminded *Paris-Soir* readers in 1936.[31] Radio stations filled evening airtime with radio plays, singing groups, and variety and game shows that men could enjoy with their families. Yet these plays, shows, and songs came with their own messages about traditional family values, showing patriarchal heads how their own families should ideally be organized. The programs maintained the power of a traditional family scheme of separate spheres that once again fed political and advertising interests.

Mary Lou Roberts's analysis of the reinvestment of meaning into patriarchal gender roles after the First World War can be helpful in understanding the ways in which both men and women were under attack on radio in the 1930s.[32] In the period immediately following World War I, in which changing fashion, a shifting gender balance, and depopulation created a fear of the "new woman," a flourishing of literature and cultural products showed intellectuals' attempts to place women squarely back into the home in their traditional gender role as wife and mother. The literary production only masked the strong undercurrent of change in interwar society, as gender roles shifted and women began taking on more powerful roles in the public sphere, and as people tried to cope with new systems of power and a failing Third Republic. Similarly, radio fiction and song promoted the ideal of the traditional patriarchal family in response to both advertisers' needs for a market in the home and the pressures of pronatalist sentiment in government, coupled with an unwillingness of political parties to take up the rallying cries of feminists and feminist causes in France.

Evening radio plays and fictional portrayals of men and women outside the scope of gender-specific programming showed the prevailing influence of the notion of separate spheres, with male heroes in the public sphere, acting the part of workingmen and heroes in French plays. These portrayals reinvested meaning into the patriarchal family, giving all radio listeners (and especially men, as the assumed general listeners) notions of ideal family behavior.

Men played the roles of heroes, risking their lives as soldiers for France and family. Women characters reflected women's place in the private sphere; as mothers and love-struck heroines in danger, fictional women were always led by their emotions, physically frail, and in constant need of rescue. Bourgeois women who transgressed their role in the private realm were brought back into the fold by the men they eventually learned to love. Even feminist bourgeois women, as we shall see, learned the folly of their radical ways and gave up struggles for equality to regain their positions as housewives and mothers.[33]

Images of male heroes dominated the airwaves, giving listeners plenty of male role models that they could follow. Families gathered around the radio heard actors and stories that brought powerful men to life. The airwaves' characterizations endowed great rhetorical power to patriarchal right and responsibility. Melodramatic songs, like Edith Piaf and Damia's renditions of "Mon Légionnaire" and "La Fanion de la Légion," featured brave soldiers dying on the colonial battlefield.[34] Wily cops understood the minds behind devilish murders in Jacques Cossin's radio series *Half-Hour of Crime Drama and Adventure*. Radio fiction depicted men as brave fighters who were willing to die for justice and country in plays like *Allô Blima . . . Ici 283*,[35] while radio depicted even nonfictional men consistently as heroes who placed nation and family above every other consideration.[36] Many of these notions of masculinity seemed to hark back to the honorable ideals of the Belle Epoque, prior to the slaughter on the battlefields of World War I.[37]

True Stories, another weekly program on Radio-Cité, which ran Wednesday evenings during the 1938-39 season, spotlighted true stories about courageous French men in difficult and often life-threatening situations. Written by Hugues Nonn, a (misogynist) playwright who also wrote plays for public radio,[38] the series featured the acting of George Colin's premier radio acting troupe.[39] Week after week, these plays gave credence to a particular vision of masculinity and nation. The show focused on what the station called "honest people," or exemplary Frenchmen that listeners could both admire and relate to.[40] A true Frenchman had courage under fire, acted publicly, and yet was always responsible to his family and to France. The show gave continual examples of the French "hero" and used the finest actors to incarnate images of the "best" qualities of French male citizens.

The plays covered events such as daring rescues and dangerous exploits, sometimes soldiers' experiences during World War I.[41] The first show featured the dangerous and difficult conflict at the Fort de Vaux, which thousands of

French soldiers died defending, losing, and recapturing during the yearlong battle of Verdun in 1916.[42] When one of the veterans of the battle called the station during the play to comment on the action heard on the radio, he forever changed the direction of the weekly program. The station called for the veterans of the battle to show up and participate in a postshow discussion of the events of the fight. In all, fifty-seven veterans came to the studio for the conference. Afterward, the writers and producer tried each week to contact living witnesses to join in postplay conversation and interviews.[43] Whenever it was possible, the actual people in the newly fictionalized drama came to present their views. Marcel Bleustein-Blanchet, owner of Radio-Cité, claimed in his history of the station that these participants "confirmed the authenticity" of the show. He thought that the show "displayed a variety of experiences, and the listener had . . . the sense of participating in the program."[44] Male listeners, then, may have seen the heroes as role models, hoping that one day their own heroic life would in turn be presented by Radio-Cité.

A perfect example from *True Stories* presented the saga of a pilot who fought to survive for eight days in subzero temperatures in the Andes mountains. The drama expressed the romance, heroism, and danger inherent in a life in aviation. Henri Guillaumet, the pilot on whom the story was based, worked with Antoine de St.-Exupery as an aviator for the post office, which gave him status and credibility with listeners who already knew of St.-Exupéry's exploits through his travel writing. For Guillaumet, personal honor was essential to his survival. He claimed that if he had died, "my friends would say I was a bastard if they thought I hadn't fought until the end." While he was risking his life for France and then awaiting rescue, his family always stayed in his mind. The character in the play cried when he believed he would die, saying, "Goodbye to everyone; my last thought will be for my wife." Both family and France were central to the play's characterization and heroization of Henri Guillaumet, as they were central to the station's message as a whole. Guillaumet himself came to the studio to be interviewed after the reenactment of his "true story," putting more emphasis on the fact that he was not a fictional hero, but a real Frenchman, to be admired and held up as an example to listeners.

Other plays, these all fictional and appearing on many stations, also equated maleness with bravery. For example, in *Helen, Divine among Women*, a play about the missing story in the Iliad of Helen's life during the Trojan War, included a speech by Helen on the merits of her husband Menelaus as opposed to Paris. She reassures Menelaus when he frets about Paris's good looks, "But my love, he was not a man! I mean to say that Paris was not a soldier, a brave man . . . like you!"[45] Helen and Louis Jean Lespine, the playwright, wrapped up ideal notions of manhood in bravery and service to the nation through the army, making Menelaus the hero and Paris, lost in his passionate thrall of Helen, a blithering idiot.

In its programming, radio also often presented traditional views of bourgeois women. With Catholic plays about nation and motherhood, and songs about fairy-tale love, radio programmers assumed that the bourgeois women who listened to the radio while they stayed at home cared for little other than motherhood, domestic duties, and frivolous passions and thought nothing of the social and political issues of the day. Like the standard women's daytime programming, these programs reinforced ideas about separate spheres, locating women inside the home, concerning their lives with domesticity, ignoring the male world of public life. These radio plays brought to life the conservative radio critics Germaine Blondin and François Jardy's visions of womanhood and served a dual purpose: entertaining women at home while giving model impersonations of desirable female behavior.

Radio was a medium in which noble women characters displayed traditional ideas about how real women should have behaved rather than how actual women behaved. In radio characterizations, women were timid mothers, vain, beautiful, and unable to control their feelings. Playwrights and lyricists defined women by beauty and chastity before intelligence and honesty. Beginning in 1935, the radio stations even elected an annual "Muse of the Radio" or an audio-radio Miss France whose voice would represent that of the perfect woman. These women were also supposed to be physically beautiful, something obviously entirely useless in a studio behind a microphone. They were to represent womanhood to all radio listeners, something that seemed newsworthy, although ridiculous, to some radio critics. Lucien Leluc, of *Le Petit Radio*, admired the second muse, Françoise Leloup-Morhange, "Muse 1937," for her figure and voice, but he thought that her election was rather silly. Understanding, however, that a "Muse" could bring new listeners to the medium, Leluc wrote sarcastically, "The Radio, like everything else in this world, alas, also needs its advertising!"[46] A "Miss Radio" made women's voices easier to listen to. After all, if one could imagine the disembodied voices as beautiful women, one might accept them on the radio and in one's home.

The first Muse, Yvonne Galli (1936), starred in *The Duraton Family*, a daily soap opera (also on Radio-Cité) that centered on the conversation at a daily family meal. She played the mother of the perfect Duraton family, a happy couple and two adoring and sprightly children. The show perfected her role as a Muse and ideal woman, making her the most popular mother in France, on the most popular soap opera, on the most popular radio station.

The Duraton Family depicted conversations during family meals that aired while families themselves enjoyed lunch or, later on, dinner.[47] Each day, the radio family gathered around the table and improvised a family meal with a famous guest, with neighbors and friends joining them when celebrities were unavailable. Perhaps fueling family listeners' table conversations, or perhaps precluding the need for mealtime talk at all, the Duratons became a popular part of radio programming and an enduring image of domestic felicity, one that lasted, with only a short break during the war, until 1954.[48]

Each family member fulfilled stereotypes of the bourgeois home: the father talked politics and news and controlled the flow of conversation, the mother dispensed daily household advice and talked about the domestic economy, the son talked sports and car racing and sometimes brought his fiancée to dinner, while the feisty daughter brought along the daily celebrity guest (usually a theater or singing star) and shared celebrity gossip and beauty advice. In her autobiography, Lise Elina, who played the daughter, categorized the family members as "a petty bourgeois functionary for a father, a housewife-mother, a sporty son and a journalist daughter."[49] She described her character, Lisette, in the Radio-Cité radio guide: "If I believe what my dad and brother think of me, I'm an unbearable ditz, and mom's advice should be welcome to me. But if my parents would let me talk—and if I dare to speak—I might just have my own little opinions. And anyway, with all of the guests at the house, I guess I'll end up getting married!"[50] Lise Elina saw her character as a typical girl teenager. Although opinionated, she envisioned a future when she would be like her mother: married and giving advice to her own daughter.

Yvonne Galli acted as her fictional daughter's role model. She saw the mother as "a homebody" who directed the family budget in order to prepare the daily meals. She liked staying in and saw her responsibility as private, not public: "After all, I need to stay in to make our small budget match the expense of feeding all the guests that come over!"[51] Galli, in an interview in *Radio-Magazine,* claimed that her favorite job was being a mother and that she much preferred her radio work as a children's story reader to that on *La Famille Duraton.*[52] In this, she let radio listeners know that even for a big radio star, motherhood and her own family took precedence over work and a successful career, and working for children's programs carried more weight for her than playacting for adults.[53]

The stability of the family had an important place in the culture of the radio. Many radio plays about women and their families supported pronatalist arguments, calling for the national obligation to motherhood. Since the late eighteenth century, the birthrate in France had been declining, and by the interwar period (after the heavy losses in World War I), the decrease in population began to be seen as a threat to security. Many in France were afraid of the low birthrates and pressed women to have large families as their responsibility to the state. In the 1930s the birthrate was an important issue for almost every political group in France. Almost every major politician (barring Léon Blum) gave speeches on the subject, out of concern for France's ability to survive as a nation, especially under the threat of another war with Germany.[54] Some conventions about radio even called for government radio programs that would instill pronatalist ideas in the polity.[55]

Cita and Suzanne Malard, a Catholic mother-daughter team, wrote radio plays about pious Catholic women and saints and, in their two-act play called *The Survivors*, even recreated Genesis in a French context to show how after an Armageddon-like destruction of the world, French life and family would continue if its living citizens held up their pronatalist responsibilities. In the play the last man and woman on earth find each other in a village and fall in love, assuring the rebirth of the French state.[56] The man and woman in the story take on the appropriate gender roles right from the start of their relationship. He asks her why she is crying, and she replies, "I am made like snow. Everything was cold in me, but since you are here I can be weak because you are strong." Here the Malards showed that strong women on their own denied their true nature. In spite of surviving alone until she meets the man, the woman relinquishes her power to him. Women needed men to be strong for them.[57]

Henriette Charasson, a Catholic activist with numerous radio plays and household guides to her credit, wrote a blatant propaganda piece called *Mothers of Paris: Around the Cradle*.[58] The play opens with an interview with Charasson as she extols the French family and women's primary role as mothers, and it continues with various women's experiences in daily Parisian life. While sanctifying all mothers by comparing their nursing to that of the Virgin Mary, this play villainizes the childless woman who is happy that she has no sons who could die in war. Her friend responded, as "The Marseillaise" played in the background: "What do you think would have happened to France if all French women had purchased peace of mind with childlessness? I bless the God that allowed me to be a mother. Even when hearing the explosions of a brutal and shaky Europe, and even in front of you women without worry and without children, nothing would stop me from crying out to God, 'Thank you, my Lord, thank you for maternity!'"[59]

This pathetic play was greatly appreciated by audiences—enough to encourage a second broadcast. An editorialist from the Catholic *L'Epoque* commented: "Too often we at *L'Epoque* critique the public stations that have neither the respect for their listeners, nor the care for their understanding. Today we have to congratulate the director of programming for the show 'Women of Paris,' which asked Mme. Henriette Charasson to replay the mother's sketch 'Around the Cradle.'"[60]

Henriette Charasson also wrote Catholic poetry that she read over the air. Poems like "Ballad to Mary" stressed domestic responsibility coupled with the divine nature of separate spheres:

> Mother of God, divine housekeeper
> Who labors in the celestial pews,
> Angelic queen, and poor while on earth,
> Always occupied with scrubbing the home,
> Cooking, fetching water from the well,
> Teach us this art of sacrifice
> Because we would be used to disappointment
> If only we wanted nothing but to gain justice![61]

As the Catholic radio plays focused on the saintliness of motherhood, others commented on women's inability to control their emotions without the strong presence of solid men in their lives. In *Marcus*, a young girl runs to the city when she has no father to care for her and eventually becomes a prostitute with an illegitimate child.[62] Helen, in *Helen, Divine among Women*, alone in Troy without the soldierly Menelaus's support, becomes obsessed with beauty and jewels.[63] In *Portraits of Honest Women in the French Novel*, a nameless man and woman discuss the characters in Balzac and Molière and come to the conclusion that when analyzed closely, women characters are never truly "honest" and "good." About Elmire from *Tartuffe* they agree, "Elmire may be an honest woman, but really she is a tease." About Madame de Montsauf from "The Lily of the Valley" the woman narrator must begrudgingly point out the character's love for Felix and her desire for a man other than her husband.[64]

The Voices from the Shadows, by Louis Gratias, shows both negative and positive possibilities for married men and women.[65] In the play, a man, Jacques, leaves his wife, Yvonne, for a career-making science expedition to the Arctic, saying, "For you, I want to be ambitious." He understands that his work and support of his family must come first, but he does not trust that his wife will remain faithful while he is away. Her women friends encourage her to cheat with a former lover, showing their true character as women saying, "Men, you should treat them as they deserve." Jacques is also confronted with temptation while on expedition, as the European men around him take lovers among the Inuit women. Yet none of the others have wives at home. Another character in the play, a doctor, has "an adventure" at every stop and doesn't blame the native women for their actions, as he knows that "they are not responsible" for their extramarital affairs.

Radio fiction writers instead connected women's honor to the successes, if not the faithfulness, of their husband. The play ends with Jacques's return and faithfulness on both sides. His wife, however, must admit that she struggled and almost succumbed to her former love. Yvonne tells Jacques, "A woman alone . . . the temptation . . ." as if without his presence she was overcome with her emotion. Although they both faced temptation, he makes no apologies for his own behavior and she never suspects him of anything but faithfulness in the face of her own mental deceit. In this play, a woman's fidelity has more value than a man's, although only the best of either sex ever seems to remain true in the face of an enticement. The family here holds firm, with a happy ending and a moral lesson about fidelity.

Dollars, by Raoul Praxy, encouraged marriage while discouraging outward feminist and independent behavior in women, taking a shot at the idea of the *femme moderne* of the postwar period.[66] In the play, a young woman named Simone compares marriage to "slavery" and tells her mother of her fears of "a man for whom you are nothing, only to realize that the day you marry he'll have rights over you. . . . No, no, mom, I really love you, I would love to make you happy, but don't ask me, please, to satisfy you by sacrificing my Liberty." Because Simone decides not to marry and will remain single forever, Praxy sets her up as the character who needs to grow and change to find true happiness in marriage by the end of his play.

Her old school friend and dramatic foil Yahne Saintoge sees men as her only option out of poverty. Having become a high-class prostitute, she uses men for their wealth and hopes one day to marry one of her "suitors." Yahne tells Simone, "A young girl, not too ugly, with a diploma, without any money, has only two resources . . . and I never had the guts to be a teacher." Yahne, an unsacrificing girl, knows that she will gain status if she gains a proper husband and understands that she will have to use her beauty and sexuality to get one.

Over the course of the play, in order that she may learn her lessons of true feminine behavior and be paid back for her frigid temperament, Simone herself gets mistaken for a prostitute (and her mother, her madam), almost raped, and locked in a hotel room with a strange man. Because the latter man does not try to rape her, Simone falls in love with him, calling him a "gentleman," finally recognizing that men are not hypocrites after all. In the world of *Dollars*, Simone has learned that as a single woman, her own morality, reputation, and social status rely on the acquisition of a good husband.

Simone's feminist sensibilities do not take much pressure to fall apart. She loses them after only one chaste night with an honest man. She, like all French women should, marries when she finds the right man. And in the play even the hardened Yahne finds true love and marriage. In a play of opposites, marriage saves Simone from a frigid life and Yahne from an oversexed one. In these two characters, the play points to the extremes of women's behavior and extols marriage as the moderate, sensible, and necessary solution for all single women. It was also the natural situation for women and the one they inevitably would search for, no matter how much they protested, as Simone did at the beginning of the play.

Perhaps one of the most blatant references to the assumed roles of the sexes came in Arletty's 1934 hit song, "Woman Is Made for Man." With a catchy tune, with a repeating musical theme with short lines and a simple lyrical structure, this song made use of the biblical story of Adam and Eve to speak about the hierarchy of the genders:

> Woman is fashioned for man,
> Like the apple tree for the apple,
> Like the bird is made for the rose bush,
> And the nest for the bird.[67]

Arletty, a woman, sang of her role in society with a happiness that reiterated gender stereotypes. Arletty's singing voice was also incredibly high and shrill, increasing the comic side to the song, while exaggerating her own femininity to a stereotypical degree. The song also had a lively dance tempo. Listeners could dance while they listened:

> Yes for man woman is made
> Like the ring for the napkin,
> Like the record is made for the phonograph,
> And the finger for the engagement ring!

Appropriately, the song places marriage at the center of the hierarchical relationship between a man and his wife.

While *Dollars* and "Woman Is Made for Man" celebrated both the necessity of marriage for a woman andthe natural patriarchal order, *Yesterday Evening* showed the ideal of French feminine behavior once in a marriage.[68] As the play opens, Marius, a middle-management businessman, does not appreciate his wife, Hélène, and belittles what she does for him at home, saying, "That's not work . . . feminine occupations." He also resents her mother, claiming that she undermines him with her constant complaints about their financial status. Hélène never complains but just continues her work, begging for a small allowance so she can keep up her housekeeping. She is the perfect domestic partner—silent and supportive.

Hélène proves herself worthy of Marius's praise when she thwarts the sexual advances of his boss, Gilbert. She is even so innocent as to believe that Gilbert's compliments are directed at her husband's work, not her own beauty. When she finally sees the truth, Hélène slaps Gilbert and sends him off, sure that Marius will be fired. Instead Gilbert gives Marius a promotion to chief of personnel with a hefty pay raise that will change their lifestyle forever, moving them into the ranks of high officials. This promotion comes not for Marius's merits in business, but for Hélène because, as Gilbert writes to her in a letter, "One does not often have the opportunity to encourage virtuous behavior." Hélène never tells her husband neither of the sexual incident of the "yesterday evening" of the title nor of the reasons for his promotion. As a virtuous, exemplary wife she gives him the credit of her success. She even gives the cheating boss a toast, calling him nice and forgiving him for his actions because they allowed her silently to give a reward to the man she loves.

Hélène's actions are all the more worthy because if she had the affair she would have been better off financially than she was with Marius, and her affair would probably have garnered Marius a promotion anyway. But by remaining virtuous she gains greater security and keeps her honor while staying within a solid family and household. Hélène's behavior underscored the importance (and seeming rarity and thus exquisite value) of female virtue. By giving Hélène (through the promotion of her husband) a reward, the play served as a lesson to encourage virtuous behavior in other unhappy wives. It reminded them that they had to live for their husbands and take pleasure in the success that would reward selfless behavior. Only with uncomplaining behavior would wives get their reward in the happiness of a secure home and satisfied husband. As Venus says to Vulcan in *Venus Justified*, after she flirts with every god on Mount Olympus, "A good wife must help her husband, using every power at her disposal."[69] And Marius and Hélène's financial security also offered them the ability to have children, thus fulfilling Hélène's pronatalist and natural role as mother to the next generation of virtuous citizens.

One popular song chose to flip gender roles for comedic effect. "It's for My Dad," sung by Georges Milton, jokingly proved to families how crazy gender bending could be. Milton sings in a baby's high voice about his family and the chaos that ensues when his mother and father swap places in the house. His father occupies the private sphere, cooking and cleaning, while his mother "enjoys herself" out with the guys. He begins with the simple line, "I have parents who are all mixed up":

> Dad is small and wimpy
> While my mother is big, pretty and plays sports. . . .
> Making fried eggs, that's for my dad,
> Having fun, that's for my mom.
> The tango, that's always for my mother,
> The broom, that's always for my father.
> Feeding the cats, that's for my dad,
> Going to the bank, that's for my mom![70]

The song ends with Milton's father taking the dog out to pee while his mother parties with her gigolo suitors! The comedic nature of the song reinvested meaning into the bourgeois idea of the separate spheres by ridiculing the father who lost control of his household and his wife. The song also privileged public over private space. The care of the house and children, a role that usually belongs to women, is drudge work while activities outside the home seem obviously more pleasant. And women were incapable of acting responsibly in the public sphere. She does not act like a man—the mother in the song does not work, talk politics, or take charge of the family accounts; rather she shops, flirts, and gossips. Surely listening audiences laughed with Milton as he sang about gender role reversal. They expected the typical stereotypes, which fit into the pattern that the majority of radio songs and plays offered to listeners.

Many popular songs played into traditional gender tropes by focusing on dream men and women as objects of desire, often including an overarching theme of unattainable fairy-tale love. As in radio plays, ideas supporting separate spheres appear in many of the songs, but unlike the fleshed-out characters in plays, many songs created dream men and women who never appear and remain imaginary ideals sung of from a distance. Dream men were to be strong protectors, who worked to provide for the women they loved. Imagined or remembered women were innocent and lovely, showing weakness and a gentle nature, waiting patiently for their princes to rescue them from the ordinariness of their lives.

Song after song showed women waiting patiently for the perfect men who remained ephemeral and untouchable. In Josephine Baker's 1937 hit "It's Him," she sang of her perfect love.[71] Lilian Harvey also sang of her true dream mate in the 1934 release "Is This a Dream?"

> I found my prince charming,
> Like in romance novels. . . .
> Could this be a dream?
> A pretty dream?
> It's too beautiful to be true.[72]

The lyric was a forebear of the later Disney tune "Someday My Prince Will Come," the French version of which was also a hit in 1938.[73] As prescriptive modern fairy tales, both songs suggest passive female behavior rather than real twentieth-century accounts of love. Perhaps the dream lover gave people hope against life lived during the deep economic depression of the thirties, but the "prince charming" image left women waiting alone and men coping with unrealistic role models. Neither men nor women could truly ever live up to the fantasy.

While female singers crooned about their ideal, princely mates, some men sang songs about the perfect marriageable bourgeois partners who, like the dream men, remained unattainable. Michel Simon let his listeners know about his one chance at happiness in the 1934 song, "She's wonderful, that little woman over there." In it he describes a brief few days with a charming woman. In a bright, happy tone he sings of her innocent personality and her beautiful physical traits: her "fine profile," "innocent, dreamy eyes," her "delicateness," her "childish air." He sings in the chorus:

> She's wonderful, that little woman over there.
> It's phenomenal what grace she has.
> She's as supple as a rosebush, as light as a bird.
> Even if she's shy and misses a step
> She's so nice she doesn't bother me.
> Among all those who are here, there aren't two like this![74]

Simon makes his ideal into a small, delicate object that, like a pretty piece of glass, might be made for his masculine gaze. Later in the number, he remembers a chat they once had but is even more struck by the way her "whole body was prettily put together." The song promoted male feelings of dominance in relationships, solidifying the importance of the male regard for esteeming the objectified female. Men were to esteem women by beauty alone, and they knew that women wanted male attention. The unnamed woman's innocence was especially important for Michel Simon's fantasy. The love affair ended after one afternoon's conversation. The relationship was never consummated and thus Simon could always call up the memory of his mystery woman's unsullied beauty. The song perpetuates an idea of the impossibility of finding a perfect and innocent woman. In all, the dream woman was beautiful, innocent, and out of reach.

Along with the fictional portrayals of married upright men and women on the radio, listeners were given an image of a moral, traditional family that upheld the idea of France and was an ideal image of the radio audience itself. For these couples were real and came from the listening public. No shows exploited traditional definitions of family more than the successful weekly game shows *The Byrrh Fiancés* and *At Least Fifteen Years Together* on Radio-Cité. On *The Byrrh Fiancés*, engaged couples competed to be named the best couple in France. Older, happily married couples would compete on *At Least Fifteen Years Together* to prove how happy their established households were. These shows introduced the men and women to the listening audience and asked the audience to vote for their favorites, those who best represented the French ideal of fiancés and older couples with families. This "reality radio" allowed station lovers to imagine themselves on stage and to compare themselves to the standard on stage.

As an incentive to participants and listeners, and in order to intensify the competition between couples and their stories, Radio-Cité offered large prizes for the winners, prizes that could, if they were careful, change the champions' lives forever. The season's winning newly engaged couple would receive a fully furnished apartment, a "dowry" of fifty thousand francs, and a honeymoon in the location of their choice.[75] The "dowry" alone gave the newlyweds a savings of the average wages for working-class men for three years.[76] The married couple would enjoy a new, furnished vacation house in the location of their choice and ten thousand francs of savings. In his autobiography, station owner Marcel Bleustein-Blanchet called the prize "the dream of all people of modest means, and the hope of every family father at the apex of his life."[77]

In the first show, Radio-Cité searched out couples with "empty bank accounts and certificates of healthy and moral lives."[78] On a public stage, two radio announcers asked them questions about expectations for married life, love, maternity, and children.[79] All the questions focused on how to make a bourgeois, upstanding couple out of two people with few means. The dream of a perfect start to married life seemed to come true for the winners. The first couple, in the 1936–37 season, an orphan and a former foster child, was married at La Madeleine in central Paris with the radio announcers and celebrities Saint-Granier and Jane Sourza as witnesses. They spent their honeymoon at a pavilion at the International Exposition of the same year, with servants at their fingertips to ensure them of a happy vacation and a perfect start to bourgeois domesticity.[80]

On *At Least Fifteen Years Together*, the winning pair was to be "the happiest couple in France" and conform to ideas of the perfect self-sacrificing, worthy parents. All candidates "of a certain age," had at least two and hopefully many children (which linked their success to pronatalist ideals of family responsibility).[81] Most were between fifty and sixty and had pasts marked by hardship and work: couples who would relish the assistance of the prizes for the happiness of their old age, in recognition of the difficult labor they had done for France and family. Winners could even offer luxuries to their families in a place to spend their paid vacations, newly legislated by the Popular Front.

The shows and the enormous prizes offered up an image of class hierarchy, giving what the station saw as the ultimate prize for hard work from the working class. But the couples that competed had to show that they deserved to win, through lives of hard work and exclusion from the mainstream and bourgeois stability. The prizes then offered the winners that same bourgeois stability. The fiancés would gain a savings account with substantial money, security, and ownership of property. The older couple would have their own dream vacation house with ten thousand francs to begin to think about retirement. The winners would then move up to the bourgeoisie as property owners, and the women would be offered the chance, because there would be no rent to pay and no extra wages needed for savings, to leave the workforce and become traditional wives and mothers. Each year, *The Byrrh Fiancés* and *At Least Fifteen Years Together* claimed they would create two ideal families from the most deserving of the underclass. Certainly the prizes would offer the semblance of uplift to each winner. The prizes were also a great attraction to listeners, reaching to their hearts, because the winnings made Radio-Cité look as if it offered a public service to the best citizens of France. The station publicly rewarded good behavior while raking in advertiser money from Byrrh and Frileuse fortified wines.[82]

In an ironic twist, a probably apocryphal story circulated among radio personnel after the second season of *The Byrrh Fiancés* ended. It was rumored that because the bride was Jewish they could not marry at the Madeleine, the central and elegant Paris church that would normally host the publicized wedding. So this was no ideal Catholic bourgeois couple from the start. Further complicating matters, the bridegroom who won the prize married his supposed sweetheart and then had her committed. He gambled and lost the prize money while on honeymoon at Nice, then sold the apartment and ran away with the earnings, leaving her behind in the asylum.[83] This story, although likely just an ironic fiction, relates an interesting tale of the reality of gendered relationships within marriage, pointing to problems with issues of patriarchal control and women's quasi-citizenship in France. Although outrageous, this urban legend and quasi–*fait divers* had potential truthfulness, as women in France had little control of finances within marriage and were not equal citizens in the state, in full control of their minds and bodies. Unhappy marriages left many interwar women with few options and no legal grounds for action. The story also illustrates the feelings that radio personnel had for the supposed dream couples that were featured on the air. They realized that behind the radio facades, couples led imperfect, normal, and hardly rewardable lives.

They also knew that the radio celebrated the idea of bourgeois domesticity, not its actual implementation. Con artists were as good for the audience, the advertisers, and the station as the real thing. Radio-Cité only gave out the prizes as the audience wished; the station did not have an obligation to monitor their use. And given the expectations of working-class mores (as we shall see in the next chapter), why would the radio personnel expect any other kind of behavior?

French radio gave little space for movement outside of the traditional home and promoted the idea of the patriarchal family as the central unit of radio listenership and market for its products. The Popular Front programmers on public radio embraced this ideal, creating plays that centered on bourgeois families and pronatalist rhetoric. Private radio created game shows and variety hours that also put the "ideal" family on display. Although bourgeois women did have moments of public time, in sparse lectures on public radio, *The Women's Forum,* on private radio station Radio-Cité, was the only successful and regularly scheduled moment of feminist or female-led political expression, and it ran during the daytime hours and was set apart from general programs. Programmers and critics alike, from both the right and the left, assumed that women were inside their homes and thus ideal, if superficial, daytime radio listeners, while they expected men's interests to take over in the evening hours. Altogether, the radio presented a traditional patriarchal view of French family as its model. As we will see in the next chapter, working-class men and women who fell outside of this archetypal family home would have little positive reflection on the radio, with little worth to radio broadcasters who saw working-class interests as marginal to their market or politics and to society as a whole.

5 THE PERILS OF THE SINGLE LIFE
Marginalized Working-Class Men and Women at Radio's Fictional Center

> Et voila comment Paulette
> Toujours très honnète
> Toujours comme il faut
> Fait le trottoir à Villette
> V'là c'que c'est d'êtr' sans défaut!
>
> And that's how Paulette
> Always upstanding
> Always proper
> Walks the streets at Villette
> That's what it means to have no faults!
> —ANDRÉ HORNAZ AND PAUL MISRAKI,
> "Paulette (Toujours comme il faut)"

Paulette, the title character in a 1938 song by Ray Ventura et Ses Collegiens, decides to leave her rural home for Paris to make her way in the world. The band jokingly tells us in the refrain that she is, like every country girl, "Always upstanding / Always proper," never stepping out of her role as a good girl and woman. Once in Paris, she easily finds work as a shop girl in a haberdashery and becomes one of a multitude of urban single working women. In spite of her "impeccable" behavior, attested to in each chorus, after many trials (and many verses), she ends her life as a cheap prostitute on the working-class outskirts of northern Paris. Although here part of a comical swing number,

Paulette's story, from when she moves to the city and finds a job to her tragic end in Villette, reflects the general and usually much more serious trend of the stories portrayed in radio fiction of working single men and women in the city.

As we have seen, radio often focused on life in the bourgeois home. Women in radio song and play had to fight against their emotional natures to stay virtuous, and women listeners were served a traditional menu of programming by broadcasters. Married male characters sometimes had affairs, but they had marriages that kept them stable and happy. Yet the lives of those who did not fit into the models of family stability, marginal figures by traditional domestic standards—the single working-class men and women in the city—fascinated radio writers and performers, who focused many radio hours both on the joys of single life and on the horrible sorrows destined to those without the protective envelope of the family. These characters served as constant reminders of appropriate behavior and provided both titillation and lessons of decency for radio listeners.

In radio fiction, young, unmarried bourgeois men and women could live out the freedoms of the single life, pursuing light relationships with the people around them and enjoying their carefree world at least until marriage. Yet these images had class limits because only bourgeois singles were shown to have true prospects of marriage after a short period of freedom. Often, the single working-class man was portrayed as a buffoon, who bragged about his exploits but never really got the girl. Radio fiction also limited working-class women in their occupations, seldom depicting them as anything but maids in the bourgeois household or prostitutes.[1] For both working-class men and women, too much time alone led to bad behavior when no patriarchal figure put limits on desire and fun. Many of the plays and songs depicted these men and women's drop into the criminal world of prostitution, robbery, and murder.[2]

This representation in plays and songs reflected socially conservative ideas about the value of unmarried men and women in France. It showed how many of those who programmed and wrote for the radio placed a moral emphasis on traditional family life, a domestic makeup that they believed would please listeners and that also held to advertiser standards for their products and for their market. In this chapter I will look at the ways radio songs and plays portrayed working-class singles and at how these ideas reflected conservative politics of the day, with no clear reflection of the realities of working-class and single life in the 1930s. In addition, the performers who sang the songs on the radio often shared the models of bourgeois and working-class lives that their own characters followed. As successful stars, some of them were able to escape from the stereotypical roles they portrayed, while others achieved fame only by following the stars.

According to some of the songs on the radio, single life could have its joys, especially for young bourgeois women who came to the city with money or for working-class and bourgeois men on the prowl. There was a sense that young people with both a job and a decent apartment in the city escaped the stodgy life of the bourgeois family. Mireille, in her songs, showed the joys of freedom for young men and women in the city. Male performers like Maurice Chevalier and Fernandel played comic working-class characters who looked for fun in light sexual relationships with the women around them. Ray Ventura et Ses Collégiens also understood the freedom that the city offered to single youth when their song character Paulette began an "honest" affair with her boss soon after she took her job, mixing pleasure with her daily grind. Her ideas about her right to youthful sexual pleasure with available men are repeated frequently on the radio.

One of the most prominent songwriters of the 1930s who rejoiced in the freedom of youth was Mireille. Born in 1907 as Mireille Hartuch, to an English mother and a Russian-Jewish father, she grew up in an open atmosphere where creativity was encouraged. Her father, a furrier, and her mother, a former stage actress, challenged her artistically. They offered to pay for her training for the stage, and she performed for a few years with the Théâtre Odéon but soon turned to writing music instead. A tiny woman, with hands too small to play classical piano, she joined with fellow actor and lyricist Jean Nohain and wrote popular operettas.[3] She accidentally scored the hit of the summer of 1933, when Pills and Tabet, a popular singing duo, recorded and released her song "Couchés dans le foin" (Asleep in the Hay) while she was touring in the United States with the theater company. The hit assured her success as a popular music composer, and she gave up the theater altogether. (The song was so popular that by 1937 it had become the slogan for a national advertising campaign for Velna fabrics.)[4] She began recording her own music in 1934, with words by Jean Nohain. In the music, her light high voice and happy lyrics jelled and made her an instant star. She chose to shorten her name to Mireille, taking on her French identity and sublimating the Jewish roots reflected in her surname. She became, in her songs and as a personality, the reflection of happy-go-lucky youth culture. Using the new medium of radio to establish a national career, she was, on air, the epitome of the modern girl.

Mireille and Nohain's songs reflected the bohemian ideals Mireille grew up with—including racy lyrics that showed the lighter side of life for young bourgeois singles, moments that she herself claimed to have experienced. In her autobiography, she remembers her father joking with her the first time she left home on tour: "You will be alone now on the other side of the world. You will receive all sorts of propositions; when you are far from us, promise me . . . not to just . . . eat anything."[5] Her modern father understood her desire to strike out on her own and did not deny his daughter a right to her own personal space and profits. Soon after, in fact, Mireille moved into her own Parisian apartment and began to entertain liberally.[6] Her autobiography reflected the perceived freedoms that came for young bourgeois women after the war. She became popular in part because she so perfectly fit the mold of the sophisticated, cosmopolitan youth.

Along with a string of hits, Mireille had her own weekly show, *Mireille and Friends*, on Poste Parisien from 1934 to 1936.[7] The show featured Mireille's hit songs, which often represented the life of the bourgeois single girl in Paris. These white-collar working girls lived in their own small apartments and were happily sexually active. In "Because of the Accountant" Mireille sings of waking the accountant who lives in the apartment below by the sounds of lovemaking in her own studio.[8] In 1933's "Almost Yes" a woman debates giving in to her lover:

> Almost yes, almost all
> My crazy eyes have promised him
> What an infinite sweetness . . .
> It's exquisite, marvelous,
> Our two astonished eyes
> Met and said: almost yes . . .[9]

In her first hit, released earlier that same year, "Asleep in the Hay," Pills and Tabet sing of a young, unmarried city couple, lost in the country, who take advantage of the dark fields to share their passions.[10] In her songs, Mireille painted a blissful world of sexual joy and unlimited freedom for France's bourgeois youth. Money, here, bought the right to experiment and the freedom to be safe and single, at least in the flower of youth. The bourgeoisie would have a heroine in Mireille and the privilege of a positive imagery of young singles not available to the working class.

While Mireille represented the bourgeois single, Maurice Chevalier was emblematic of the less successful, yet still optimistic, male working-class character on the radio.[11] He exploited the character of the sexually free single working-class male throughout his career. Chevalier was the model of a successful twentieth-century entertainer, working well in all the new media that the century offered, from stage and film to radio and television. He was born in 1888 and began his career when he was a teenager, getting his first Parisian stage role in 1910 at the Folies-Bergère in 1910. He worked side by side with the popular music-hall star Mistinguett, with whom he engaged in an affair. When "talking movies" first appeared, Chevalier recognized the potential of the new medium and traveled to Hollywood, giving up his stage career for a while for a more lucrative paycheck and a wider international audience. He starred in numerous American films and then in 1936 returned to France to make movies and tour.[12]

Chevalier had tremendous success in America, and the movies he made there exported his working-class charm around the world. An entertainer who understood the desires of his audience, he became a signature playboy, trying to make his move, always singing and never without his straw hat.[13] He appeared in musical films like *The Playboy of Paris* in 1931 and, in 1932, in the film *Love Me Tonight*, directed by Rouben Mamoulian. In it, he played a poor young tailor who falls in love with a baron's daughter and acts the part of a French baron to win her hand. Near the end of the story, in the character of the baron, Chevalier sang the thrilling song "The Poor Apache," with lyrics by Rodgers and Hart. In it, Chevalier describes the life of the "apache," or the Parisian thug of the Belle Epoque, thrillingly (and ironically) depicting his own life on the working-class streets of Paris.[14] The character in the song linked him with a traditional image of the working-class youth in Paris by drawing a direct parallel with a character from before World War I. With the portrayal in 1930s popular song, the image of the violent, sexually free working-class man earned its place in Parisian history. The brash lyric of the song further solidified Chevalier's rough playboy image, a character that he would cultivate throughout the 1930s:

> Wear a muffler when you wear a collar and tie?
> Why not? I'm an apache!
> A thing that makes me happy is to make a woman cry!
> Why not? I'm an apache!

> My sweetheart's a shop girl, she's a treasure,
> I am a gentleman of leisure,
> When I grab her wrist and twist it,
> No woman can resist it! I'm an apache!
> I'd love to treat her pretty and take her round the city,
> But what's a poor apache got to do?
> With one big sigh I must black her eye . . .
> I'd love to buy things for her,
> And tell her I'd adore her,
> But what's a poor apache got to do?
> With one good kick I make her pay me quick.[15]

The brutal sexism in these lyrics shows the working-class man's treatment of the prostitutes he cannot afford to pay. The violence translates sexually in the mythic working-class history of the song. The song does not depict the criminal behavior of the apache but focuses solely on his sexual violence. Working-class sexuality becomes the key to Chevalier's character. And it is because he plays the role of the working-class rake that Chevalier can get away with overtly sexual behavior. And the women he sees are worse than he—they sell themselves for sex and so can be treated like chattel.

> She comes and whispers sweetly:
> "I love you so completely!"
> And then I gently whisper to her:
> "Nuts to you!" That's how I say "I love you, too!"
> That's the truth, what a poor apache must do!

In a conservative worldview that valued married women and mothers, loose women would be exploited by working-class men around them. And Chevalier's baron-tailor could attract wealthy women with the power that this abuse represented. At the end of "Love Me Tonight," Chevalier, as the tailor-revealed, wins the girl.

The extremely brutal lyrics in "I'm an Apache" were those of a very popular song. Chevalier would continue to play "the poor apache" for his European stage theater and radio audiences throughout the thirties.[16] The dramatic stage number, which used plays of light and shadow to accentuate the shady nature of the working-class character, was one of the favorites in his 1936 stage tour.[17]

Perhaps the audiences liked to witness their own fantasies of illicit behavior acted out before them in song, behaviors they knew from paraliterature, or pulp fiction, and the *fait divers* in their newspapers.[18] Certainly Chevalier could not behave this way outside of the boundaries of a character from the working class. In their public lives, bourgeois men could not be this open about sexual violence, but they could revere the working-class character on stage and radio that spoke to their inner sexual desires.

Chevalier believed that his American film career would lead to a triumphant return to French film in 1935. Instead, he would never be the film star he imagined and made his fortune with recordings and radio and stage performances. He relied on the radio, in both recorded concerts and variety-show appearances, to remain in the public eye. In 1935 and 1936, Chevalier made three relatively unsuccessful films with director Julien Duvivier, including *L'Homme du jour*. Although only moderately popular at the box office, it yielded one of Chevalier's big radio and stage hits of the thirties, "Ma Pomme." It was radio, and not film, that made the song a hit. The song was about another rascal who lived on the fringes of society and relished his less-than-"civilized" lifestyle. The upbeat tune had memorable lyrics about a typical working-class character. In the first stanza Chevalier makes his class status perfectly clear, to let audiences know where the song will take them:

> I might not be known by the nobility, or by the snobs.
> If you want to find me you'll have to ask in all the little bars.
> You'll see my name on all the mirrors
> And on all the *bistrot* tabs.
> The corner tobacco shop is my palace
> Where, in the evening, I find all my buddies.

The character is in place for the long and rousing chorus:

> Ma *pomme*!(My mug!) It's me!
> I'm happier than a king!
> I never work myself into a lather
> I quietly just get by!
> I've heard that some men hang themselves with worry.
> Why bother?
> Because to be happy like me,

> My mug, my mug,
> All you gotta be,
> Is as easy-going as me!

Throughout the song, Chevalier uses street slang to help create an urban working-class character. With words like *pomme*, which means mug, or face, *ardoise*, or unpaid tab, and *potins*, or buddies, Chevalier places himself into a shady milieu of the urban poor.[19] His audience can take his words as part of the working-class character and thus enjoy the images he presents them. And how could he resist a little denigration of the neighborhood women around him? Here his working-class character displays his openly predatory nature:

> Women? I need them like everyone else does.
> Oh, but I don't make a big deal about it.
> When I want a brunette, or better, a blonde,
> (Whistle) I choose when I'm ready.
> 'Cause I don't have any dough,
> I can easily promise them anything they want.
> But when I move on, I'm a true prince,
> As I go, I leave them my picture![20]

Chevalier retains his image as a rake who leaves women (or prostitutes) behind him. The character here is not as violent toward women as his "apache" but shows many similar character traits. He comes from the poor streets of Paris, he does as little work as possible, and he mistreats the women he meets. He, like other working-class characters that we will meet later, does not get tied down to a family and home.

Chevalier could not sing these songs without donning his working-class image. In 1936, when he had finished his films, he began a tour of France, assuming a more sophisticated, wealthy image by appearing in formal wear while singing his regular repertoire, including "Ma Pomme." The beginning of his tour was not a success; he could not sell any tickets. The music-hall crowds would have none of this new "classy" image. They knew Chevalier as a working-class rogue—his song lyrics showed it. And his life reflected that image as well. His many affairs with fellow stars were quite public (with Marlene Dietrich, Nita Raya, and Mistinguett, as well as others), as was his divorce from his wife Yvonne Vallée that same year. When Chevalier finally agreed to redon his straw hat, the tour sold out. The working-class rogue who could get away with singing brash lyrics was back.

In all of his songs Chevalier plays the young charmer who lives day to day on the streets of the working-class neighborhoods of Paris. From details from Chevalier's autobiography and songs, literary critic Adrien Rifkin argues that Chevalier's life showed audiences the image of the working-class man who made good.[21] Perhaps this was actually the reality of his life. After all, Chevalier worked his way up the class hierarchy, even ending his life with his own chateau. Yet in song and film, Chevalier always played the working-class rascal who was happy but unsuccessful. His comedic songs portrayed the urban youth in the northern and eastern faubourgs of Paris. Realizing that this working-class image made him successful, he continued to record hits that, in story and slang, reflected these characters: "La Petite Dame de l'Expo" (The Little Lady at the Expo), "Ah! Si vous connaissiez ma poule!" (Ah! If You Only Knew My Chick), and "Appelez-ça comme vous voulez" (Call It What You Want).[22] His popularity on the radio increased as well, and in 1937, as we saw in chapter 2, he played godfather to the new private radio station in Paris, Radio-37. He was the first to speak into its microphone to dedicate the station.[23] His appearance at the event was a move by station owner Jean Prouvost to make the new station a hit from its very inception, and Maurice Chevalier's appearance had the star potential to guarantee that success. He was the perfect image for a fun-loving Parisian station. Like the station Chevalier appeared to have no grand illusions or notions; he was only there to entertain. Even more, he, like those who heard him, appeared to represent the Parisian audience, as an everyman or "everycitizen" who would listen to the station. His blessing on the station appeared to come from Paris itself.

Using this everyman image, Chevalier had continued success throughout his life, becoming one of the most adaptable performers of the twentieth century. He began his stage life performing with Mistinguett, one of the most treasured women of the Belle Epoque and Jazz Age, worked with director Vincent Minnelli after World War II, and ended his career with performances on Ed Sullivan, the 1950s and 1960s icon of television. With his working-class character and jaunty style, Chevalier was able to move from mass medium to mass medium, something which most performers, including the ever-less-popular Mistinguett, found impossible.[24] Maurice Chevalier retired in 1968, the year of the student riots in Paris, a year that marked the end of the modern era.

Five years after the dedication of Radio-37, in the midst of World War II,

Fernandel, another radio and film star, would use the image of the working-class rascal in his own way to great success. While the smooth-talking, attractive Chevalier had some sexual success, horse-faced Fernandel became the true comic character, never quite able to impress women. With an ugly face and a silly demeanor, he wanted to be a cad but, in spite of his desires, maintained his innocence. In "For You to Have Said Yes," a 1941 hit, the narrator plays an unsuccessful lover who stalks his prostitute girlfriend and masturbates outside keyholes as she meets with her clients. He sings a tango about his unrequited love in past conditional and subjunctive, making fun of the proletarian roots of the character by using language far too snooty:

> For you to have said yes to me
> I would have had to have asked you.
> For me to have asked you
> I would first have had to have dared it.
> Our hands would have had to have clasped,
> You would have had to have shivered,
> I would have had to have made vows to you.
> You would have had to have liked me
> Ah! But I didn't dare, dare, dare.[25]

Both Fernandel and his would-be lover act in the sexually free manner that listeners expected of single urban working-class characters in song. Throughout the 1930s, audiences loved to laugh at ugly Fernandel's exploits (or near misses). Radio-Cité, a private radio station in Paris, hired him in the 1937–38 radio season for a weekly comedy show called *Fernandel and Company*.

Other songs showed the life of the single man on the prowl, from "Eteignons tout et couchons nous" (Let's Turn the Lights Off and Go to Bed), sung by Jean Sablon, to "Sous les ponts de Paris" (Under the Bridges of Paris), performed by Georgel. A drunk man in a courtroom in Ray Ventura's "C'est dommage que je ne puisse pas vous le montrer" (It's Too Bad I Can't Show You) sings of the lovers who take advantage of the parks of Paris at night:

> In the Meudon woods, lying on the grass,
> A lady and a soldier were making love in each other's arms
> But a policeman came to ruin their fun
> And me the next day, I was called as a witness.

What were they doing, they asked me.
I said, intimidated:
It's too bad I can't show you, your honor,
It's too bad, but there's no way I can show you here.
When people get undressed
In a little wooded corner
It's not to play marbles
Or to do crossword puzzles.
It's too bad I can't show you, your honor,
But know that in any case
They weren't bothering anyone![26]

Working-class people in song, in apartments, in hotels, and in the parks, were portrayed as sexualized beings, always getting caught with their pants down.

The lives of real working-class men and women were much less humorous and fun. The economic crisis had hit hard by 1931, and jobs were scarce. Unemployment rose steadily through 1935 for both men and women, and many had to be satisfied with whatever work they could get. After 1935, for men, however, employment possibilities brightened. Working-class men even began to see their prospects change with the election of the Popular Front in 1936, as they saw themselves and their politics represented in the left-wing coalition. The communists and socialists bonded together with massive strikes that brought about political and social change. Yet by 1937, another round of strikes brought down the very same government as it stalled on many communist demands.[27] It was not until the 1950s that France's economy, and the prospects for working men, regained the momentum of the 1920s.

For women, the picture looked especially bleak. Job opportunities were scarce, and choice even more rare. Many women worked in factory jobs, and very little pink-collar work was available apart from secretarial positions and shop clerks.[28] In a feminist tract from 1935, Suzanne Cordelier bemoaned the job market for bourgeois women, pointing out that women had little choice in the work they pursued. She then described seventeen careers in which women had some success and tried to encourage her readers to begin there. The options she laid out were the standard jobs for educated women, correct within their nurturing sphere—from hospital nurse to librarian.[29] Cordelier imagined such careers only for bourgeois and educated women (like Mireille). She offered no hope or prospects for working-class women.

Working-class women took what jobs they could find, looking for extra money to support themselves and their families at home. Paulette, the fictional heroine of this chapter, worked as a shop girl in her youth:

> She left to make her living
> Always very politely,
> Always properly,
> At a bonnet shop that also sold girdles wholesale.

This image of the single working-class woman as youthful was realistic. Most women worked only until they married. Age restrictions on hiring practices limited the number of older women who could work. For example, the average age of a telephone operator, one of the jobs that was almost exclusively female by 1900, was less than twenty-five.[30]

Right-wing Catholic groups, which had gained some power over public radio broadcasts with the 1937 radio elections and had their own playwrights in Henriette Charasson and the Malards, fought against all female labor, especially that of married women. In 1931 and again in 1937, the Catholic women's groups the Feminine Civic and Social Union and the League of Stay-Home Mothers participated in congresses calling for the abolition of female labor outside of the home.[31] Working women, then, although playing central roles in the economy of their families, were under siege from the more conservative groups in France.

Radio, too, with its reliance on the family group as its listening unit, became a site for fears about unsupervised working-class women. In the vast majority of the working-class women characters they created, programmers and writers traced single women into downward spirals. Radio artists, as we have seen, portrayed womanly virtue as a hard-won trait and in their songs and plays declared virtuous women difficult to find. The working girl in songs and radio plays, alone in the city without father or husband to steady her, found herself repeatedly taken advantage of by the men around her. Hers was an easy sexuality, and in radio fiction she was understandably used and left by lecherous men. As the title character says about his daughter in Hughes Nonn's 1937 radio play *Marcus*, "One day a man took her with him to the city. Where we live, we know what that means. A woman doesn't go to the city to work, that's for sure."[32] Radio plays and songs portrayed the working girl as a victim of her passion for unscrupulous men.

The most prominent working girl in French radio plays was the maid to the bourgeois family. She appeared over and over, leaving the listening audience as a witness to her base moral judgment. By focusing so much attention on the domestic servant, the radio portrayed a stable French bourgeois society at a time when many families had to discontinue live-in household service for a lack of funds.[33] Although usually interpreted as an innocent, the servant girl was easily led into bad behavior by the men around her, whether her working-class boyfriends or her lecherous male employers. In a city alone, left unprotected by men in her own family, only age and loss of looks could save her from sexual advances.

In some ways, the character of the maid criticized the atmosphere that these women may have faced in their houses. In radio plays, male employers took sexual advantage of their domestic servants, while their female employers sometimes assumed bad moral conduct that never really occurred. Whether she had behaved immorally, the fictional maid lived precariously in French fiction. Guilty until proven innocent, the radio's maid led a frustrating life in an untrusting, untrustworthy world.[34] And whether right or wrong, a maid rarely escaped from her job unscathed.

Annie, the pretty maid from Canada, does not escape her bourgeois employer's assumptions about her willingness to have premarital affairs. In the radio play *Samedi soir* Annie's fiancé comes to Paris for a hockey match the day before she is to leave with her employers for her native Quebec.[35] Her mistress, surprised that she had not yet seen him, gives her the evening off to do so. Annie attends the hockey match, and, when her fiancé's team wins, follows them to the postgame celebrations. She trails unhappily along with them as they party until eight o'clock the next morning. She knows that she should not stay, but she wants to spend as much time as possible with her fiancé. Annie also has no means to return home, as a young woman cannot wander the streets of Paris alone. When she finally does come back, her mistress assumes the worst, crying,

> Well, Annie! You think that you can come and go as you please? . . . It's at this hour that you come home? You could have at least saved appearances and let me go on thinking that you slept at home! . . . The joys of Saturday night, huh? . . . I wouldn't have thought it of you! No reserve, no modesty! I should leave you here [in Paris], with your debauched friends, to your debased evenings! I don't know why I should bring

you along after what you have done: . . . Or, rather, yes, I know. I'm too good. That's it! You don't know how lucky you are!

Annie is left hurt and lonely, forever sullied in the eyes of her mistress. Annie behaves beyond reproach, but her mistress reaches the only conclusion she can when faced with a maid who was out all night. Society (and the limits of French radio interpretations of working-class women) tells the employer that Annie, pretty and working-class, could not be assumed innocent.

Bijoute, by André-Micho, shows the results of the fall of the working girl, with its portrayal of a sexy young maid and her foil in the appearance of her hoary replacement. [36] These two characters frame the ongoing argument between a lecherous husband and his shrewish wife. The young hired maid causes stress between husband and wife, as the man of the house cannot keep his hands off her. He tells his friend, "For me, without any bad intentions, I found it relaxing and agreeable to see that sweet young child around the house; and my eyes happily fixed on the young, pretty face." Unfortunately his attentions do not stop at simple looks, and with his jealous wife looking on, things progress badly. He continues:

> Emilie, of course, who saw my caring behavior toward Léa, took offense at it and without my being aware, watched over my actions and gestures with a vigilant eye. So well, that one day, as I was offering a caramel to the little one, and as I gave her a paternal tap on the cheek, the door opened brusquely and Emilie surprised me in the middle of the gesture. . . . Ah! my friend! . . . what she imagined!

We can only assume what Emilie imagined between her husband and her servant, but Léa is fired for the husband's behavior. Due to her already aroused suspicions and the randiness of her husband, the wife must believe that the maid has been indiscreet. Because the wife's reaction is so strong, the listeners might also assume that Léa is not the first young, pretty maid to have tempted the monsieur. The radio stereotype demanded a belief in the immorality of the working girl. Léa was cursed from the start. We, the listeners, are not privy to the fate of the now-unemployed maid, but in the next scene we are given the chance to meet her older double, the now-haggard woman who replaces her in the house.

Emilie thinks herself crafty in deciding to hire an old, ugly woman as the new maid who will neither excite her jealousy nor tempt her husband with the loose morals and sexual attraction of a young working girl. Unbeknownst to Emilie, the woman she hires turns out to be a former lover of her husband's—long ago a young maid who was ruined by his amorous attentions. During their earlier affair, the husband called her "bijoute," or jewel, because of her beauty. The sight of his jewel as a haggard old woman shocks him. In disgust he asks her, "How did you become so. . . . I mean, what you've become?" She responds, repeating the trope of the fall of the working-class girl: "How? Oh! That's easy: I descended quickly, from rung to rung, until I dropped even further. And when a man abandons you, it's crazy how quickly you descend. . . . And now I have to wipe up at my former lover's house!" Her response gives the image of an old housekeeper, perhaps a former prostitute, who has no more sexual worth and is detested by one who formerly loved her. "Jewel," no longer the overtly sexual young working girl, is left with nothing at all. The consequences of being a single working woman are spelled out in her return to her lover's house. Sexual availability might be lovely in youth, but for working-class girls it leads only to ugliness, poverty, and ultimate humiliation.

This image of the easy sexuality of the working girl makes the typical housewife very suspicious of her maid's behavior. Emilie may perhaps be an exaggerated stereotype of a shrewish wife, reinforcing the comedy of the play when she catches her husband giving a "mercy" kiss to his now gaunt "Bijoute," but Emilie's fears about the easy virtue of her maid were still understandable to a 1930s listening audience confronted by these repeated sexual images of the single working girl.[37]

Radio fiction relates even the unfulfilled sexual desire of the working-class woman. In another play, *Le Théâtre Express: La femme de ménage*, a housewife, Madame X (read any-bourgeois-woman), and her maid, Marie (any-maid), are talking while preparing that evening's dinner.[38] Marie is described in the cast list as over thirty years old and ugly. Thus we are left to assume that Marie does not fit into the category of the pretty working girl, but assumptions about her unchaste behavior still hold. Marie tells her mistress the story of her son Louis, who lives in Paris. Madame X assumes the worst of her maid, shocked that Marie has had an illicit affair outside of wedlock. Perhaps our bourgeois housewife would not have hired a pretty girl as a domestic servant, but with Marie, an ugly woman, she should not have been faced with a girl with a questionable sexual past. But if the unexpected had happened and Madame X found that her maid was an unwed mother, the transgression must have been under illicit circumstances. Madame X has overestimated the seducing abilities of her ugly maid, who loved Louis's father but was not pretty enough to tempt him, even after agreeing to let him have his way with her (so she is debauched in spirit, if not in body). Instead he married another, prettier woman and died soon after. As the mother died not much later, Marie generously brought the now-orphaned son up as her own. Madame X, in her assessment of her maid's honor before learning the true story, shows the bourgeois assumptions about the free morals of the working class when she assumes the worst of the now honorable and generous Marie. Yet in a way her servant fits those assumptions: we learn that she wanted Louis's father as a lover. Ugly Marie, though not from lack of trying, cannot fulfill male desires for the pretty, expendable working girl, but her own ambitions to take a lover belie her looks. Even the chaste working girl has loose morals, a virgin only from circumstance, not desire.[39]

The working girl's inherent lack of innocence in the eyes of the radio fiction writers could, in the worst cases, lead to violence within the bourgeois household. In Jacques Cossin's *La Peur*, the play that began this book, a maid has a sexual relationship with a robber, whom she invites into the house every evening.[40] Her mistress has presentiments of horrors that will occur in the house, but perceived as a hysterical female, she is ignored by all the men around her.[41] One evening, the maid's lover comes to the house with the intention of robbing it. When he finds the wife alone in her room, he brutally murders her. Thus, although the maid herself was innocent of the crime, her corrupt morals allowed the entry of evil into her employers' home. Working girls could never be fully trusted because of the failings of the working-class men they frequented.

Another maid, in the radio play *La Démarche,* anything but innocent, shows the worst of working-class female behavior.[42] The maid is unnamed, and we only hear secondhanded about her from those to whom she has behaved badly. She has stolen one thousand francs from her mistress, Madame Greville-Morand. When accused, she threatens her mistress with blackmail; she knows that her employer has been having a long-standing affair. The wife feels unable to act, even after her husband accuses one of his clerks of the crime. Her lawyers save the day, however, when they realize that the husband had conducted his own affair with the blackmailing maid. The lawyers tell M. Greville-Morand about the crime and the maid is summarily fired. Because she is no sexual innocent herself, the husband can fire her with no knowledge of the original blackmail attempt. The maid is left powerless. Neither member of the couple is any wiser about each other's extramarital affairs.

The unnamed maid had apparently been stealing and blackmailing for quite some time and represents a criminal character who has taken advantage of a bourgeois, and thus in the radio's class system, inherently honorable, husband and wife. The working-class maid, on the other hand, steals what she can after winning the trust of the wife (she delivered the love letters between wife and lover) and seducing the husband. But all may not be as simple as the playwrights would like. We know that the maid is no longer an innocent, though perhaps she was before the affair with the husband. Did the husband act much like the employer in *Bijoute*, seducing her and then leaving her with nothing? Has she sunk in character only since her innocence was lost? In any case, she is punished while the others go free. The maid loses her job (and will probably get no other), but husband and wife stay together and maintain the appearance of a perfect bourgeois household. The ideal French family is saved.

Songs, too, played into the stereotype of the sexual(ized) French maid. Even Mireille, who normally celebrated sexual freedom, wrote a popular song about the easy maid recorded by Pills and Tabet. In "C'est gentil," a man sings of his affair with a hotel maid whom he visits whenever he is in town.[43]

> Of course there's the little maid.
> She kisses you as soon as you call for her.
> Her room's at the end of the hall.
> I visited her there yesterday evening.

The song implies that the maid sleeps with every young man who stops through, since she is the only real pleasure that the ratty hotel offers its clients. Unfortunately her *patronne* also wants to share in the pleasure:

> I wanted to see the little maid again
> And I came across her boss.
> Her body aflame, she said,
> "Come, I'll take you to paradise."

When the singer no longer thinks the maid is worth the trouble of her oversexed boss, he easily gives her up and switches his business to the more comfortable hotel across the street.

Outside of bourgeois influence, and unprotected, the stereotypical Paulette, too, although not a maid but a shop clerk, follows the pattern of working-class sex and criminality. First she cheats on her boss, and then "she left with the cash register, always without weakness, always properly." Her slide does not end there, as she begins affairs with numerous men. Ventura sings, making fun of the fictional trope:

> Then she became the mistress of a metro conductor.
> Then a general was her lover,
> Then two lieutenants,
> Then three sergeants.
> Pretty soon she gave herself to the entire regiment.
> Yes, but always chastely.

Paulette has fallen from an aboveboard working girl to a member of an underclass, defined solely by those with whom she has affairs and the men who become, for a moment at least, her sexual and monetary protectors.

Many other single working-class women portrayed in popular song had only sexual identities, sometimes as mistresses who may or may not have also worked as wage laborers. In Mireille's "23 Acacias Street," a young bourgeois man sings of his love for the woman who lives at that address. He laughs about her apartment with its tacky decoration, "A portrait of Marie-Antoinette and color pictures of naked women / And two rustic chairs, a fish in a bowl / A music book, an admiral's sword," probably from some previous sexual relationship. But his interest in this single woman is also purely sexual. He sings:

> But only the bed interests me
> It's from a store in Barbès.
> It's where Ida, my mistress, sleeps.
> Great luxury leaves me cold.
> There's only one house I always dream of,
> One floor where there's crazy love,
> One bed in all of Paris,
> It's where Ida's bed is:
> 27 Acacias Street![44]

Ida is not the only single woman who inhabits ambiguous territory. In "No Money at All" a woman sings of her happiness despite her poverty as long as she has "her lover in her bed."[45] Another of Mireille's hits, "My Grandmother

Was a Train-Crossing Guard [*garde-barrière*]," portrayed the singer's grandmother as an easy woman who had sexual relations with all the men who worked the train:

> The lantern wavers came to visit
> The ticket-sellers and the conductors
> Were always around.
> What playful eyes!
> She welcomed with no pretense
> Everyone who was connected with the train
> And they said that the entire company
> Had paraded in front of her bed.

As a working woman, the grandmother was sexually active, especially since she had no male supervision in her guardhouse. We learn, however, that she is married and so has limits on how far she will go with the men of the train company:

> When her husband wasn't around
> More than one date was set
> And there were lots of caresses
> Between the local, the rapid and the express.
> But when her lover became too pushy
> She lowered her eyes in a decent manner.
> "Please," said grandma, "I need to close my gate!"[46]

But even with her modesty (and who could expect less of a future grandmother), the absence of a patriarchal figure left the working woman room to maneuver sexually.

On the radio, this kind of behavior could have no good end. With working-class men, as with the maids described above, in noncomical plays and songs, free sexual behavior and assumptions of immorality often led to criminality and almost always led to disappointment. For working-class men in radio fiction the fate was not the happy-go-lucky easy life portrayed by Maurice Chevalier and other comic artists. In many songs and plays the single working-class man's free behavior, like women's, led him into a life of crime.[47]

"Browning," a song performed by Edith Piaf, a celebrated radio artist, shows the missed opportunity and criminality inherent in the working-class single man's life. In the song, a young Frenchman has had the opportunity to travel to America to begin a new life. Instead of seeking employment and a new chance, he returns to France having learned the wrong lessons. He brings a gun home with him (the "Browning" of the title) and brags of his prowess, learned at the side of American gangsters. Tragically, he accidentally shoots himself and dies in front of his cronies on the floor of the local café. His story of criminality and death is a typical one on French radio. Other realist songs, like "Dans un port" (In a Port), "Mon vieux pataud" (My Old Dog), and "L'Etranger" (The Stranger), depicted the criminal side of single male behavior, drawing a picture of the underworld that the working-class men inhabited.[48]

In a comic turn, Fernandel poked fun at the criminal working-class gangster and the songs that exploited the idea, in his hit "A Hard One, a Real One, a Tattooed One." The song character uses slang and threats to try to "scare" his audience into believing in his wicked and violent nature. He lists his crimes and bad behavior in the chorus:

> I'm a hard one, a real one, a tattooed one!
> I don't run away, what does that get you?
> I'll get even with you,
> Don't try to play me,
> I'll take you out, you catch my drift?
> I've munched on cannibals,
> I've taken bullets.
> I gotta get outta here,
> No discussions
> 'Cause the African battalions
> I wear their maker's mark
> And that's the whole portrait
> Of a tattooed one, a hard one, a real one![49]

Radio plays, too, often exploited the stereotypes of criminal male working-class behavior that came from men unrestricted by strong patriarchal influence.[50] *Le Retour dans la nuit* (Return in the Night) shows the inevitable downslide of the children of the working class in the return of the prodigal son.[51] An unnamed father and mother who live in a provincial village have a son, Gilbert, who has left home and gone bad. When the son returns to them on Christmas Eve after having escaped from prison, the father claims he will shoot

Gilbert if he doesn't turn himself in to the police. The criminal behavior of the unremorseful son has shamed the father in the eyes of all his neighbors. Yet when the police come to the house searching for Gilbert, out of a sense of guilt and some small residual paternal love, the father does not reveal where his son is hiding. But the father's sense of responsibility for his son comes too late. Gilbert has run off, expecting the worst from his father. Later the police shoot the son, and he dies without his father's forgiveness, leaving the father feeling guilty for not having loved his son enough to save him. In this play, poverty in the paternal home and the father's lack of love for his son lead to criminal behavior.

Paternal irresponsibility often plays a large part after the breakdown of the solid working-class family and sons' drop into criminality. Although culpability for bad parenting motivates failing parents to make enormous sacrifices for their sons later in life, this behavior usually has no positive result. In *Cellule 29*, by Georges Avryl, a guilt-ridden father guards the prison where his son, a murderer, has come to await his execution the next morning.[52] The now-imminent death of the criminal son is linked directly to his father's absence in the home as the prisoner shows when he accuses his father who comes to see him in his jail cell, "Mother died six months ago. . . . Since your divorce she wasn't the same. . . . You know how weak her lungs were. . . . She no longer wanted to take care of herself . . . and so. . ." It is the father's fault that his son had taken a bad path after he was left alone with a sick mother, in this breaking apart of a solid family. Perhaps another woman made the father abandon his family in the midst of an economic crisis; perhaps he no longer wanted to take care of an ailing wife. Yet the father refuses to accept full responsibility for his son's actions. The son replies to his father's query about his life, "Since my return from army service, I haven't been able to find work as a mechanic. Unemployment came . . . and I let myself go." He goes on to explain that he couldn't ask his father for help, being unsure about his love after he left the family. The play places the problem squarely on the working-class father's shoulders. According to the son, if the family had had patriarchal control, no criminal acts would have occurred. In this instance, when the family fell apart, as it was a working-class family, there was not a long way to slide for the son to turn to criminality. For the lower classes there was no buffer for mistakes.

Unhappiness inside the working-class home is nowhere more evident than in the play *L'Enfant* (The Child) by André de Lorde.[53] But the poverty of this family and the slide into criminality of the son are shown both as the fault of the parents and as an inevitable genetic path of working-class men. The first scene takes place in a peasant cottage where the Bonnard family takes in wealthy infants for a small living fee. Although they love the children they keep, they despise the parents they serve who refuse responsibility for their proper children. The husband says, "All these people, these parents, couldn't they have raised [the children] themselves? But that would annoy them, they preferred travelling, having fun. . . . But me, do I have fun? All the same, these little ones, they weren't born of unfortunates like ourselves. They'll have a different kind of life."

Monsieur Bonnard also knows that when the parents return they will take their now older children away to lives of plenty and he wants to offer that possibility to his own child. When one of the children dies of a fever, the couple replaces him with their own son, who looks much like the dead child, trying to give him a better life in a bourgeois household. Unfortunately, the Bonnards leave a hereditary mark on their son that will determine his future. He, as the son of poor peasants, cannot turn out well as the son of rich bourgeois. The play will show how the mixing of classes is impossible.

As expected, the son turns out dissipated and spoiled. After his wealthy false parents die, unable to understand the value of money, he accumulates vast debts. Eventually he even murders a wealthy man and flees justice by running to the Bonnard household. Is he subconsciously aware that his true place is with the Bonnards and that they, as his real parents, will offer him safety? Madame Bonnard takes him in, but the police follow his trail. They capture him and bring him to trial.

His mother feels excessively guilty for her actions, so at the trial she reports to the court what she had done twenty years before. In his jail cell, her son berates her saying, "You should have left me how I was, where I was. I wasn't made for this situation in life, for these riches. That's why I never understood how to profit by them, why I wasted them. And then all that I stole . . . like you stole the trust of those who thought me their son." Her son realizes that he could not escape poverty. A solid consciousness about the value of money could not be genetically passed down to him from poor parents. A poor man's son did not have the physical equipment to learn how to live with money. The bourgeois character, handling the responsibility of wealth, proves in this play to be genetic, not environmental.

Because of his mother's testimony, he is sentenced to "only" twenty years hard labor in French Guyana, which would effectively be a death sentence. Did his true mother's testimony work against him here? Would he have been as harshly sentenced if he had proven to actually be the biological child of respectable bourgeois parents, instead of a poor, lying woman's son? As he leaves for the colonies, his mother commits suicide, wracked with guilt because of the fate she gave her son. She jumps off of a cliff in front of the boat because she could not save her son from his genetic inheritance of poverty and criminality.

If Bonnard ended up doing hard labor in South America, the fault was not entirely his own. For many working-class male characters, the fictional breakdown of their radio families left them no stable life to fall back on. Inevitably, their criminal life ended tragically because their families offered them no support in their time of need. Radio plays expressed that the working-class family was never a stable unit that could offer its sons the lives they desired. On the radio, these families were always in a turbulent state, where the patriarchal system had broken down and children and wives made the economic and political choices for the household. The working-class single men suffered because of the breakdown of traditional hierarchies. Sometimes the radio fiction even suggested that this collapse was hereditarily inevitable, for even when offered a life with money and opportunity in adoption, the single men made the wrong choices.

If single men on the radio often ended either in jail or dead, working-class women, too, suffered for rejecting the stable, patriarchal household. The last stages in the life of the single woman are detailed in a genre of song that became exceedingly popular on 1930s radio—the song of the prostitute, or *chanson du trottoir*.[54] These prostitute songs were easily recognizable to the listening public. In order to capture the public imagination in three minutes, the songs had many similar traits and fell into a type, or genre.[55] All of the songs were sung by women, who usually played the role of the prostitute.[56] The songs had no vast orchestration but were sung with accordion accompaniment. The accordion was an instrument that street performers used at the time, further stressing the atmosphere of the songs as sung from the sidewalks where the prostitutes plied their trade. The most successful female singers like Damia, Edith Piaf, and Frehel all had husky voices and timbres that relayed how hard the women portrayed had lived. And because the prostitute's song was often tragic, the pacing was slow and the singer sounded worn out. Many of the songs ended with the prostitute/singer (and hopefully the listening audience as well) in tears.

These songs come from a music-hall tradition that stems back to the late nineteenth century. As prostitutes became more "visible" in Montmartre night culture, the songs about them and the culture that concerned them became more prominent as well. Montmartre culture mixed the social classes, bringing the prostitute into open contact with bourgeois men and women who enjoyed the new Parisian night life. By the 1890s, however, the country's leaders felt that this culture had to be tamed and commodified, and it became a show more that a reality. Elizabeth Menon argues that prostitutes became more powerful as they became more visible at the turn of the century, linking the space between pleasure and danger.[57] By the 1930s, however, the prostitute that may have earlier been "the primary focus of male fantasies of female sexuality" moved from siren to victim, still titillating, but no longer particularly powerful.[58] The culture of Montmartre was no longer the domain of men and forward women. On stage and in film at least, Kelley Conway has shown, the women who portrayed these characters had the ability to use their lives to give these women an agency they otherwise would not have had. Frehel, especially, used the songs to reinvigorate a languishing career, eliciting sympathy and respect for the characters she portrayed.[59] On the radio, all could share in the imagined edgy haunts of the prostitute as well, but the songs did not stand on their own in intimate concerts from women who were known for their craft. Instead, they came in the context of an audio culture that placed them into a world where there was no relief from the condemnation of working-class women's choices. The voices came disembodied, singing only pain and bad luck. Radio was not film, in that there were no positive examples of working-class heroines to serve as foils for these pitiful women. The loose women depicted on radio were the women of the working class. They became tragic life lessons perhaps, but more likely they were fascinating specimens of otherness to the families who listened in their living rooms to these sorrowful tales.

The women in these songs never called themselves prostitutes (*prostituées*) or any other standard slang term such as *pute* or *putain*. The term "prostitute" was either too direct or too derogatory and showed too much knowledge of the place these women held in the labor market. Rather, they referred to themselves using the euphemisms of "dolls" (*poupées*), "playthings" (*jou-jous*), and, most often, girls (*filles*). In a few cases, the women called themselves *catins*, which roughly translates to harlot, but the derivation of the word points to a root of "Catherine," which in Québeçois slang meant doll. All of these terms objectified these women either as toys or as children with no real control over their bodies or their destinies. The men who frequented them then controlled their sexuality once they paid for a prostitute's services.

The setting of the songs was equally important, showing the places where these sexual creatures plied their trade. There was little romance or beauty in the lives of the characters. On street corners, in cafés, in dance halls, waiting by entrances to bars and at ports, the "girls" "ogle [*lorgnent*]" and "trap their prey [*guettent leur proie/leur gibier*]."[60] They become animal-like shadows of the night.

The songs suggest that all men had easy access to prostitutes. The French singing star Damia sang that "Men like us when we say 'I love you' / Whether they're broke, filthy rich, brown-haired or blonde."[61] In "The Village Harlot," Yvette Netter told audiences that "All the guys have been on top of me [*tous les gas ont passé sur moi*]," and continued with a litany of the men she serviced:

> The very timid teenagers, I guided them in their first pleasures,
> And I shared the last desires of the old men with their wet glances.
> Long ago, I gave hope to frank soldiers returned from the carnage.
> After lovemaking, full of courage, they left proud without fear.[62]

Any man, of any age or class, who could afford the prostitute could have a girl for a night and could have his ego restored while soothing himself in necessary sex.[63]

The economics of the profession were often mentioned in the songs but always in the control of the men who made their choice. In "The Dolls of Midnight" Berthe Sylva sang of the prostitutes, "They are beautiful playthings / That a man buys for one night."[64] The woman who sang "The Tango of the Girls" let men know that "between our arms anyone can find his pleasure / Without worry. With us, one price means two desires."[65] The customer's desire for sex could be fulfilled here and, in the song, the prostitute could do nothing but comply with male desire and take the money he offered.

In spite of their monetary concern for sex, most of the characters depicted in *chansons du trottoir* still believe, or once believed, in love. This hope helps them live through each day but at the same time underlies the problems these women have. For example, Frehel, an aging music-hall star, sings of the sadness of the prostitute's life but ends with "And even so, as soon as a hopeful moment occurs / All of them still believe in love."[66] But it was this false sense of love, and a willingness to express that love in sexual favors, which led these women down the wrong path in the first place. Mirane Esbly tells listeners in "Listen up, honey . . ."

> Sometimes I think it's better just to die,
> A woman can never get up from her first fall.
> And from fall to fall,

And rising to try to find a way to crawl up,
Until they push you down again.
She gives her heart away for a trusting vow,
For the promises of a lover who moves her, ha!
When love is nothing but a big bazaar with crooked aisles,
Full of junk.[67]

The plots of the songs included this lost love and became small tragic tales of the streets. Single women gave in to their baser instincts, trusted unworthy men, lost their own innocence, and followed the natural downward spiral, eventually becoming prostitutes.

Many radio stars made their fortunes singing these tragic tales, including Damia and Frehel, but one star outshone them all, becoming an icon of French song in the latter half of the 1930s. Edith Piaf perfectly represented French radio's vision of the single girl, both in her performances and in her life. In her songs she portrayed marginal characters, whose position in society allowed them more freedom of sexual expression in their lyrics but always at a price. French society expected Piaf to carry this lifestyle over into daily life or else suffer a loss in popularity.[68] Piaf came to the stage and radio directly from the street. She grew up in Ménilmontant, one of the seediest neighborhoods in Paris.[69] To survive, she may have spent some time as a prostitute. She also sang on street corners to pick up extra cash. There she was spotted by Louis Leplée, a gay night-club owner, given a new name, and put on stage.[70] Her management would not allow her to become too much of a sophisticate on- or offstage. Piaf came from the streets, never lived a domestic existence, never sustained long-term relationships with men, and never had children.[71]

Piaf began her professional singing career as the *Môme Piaf*, a kid or bird (with the same literal and slang meanings as in English), who performed onstage with her accordion. Leplée called her *môme* because he hoped she would captivate audiences who would admire her tiny "bird-like" body that held such a tremendous singing voice. This same small form and thin face made her an impossible market for cinema. The slanginess of the name also had the connotations of the street, for Piaf was a poor girl trying to make it on the stage and in song, an image that could only enhance her performances of the *chansons du trottoir*. The combination of her rough, emotional voice, her shady background, and her ability to convey the sadness of the stories in her songs virtually guaranteed her stage and radio success.

In 1936, Piaf got her big national break, moving from the local Parisian nightclub scene to perform on the station Radio-Cité, in one evening episode of a program series for singing hopefuls called *The Music-Hall of the Young*. Jacques Canetti, artistic director at the up-and-coming Radio-Cité organized the show and recognized Piaf's talent right away. Broadcast originally from Paris, the show was replayed nationally by other private stations. Canetti immediately signed Piaf to a contract with Radio-Cité to appear weekly before live audiences as the warm-up act for the evening programming. He also signed her to a recording contract with Polydor in order to get her behind the microphone with marketable music.[72] Due to Piaf's rising popularity, Canetti encouraged her to take lessons in being a star, to smooth out some of her rough street edges, and make herself more palatable for a national audience. Thus, at age twenty-one, Piaf was taken from the street and shown how to act the part of the experienced female entertainer. Her managers taught her how to address an audience and showed her how to make the most of her simple appearance. She was taught to accentuate her poverty and the poverty she sang about in her songs. Her voice was rough and spoke to experience that far surpassed her twenty-odd years. With her newly refined image, Piaf soon took all France by storm, making hit records with Polydor by the end of 1936 and becoming the icon of the realist song singer. Raymond Asso, the foremost lyricist of realist songs, began to write exclusively for her, dumping other singers, like Germaine Sablon and Marie Dubas, who he had often written for before.[73]

Piaf always sang in the role of a single working-class woman. One of her first hits was "Mon Légionnaire," which was written for Marie Dubas by Raymond Asso in 1936. A lonely, tragic bugle call sets the scene. Piaf, as a husky-voiced single woman, pledges love to a heroic French Legion soldier. She spends one wonderful night with him, giving her character the ambiguous role of the single working-class woman—is she just sexually forward, or is she a prostitute? The love affair is illicit, but the soldier is quite beautiful. What single woman could resist?

> I don't know his name, I know nothing about him.
> He loved me all night long, my legionnaire.
> Leaving me to my destiny,
> He left at first light in the morning.
> He was thin, he was handsome,

He smelled good, of warm sand, my legionnaire.
There was sun on his forehead,
Which put light into his blonde hair.

Piaf regrets that she never tells him that she loves him, and he goes off to North Africa and is killed, never knowing her feelings for him. She sings in despair:

They found him in the desert, his eyes still open,
Clouds passed in the sky.
He showed his tattoos,
And laughing he said,
Showing his neck, "Not seen, not taken."
Showing his heart, here, "No one."
He didn't know, I forgive him . . .

Piaf is the victim of an illicit love (or at least a sexual) affair. Like the prostitutes in their songs, she loves a man who cannot love her back. After she sleeps with him once, she is left dreaming about him forever:

I dreamed anyway that destiny
Would bring him back to me some beautiful morning, my legionnaire
We could stay together
In some marvelous country full of light.[74]

Piaf's character dreams of a place where she can go to escape her dreary, inevitable existence as a lonely, single girl. For listening audiences in 1936, used to the tuneful laments of single working-class women, the pathos of the song must have been obvious, and many who heard Piaf sing were moved to tears. Even Mistinguett, who in 1936 saw Piaf as a professional rival as well as competition for Maurice Chevalier's affection, claimed to have cried at Piaf's performance. The song became one of Edith Piaf's greatest hits and a standard in radio and stage performances.

Another big hit came in 1937 with a song entitled "Stay," written by Jacques Simonot and Pierre Bayle. The song takes place after a love affair ends and is the heroine's attempt to win her love back by helping him to remember their pleasant past on the last night they will spend together:

> Now that it's really over,
> And our hearts have recovered,
> Stay, so that we can talk a while
> Of the time when we were happy . . .[75]

Piaf leaves us with more sadness of loves lost and a world beyond her control. The single girl's sexual passion has become the sole focus of her life.

Edith Piaf also sang many of the *chansons du trottoir,* whose traits fit her singing style. With her past on the streets and her throaty voice, the prostitutes' songs became Piaf's forte. Of the fifty-six songs she cut between 1936 and 1940, thirty were *chansons du trottoir.*[76] The others, like "My Legionnaire" or "Stay," told tales from the city streets and seedy ports. Piaf, with her remarkable voice and her own questionable past, which itself became the talk of the French tabloids, could play only characters who provoked pity or lust from her audience.[77]

In the *chanson du trottoir* "She Hung Out on Pigalle Street," she sings of a girl who wanders the streets of a seedy neighborhood in Paris (much like Piaf herself may have been in her own youth), making money by turning tricks. She leaves the streets when she falls in love with a man who in turn dumps her after a short while. In true single-girl fashion:

> She returned to her Pigalle.
> There was no one left to hold her back.
> She found her old sins, her shadowy places, her dirty sidewalks
> But when she saw lovers walking up the street hand in hand
> There were tears in her big blue eyes.[78]

For this impure woman, the lack of a permanent male figure in her life has left her with only one option: life on the street.

Edith Piaf played the sexually active single girl in French film as well, but this time a bourgeois woman who had fallen astray. In 1937 she acted in the title role of the movie adaptation of Victor Margueritte's popular 1922 novel *La Garçonne.*[79] The *garçonne* was a flapper torn between a life of gender ambiguity as a "new woman" with sexual freedom and settling down with a husband and family. Piaf sang the song that typified the *garçonne*'s loose behavior, "Even So."

> I walk to the door of the bar, where I drank to extremes.
> They pick me up somewhere, my burned body on a stretcher.

> Even so, I drink
> Everything, especially drugs, ecstasy upon supreme ecstasy.
> I'll do anything with no fear, until I go crazy.
> Even so, I take them.
> I act like a *femme fatale*, in the arms of a troubling lover
> And when something bad happens to him, he dies in a hospital bed.
> Even so, I love.

She cannot sustain this hard life for long. In a happy ending, she chooses family over freedom, respecting "normal" gender behavior with stable marriage and the promise of creating a family.[80] Edith Piaf, a dangerously ambiguous figure of the thirties, is, by the end of the film, transformed on screen into the model of bourgeois purity and stability. In the film, the *garçonne* comes from a bourgeois family and can return to it. This option was not available to the single working-class women Piaf portrayed in song.

Edith Piaf's career was brief. She died of hard living at age forty-eight. Yet before her untimely death in 1963, Piaf became a star of immense proportions. To achieve this success, Piaf used standard gender molds of single working-class girls and prostitutes and adapted her songs into an acceptable character on the fringes of ordinary life, the sexual victim who paid dearly for her immoral behavior. And to please her French audience and fit into the atmosphere of the radio, film, and stage characters she created, she paralleled the life of this character off the stage. Piaf gave up her own domestic life both publicly and privately.

In response to the French song trope of the good-hearted prostitute, Ray Ventura wrote his brilliant parody of the *chanson du trottoir*. In it, Paulette continues to follow the sad fate of the single working-girl. Paulette begins to drink, do drugs and falls into sexual perversion:

> And then she began to drink,
> Always sagely,
> Always properly.
> Every evening she needed many straight mint drinks.
> She drank as many as fifty,
> Always blushing,
> Always properly.
> When she'd had enough of the mint,

> She'd order herself some coke.
> She offered herself all the passions,
> Obsessions,
> Objections.
> She knew about the most perverse things,
> Lengthwise,
> Widthwise,
> And upside-down.

She then turns to prostitution to support herself, ending up walking the streets in the seediest part of town, "Villette," on the margins of life and literally on the margins of the city.

The comic litany of bad behavior in "Paulette" mocks the characters in the *chansons du trottoir*, but Ray Ventura does not stop there. He makes light of the idea that in spite of all these activities, Paulette was "without faults" and still a caring woman. Here he rips apart the idea that prostitutes still believed in love and were dragged into the profession by wicked men. For Ventura, it was obvious that the women who ended up as prostitutes had to take the blame for themselves. Ventura, while taking the "good-heartedness" out of the whore, reminded his audience that most working women did not automatically follow Paulette's path and that that path should not have been the only one that was expected for them. For Ventura, the characters of the *chanson de trottoir* were not the victims of rotten fate but rather the victims of a conservative and silly song genre that gave an old-fashioned moral lesson in the midst of a changing world for urban youth.

Ray Ventura's "Paulette" shows a strong critique of French culture's rejection of the young working-class single and is itself a refutation of the inevitable downward spiral that was depicted for single youth. Writing and performing songs for young audiences, Ventura and his band had different ideas about what could be a stable and happy life. Many of the other young writers and performers, like Mireille and Fernandel, embraced and enjoyed the freedoms that they saw embodied in single life. And although working-class lives in the 1930s looked nothing like the joyful characters portrayed in their songs, their radio offered a happy distraction to the drudgery of youth during the financial and political crises of the decade and the increased fears of the changing gender roles in French society.

Yet conservative assumptions about the problems of working-class life also often played on French radio. In spite of some happy portrayals of young bourgeois love and lust, nowhere in radio fiction do working-class women and men appear as positive role models. Paulette's life follows the stereotypical melancholy path that was set up for almost all single working women in 1930s French radio fiction. Working women began by having affairs with their employers, sometimes brought criminality into their homes, and ended up singing about the tragedy of their lives on the streets. Single, working-class people were always assumed to be led astray by their passions because they had no support from husbands, fathers, or stable nuclear families. While a titillating fascination with the underworld helps to create a genre of working-class life, ultimately the standard, conservative lesson of radio fiction was clear: to avoid tragedy and lead happy lives, women and (less so) men had to move directly from the care of their fathers to the care of their husbands or new families, maintaining the ideal of a stable, patriarchal French household.

6 BOA CONSTRICTORS, MAN-EATERS, AND *LE CAFARD*
Colonial Landscapes on Metropolitan Radio

In 1936, a Jacques Cossin mystery, *The Enigma of the Night of the Fourth*, featured an innocent country farmer murdered cruelly in his sleep by a neighbor's boa constrictor brought back from Java.[1] The radio play underscored the horror of the killing by making the assassin a snake from the colonies and the retired country farmer an exemplary French citizen before his untimely demise. The lesson of the tale was simple. The exotic features of the colonial world had to stay in that world or they would pollute the fabric of the home, even killing the nation's best citizens. The mystery brought to life a worrisome tale that could shock the radio listeners with its exotic and deadly invasion into their own homes and assumed safe spaces.

As revealed by this play, radio, the electric mass medium of the home, had a particular relationship to the depiction of the colonial space. In spite of a fascination with the exotic, scenes of the colonies had to penetrate into, but not alter or degrade, the safety of the home. In order to protect the integrity of that home, the stories of the colonies focused not on satisfaction and happiness outside France, but rather on the danger that lurked beyond the national borders. After all, colonial subjects did not reflect back the image of bourgeois patriarchal morality that radio producers saw as their ideal. The colonies could show only a poor reflection of the best that was France and make the metropole and French home more glorious in comparison.

Metropolitan radio often depicted life in the French empire in songs and plays. This interest reflected a fascination for representations of the empire during the decade, as the 1930s saw two major celebrations for "Greater France [*la plus grande France*]" in the Colonial Exposition of 1931 and in the International Exposition of 1937, with the Ile des Cygnes in the Seine set aside for colonial exhibits. Some of the radio's airtime was spent in similar reverence, but in spite of all the emphatic love of empire that came from the government propaganda in its expositions, the radio's representations of the colonies showed a much more ambiguous feeling toward France's relationship with its satellites. On the one hand, the French felt they had much to be proud about in their heroic and conquering imperial past. They had brought civilization to the "savages" in the guise of the railroad, industry, and colonial governments and an official civilizing mission. On the other hand, by the late 1930s, France's colonies posed many problems for the government and the economy. Aspirations for the colonial *mission civilisatrice* were not high, and morale in the colonies was low. Furthermore, the rumblings of rebellion were becoming louder in both Indochina and North Africa.

Radio plays and songs reflected an unclear relationship to the empire, attesting to both the patriotic up side of "the civilizing mission" and the horrendous difficulties that faced the French once they were abroad. The colonies were exoticized for listening audiences and provided much that was unusual, magical, and mysterious. For the most part, however, radio's colonial story exhibited great disappointment in the project. From horrific slaughters to extreme boredom, the colonies held no appeal for those who traveled there in radio fictions. Even more disappointing were the images of the natives who were to be civilized by the French. All of them appeared as strange stereotypes on the radio, characters that the listeners would probably already have been familiar with from movies and novels. The colonies had nothing to offer French citizens back home, except for economic boon. According to radio fiction, metropolitan culture could reap no benefit from contact with its empire and all of the cultural and social advantages traveled in the other direction.[2]

Both public and private radio thus created images of the empire that served for a specific listening audience. Both the government and private radio interests described a highly stylized "Greater France"—one that never actually existed on the ground.[3] The large majority of the audience would never hear more than scattered news reports about the colonial unrest. Public radio had ten-minute, biweekly reports about activities in the colonies, but there is no way to know how much political and social turmoil was featured in the programs.[4] The citizenry's image of its colonies came either from the expositions or from books and radio. The colonial expositions, the first in the Parc de Vincennes on the outskirts of Paris in 1931 and the second on the Ile des Cygnes in the Seine at the International Exposition of 1937, attempted to introduce the French to their empire by showing them displays of life for the natives as well as giving them lessons on the economic development the colonies offered to France. Of the 60 or so million inhabitants of the empire, only 2 million were European, and of those, only five hundred thousand were French.[5] Most citizens knew the empire existed but would never actually see it. And the vast majority of those who did go abroad would travel across the Mediterranean to North Africa, and no farther. West and Equatorial Africa, Indochina, and Madagascar were imaginary spaces to the vast majority of French citizens.

In this way, the colonial sound images in radio had to invoke a background much more clearly than those of plays taking place on home soil. Metropolitan listeners needed description in sound that could allow them to imagine what the actors or the reporters saw around them, thus the sound image. From the calls of the muezzin in the Algiers Casbah to the rumbling of native drums in the upper reaches of Indochina, sound decor gave the listener a specific sense of place in an unknown world. Even the foreign tones of Arabic or an African pidgin French told radio audiences something about the people depicted in the colonial setting. The sound images presented on the radio became an important part of how most of the French envisioned their relationship to the empire and its inhabitants. Without the sound, the stories lost their exoticism and could have taken place in the metropole. These stories, through sound, were rooted into an empire of colonists, colonials, and foreign landscapes.

This relationship of sound and colonial story was very clear in a series presented on Poste Parisien during the 1937–38 season; it was called *A French Imperial Voice: From North Africa to Black Africa through the Sahara Desert*. In nine hours of radio recordings, presented each Monday, Wednesday, and Friday from March 21 to May 2, 1938, French listeners heard the sounds of the French empire as recorded and reported by Paul-Edmond Décharme and engineered by Robert Biart. To show the French their African empire, Décharme interviewed colonial governors and tribal chiefs, took his microphone to colonial schools and Foreign Legion parades, and most important, revealed African ceremonies to his audience back home. Décharme and Biart became a new, radio version of the great explorers of Africa from the nineteenth century. Now, with the civilized technology of the interwar era, two men could intrepidly tour Africa and bring back sound for the public. These sound images superseded the visual images that those in the hexagon may have seen in newspapers and on film. The "true" experience of the hero-reporters brought a new Africa to audiences, one that added immediacy to the colonial experience.

Although the recordings have long since vanished, a review of the program gives a sense of the impact that sound recordings had on metropolitan perceptions of their empire. It was praised highly by *La Semaine Radiophonique*; the journal claimed that "two earnest men, desirous of serving the French cause, have made a work of art, an aural reconstitution that words can hardly describe."[6] The reviewer marveled at the ability of sound to recreate the atmosphere of the empire, giving the listeners a sound glimpse of the most exotic practices: "Paul-Edmond Décharme and Robert Biart made a crossing to southern Tunisia to gather the strangest recordings imaginable: for the first time, and after many negotiations: the microphone entered the Kairouan Mosque, the holy city; it also traveled to the island of Djerba, where, for twenty-five hundred years, the same customs have prevailed." In a later review of the series, Antoinette Roland underlined the unusual nature of African practices and the amazing engineering feats of the two radio employees, outlining the recordings she had heard over the course of the programs:

> We are not just stupefied by the audacity of [these] travelers, but we can also imagine the technical difficulties and literally identify with our heroes' impressions. Along with them, we feel fear from the sound of Simoun's song; like them, we risk capsizing in their raft; following them, we listen to drums and, even better, the mysterious Touareg woman's one-stringed violin, which we have the advantage of not having to see; finally the interview with the black king and his cry of "Long live France!" is as moving as the silence of the disciple of Father de Foucauld, who evokes his protector and saint while babbling in guttural tones.[7]

The series becomes a report about the truth of the empire. The sounds give the reviewer the impression of unfiltered reality. Roland continues, "This report is appealing for more than its truth; it is a far-off reality which becomes our own during the entire program." Audiences could listen to the recorded empire and feel their ownership of the territories beyond their view. Sound functioned as the method by which audiences understood their place in the center of a vast regime. The real empire could be translated in its sound and enjoyed by audiences safe inside their metropolitan homes.[8]

This "real" sound background was rare on the radio. French listeners most often learned of the colonies in fiction. The radio sometimes used worn-out descriptions familiar to most listeners from the expositions, novels, and museums.[9] The North African and East Asian parts of the empire were always described with an orientalist slant, full of spices, sun, and magic. In *The Viceroy of India's Daughter*, by François de Teramond, the story travels through the markets of Calcutta into the soaring heights of the Himalayas, with descriptions and sound backgrounds woven through the action.[10] In the orientalist radio tale, the decor was always fantastic.

One of the plays is a magical fairy tale that took place somewhere in India. There, fairies and witches and supernatural phenomena ruled the land. In *The Story of Prince Ahmed and of the Fairy Pari-Banou*, all the trappings of a classic Arabian Nights tale were present.[11] Our hero, Prince Ahmed, was forced to fight the evil sorceress and two viziers in order to rule his kingdom. He received help from the fairy Pari-Banou, who, through her magic, fooled the three villains, killed them, and married the prince.

Most of the decor depicted here reflects a European interpretation of the Eastern. The sound background to the play was a selection of classical pieces written by Western composers. "Scheherazade" by Rimsky-Korsakov plays a central part, harkening back to Burton's translation of *Arabian Nights*, still popular in the 1930s. An oriental serenade by Schubert underscored the love scenes between Ahmed and his fairy princess, and the more action-packed sequences are punctuated by a Turkish march. It obviously did not matter to the playwright, René-Paul Groffe, what part of the East the music was written to represent. In 1935, *Le Petit Radio* vaunted Groffe for his ability to create wonderful backgrounds to his plays: "What we call the 'aural décor,' which is the creation of an ambiance, an atmosphere, that takes all of his attention."[12] Any Eastern-sounding melody set the praiseworthy context for the "Indian" fairy tale. And certainly no "authentic" music was needed. Any familiar, but exotic, Western music could set the orientalist scene.

Unseen props described by the characters also give the story its oriental and mysterious flavor. The prince has flying carpets and magic fruit locked up in his palace safe. India itself is described by a chorus as "the land of roses," with perfumed smells as central to the notion of the East. Jewels, too, feature prominently, as a woman sings:

> Our diamonds are innumerable
> The pearls in our seas, too many to count
> It's India, land of wonders!

During the course of a marriage ceremony and celebration in this marvelous land, there are jousts on the backs of elephants, tiger hunts, pearl diving, and of course snake charming and fire eating in the main square. The elephant jousts make a maladroit reference to a European medieval experience, having no historical place in an Indian one. It is also evident, later in the story, that Groffe had no conception of the flora and fauna of India, as he placed four lions as guards of the healing fountain of his heroine-fairy, animals that belonged squarely in the African Serengeti. With audio, Groffe paints the perfect orientalist painting. For Europeans, already aware of orientalist imagery, the play recreates a glorious, mysterious past for an India that, in spite of the colony's continued use of pungent spices, is all but lost to the Europeans by 1937.

In radio's imagination, the mystical oriental still ruled over a kind of sorcery, although magic was by 1937 considered pure superstition by most radio listeners. For radio fiction, the use of magic was not confined only to an orientalist past. In *Taipan*, a Vietnamese farmer uses magic to kill a white Englishman, committing suicide by shooting himself in the heart, while at the same time killing his adversary by exploding his heart.

Barring magic, the orientalist backdrop is used for almost every play that takes place in the French colonies. The narrations in the beginning of plays describe scenes as "spicy" or "mysterious." In *Two Men in Morocco*, a ship approaches the Moroccan shoreline and a man on it explains what he sees in terms that metropolitan listeners could envision, "Morocco, its colors, its veiled women, its flat roofs . . . all like in the movies."[13] During their stay in Morocco they encounter no natives at all (at least not within the confines of the scenes we hear). They were white men within a white colonial Moroccan landscape. They talk about the Casbah, but they never enter it. And they never have any conversations with the natives. In the play, the Arabs serve only as background noise and decor.

In spite of the mystery that the North African and Eastern colonies offered, radio fiction, when not representing the legends of the East in the style of *Arabian Nights*, portrayed the colonies negatively. Aside from a few military songs that centered on the centennial celebration of the Algerian conquest and the Colonial Exposition of 1931, radio gave its listeners little incentive to travel to the colonies.¹⁴ The faraway exotic lands of the empire were no escape from the realities of French life in the thirties. According to the vast majority of radio plays and songs, travel to the periphery, while heroic and courageous, could, in the long run, bring only depression, degeneration, and despair.

One of the major problems in radio stories came from the natives who lived there. Radio fiction always depicted the natives stereotypically, giving characters the qualities that listeners expected. The Asians were always honor bound, the Arabs vindictive and comic, and the Africans naïve and childlike. All of the characters encountered in the colonies were male. Native women did not fit into the world that radio created. This may have come from a fear of radio writers to promote miscegenation, or even to hint of the possibility of sexual relations between white men and native women.¹⁵ By the 1930s, white women were a common presence in the colonies, one that had the responsibility of maintaining the boundaries of assumed civilized behavior. The radio plays, then, have limited casts and, for the most part, create a homosocial environment in the colonial world they describe. The only characters in radio plays and songs that provide heterosexual interest for male colonists were the European women they either brought with them or met once there. For example, the hero in *Two Men in Morocco* falls in love, not with a Moroccan woman, but with a beautiful Spanish refugee he meets at his work site.

The French citizens who traveled to or worked in the colonies constantly battled against the problematic nature of the native men they met on their journeys. Not quite civilized and not quite adult, each native group proposed its own challenges to the French characters in colonial radio plays. Although native men played the roles of servants, part of the colonial home, none could quite be trusted in the dangerous locales of the action, which increased the sense of suspense, as French and European homes were constantly under threat from the colonial subjects housed inside them.

One of the prominent Asian stereotypes was that of the honor-bound vengeful man who never forgot a slight. He would wait years to avenge his anger upon those who hurt him. For example, the rebellious Indian Buddhists in *The Viceroy of India's Daughter* did not fight against the British out of a desire for freedom but rather to revenge themselves upon the British empire. In unison they cry out, in a very un-Buddhist fashion, "Vengeance! Vengeance!" while making their plans to take over the country.¹⁶ This theme is repeated in other plays, two of which deserve a closer look. In *Jekko the Malay*, he takes the form of a servant to a newcomer in the colonies, while in *Taipan* the Asian is an indebted Vietnamese farmer.¹⁷

Jekko, in his eponymous tale, is a "good" manservant to Brichet, the head of a tobacco plantation in Malaya. Brichet himself is described in the cast of characters as "generous . . . but strict," and it is this second trait which will be his downfall. Brichet, unhappy with Jekko's performance as a servant, says to his white friends, the Fammys, while at tea, "He is terribly curious and I don't want . . . or what I really want is to train him to be more discreet." And when Jekko spills tea on Madame Fammy, Brichet, perhaps as part of his "training," slaps him. The Fammys are disturbed by this extreme behavior; after all spilling tea is not a great offense, and Jekko leaves in silence. Brichet, instead of apologizing to Jekko, excuses himself to his guests, saying, "I don't know what came over me all of a sudden . . . but I've never hit the poor devil before." The Fammys leave, more worried over Brichet's mental state than Jekko's wounded pride.

Over the next few months Jekko is more attentive than ever, even once saving Brichet's life. But he is only waiting for his moment to strike. When the Fammys leave for Europe he attacks Brichet with a knife. Luckily, a former servant of Brichet's, the Chinese "boy," kills Jekko with a rock before Jekko can hurt his master. And why does the Chinese servant kill Jekko? The servant was not more honest or rational than his counterpart. The listeners learn that he, too, held a grudge, this one against Jekko for having replaced him in the house when he himself was fired for being lazy. Monsieur Fammy, being unavoidably detained before leaving altogether, comes back to witness the scene and says, "The Malays! . . . Those people never forget!"

This image was repeated in the remake of Somerset Maugham's *Taipan*, rewritten for radio by Maurice Zeller Denis.[18] In it a white man, Archibald Horner, or the Taipan, an Englishman in Saigon, is murdered by a vengeful Vietnamese, Van Kinh, whose property he stole in a business deal. Van Kinh tells him, "You know, Ong Taipan, that my race never accepts dishonor? You know that only death can purify them [our ancestors]?" When Van Kinh says this to Horner, he uses the familiar form of speech or the "tutoiement," expressing his lack of respect for the white man's behavior. Horner's friend, noting the exchange, says to the Englishman, "You should never have acted like you did. . . . You know the yellow people." But the Taipan, feeling powerful, laughs it off—until he is magically murdered for his deeds. In this way the play exhibited the Asian "type"—the vengeful killer who remained a constant mystery to his white colonial masters until he found the perfect time to strike. And when he killed or revenged himself, he did so in a typically Asian and magical way.

Unlike Asian lands, Sub-Saharan Africa and its colonies were rarely heard from on radio, and its native peoples even less so. They appear infrequently in radio plays and only occasionally in popular song. The climate and geography of Africa played a much more important role in the plays and songs than did the *indigènes*. For the most part, Black Africa remained a blank slate on French radio, with little attempt to tell stories about the continent. The only Africans who did appear were depicted as ignorant and childlike.

One of the plays mentioning Sub-Saharan Africa was *The Caprice*, in which one of the characters, Jean-Claude Dutillier, had returned from Senegal to France.[19] Describing Africa to a woman he met on the Côte d'Azur, he chided himself for having believed reports about Senegal before he left, "It's not at all what I imagined it would be, after all the books I read. I dreamed too much, you see." His Africa gave him only heartache. The climate was "the most difficult," and boredom led only to *le cafard*, or depression.

He mentioned native Africans once when he praised his partner, Bernard, for his contributions to the uncivilized peoples they had found, "The negroes, if you only knew what thanks they give to him, for all the good he has done for them!" It is unclear whether he uttered the comment earnestly or sarcastically, but either way, the white men from France, despite the fevers they got, despite their frequent voyages to France and their fights against "le cafard," had done only good by the ignorant, uncivilized natives.

In *The Child*, by André de Lorde, an old French couple speak about a biracial child they took care of. The mother exclaims, "Wasn't he cute!" while the father is more cynical, "Yes, he was quite cute. I would have called him a little animal."[20] In the story, this child is used as an example to show the variety of children this couple has taken care of. He is an oddity, as mixed children would have been in the metropole, and cute but certainly not French. In spite of having one white parent, he displays the stereotypical traits of the African, as he is "a little animal" and not even human. His blackness trumps his whiteness in the story and points to the inherent problems of miscegenation.

The Africans are represented no differently in the few songs in which they appear. In one play, two children sing a song that earns them some pocket change, exhibiting the silliness of a native boy who fears even his everyday surroundings:

> The little negro boy
> On his big boat
> Going downstream

> On the Congo
> Sees some reptiles
> And big crocodiles.
> He gets very scared
> The little negro boy![21]

Another popular song that was sung by many different stars, including Edith Piaf and Suzy Solidor, was "The Great Voyage of the Poor Negro," which included lyrics in a Pidgin French ("Me want home").[22] It depicted the story of an African who is taken from home and forced to work on a merchant ship. While in the South Seas, and miles from the visible shoreline, he jumps into the ocean and dies while trying to swim back home. The character is quite pitiful, innocent and simple, and offers no physical resistance to his captors other than moaning half-French complaints. On radio, Africans, in general, were too ignorant to do much harm.

Like the African, the Arab in French songs causes no great harm. He appears in order to make the audience laugh. The differences between French and Arab culture are put into relief to create comedic situations in the narrative of the recordings. A different, and harsher, Arab stereotype appears in the radio plays. The Arab is someone to be feared by those who work with him. He is generally used a foil for the more "just" French characters.

In the play *Calling Blima . . . From 283 . . .* , two men on assignment in the Sahara have a young Arab boy as their servant.[23] Bernard, the older of the two French soldiers, describes this boy to his partner, "You've always got to have an eye on Ali. He never stops looking at you. Look at him. He devours you! Only figuratively, of course! He's not anthropophagous yet." Of course Ali never becomes a man-eater, for in fact he does not pose much of a threat. Not only is he a young boy, but we find out he is also mute. Bernard lets us know that this prevents the servant from either saying "stupid things" or lying to them. The silent Arab is a reduced figure here, but he remains a mystery, for we never find out how he lost his voice. Perhaps the French listeners assumed it was due to some barbarous Middle Eastern punishment. The muteness also allows Jacques Cossin to write a play in North Africa without any audible native characters. He literally silences the Arab inside the French army post, giving his two French soldiers full control of the aural scene.

In many songs the Arab is quite verbose, specifically noted for the strangeness of the sound of his language. Arabic-like tones help to set the scene of many songs within the Arab villages of North Africa. Singers make many jokes using the guttural nature of Arabic, showing how "unFrench" it sounds. With whining clarinets and gongs behind them, Alibert, Rellys, and Rivers Cadet used common Arabic words in nonsense order ("arbis, couscous, loubya, barkah" or "arab, couscous, beans, enough") to sing their rousing chorus in "Come into My *Casbah*."[24] In "Living with the Bedouins" and "Le Radabi-Nacou-Naha," the guttural sounds of Arabic become the butt of the joke in the songs.[25] By taking the strange and perhaps frightening and making a joke out of it, the songs placed it out of the realm of what could harm. The Arab was further compartmentalized in "Madame the Marquise Voyages." When Ray Ventura's band "traveled" to North Africa in the song (after passing through most of Europe and America in other verses), the Arabic style they played was easily recognizable, Europeanized "oriental" music.[26] The Arab is reduced from a possible threat to a funny moment in song.

The natives in the radio plays and songs have little real impact on the lives of the French who live there, and their characterizations are sketchy at best. They are reduced to children who should be controlled by the colonists. Picking up on the anglicism, the French colonists constantly refer to men of color in their presence as a "boy" and have no respect whatsoever for the people around them as adults or responsible people unless they have French supervision. Yet this condescension leads often enough to the problems that occur in the plays. As parents, the colonists must themselves act responsibly and treat the colonial subjects with care. When Brichet hits Jekko in an exaggerated form of parental discipline, he almost pays with his life. The Taipan experiences the same problem. The lack of desire to communicate with the Arab who lives with them at post 283 leaves the two Frenchmen without companionship. They certainly make no real overtures to their mute servant boy. Natives are untrustworthy servants and never friends because they are not white and cannot have adult relationships with their masters.

Yet if the best of these natives can be hired as useful, if not entirely trustworthy, servants in white colonial homes and offices, the worst of the colonized peoples are no more than murdering savages. The fears of colonial uprising and the necessity of the French empire as a parental controlling force seem apparent in the plays that deal with calamity in the colonies. These plays honor the French citizens who founded the empire, and they reiterate the need for French supervision that the radio programmers thought natives had.

K-247 typified the idea of the savage on the outside of French civilization and deserves a closer look.[27] The story unfolds on a train to Paris, where two men discuss their experiences in the colonies. One is on his way back from Indochina and has a terrible story to tell. The scene then shifts to the outpost K-247, where European engineers are constructing a railroad bridge. One, Lechaume, the head engineer, unthinkingly brought with him his wife, Sophie, who enjoys daily rambles in the surrounding jungle. The other, Weber, in charge of the encampment, explains the difficulties of the area, including the surrounding hostile natives. Ignoring this threat, Lechaume continues his work and his wife continues to hike in the forest. Eventually she is kidnapped and killed, Lechaume beheaded, and of the twenty-five men in the camp, only Weber makes it back alive, but his horrific experience has driven him insane. Months later, the doctor who treated him in the asylum tells the tale to his companion on the train to Paris.

Already claiming that his tale took place in the farthest reaches of the colonies, the author, Marc Denis, distanced his listeners even further from the location of the massacre. First, in a voice-over, he alleges that the story is real but that he has changed the names of both the characters and the geographical locations to protect his sources as well as the identity of the lone survivor. He then creates a narrator that separates the story from the audience by another level. This distancing allows Denis to tell a horrific colonial story, removing it as far as possible from the safety of the French metropolitan home. Further, by claiming the changing of names, Denis manages to convince his audience that the horrifying story was true, and his distancing protects his audience from the imagined evil of his story. When the play aired, a reviewer for *Radio-Liberté*, taken in by Denis's fictions, wrote: "Maybe those who lived through those anguishing hours evoked by this play are still alive today. We understand that for this reason the names of characters as well as rivers and places that provide the theater for these dramatic events have been modified."[28] Denis drew the radio reporter into his game to see the horrifying (and obviously fictional) events that occur on the outskirts of the empire as real.

Denis further dislocated his listeners by giving a story within a story. The play begins on a train from Marseille to Paris, where two men in a cabin share their experiences in the colonies. Both, by travelling on this train, return from the periphery, the colonies, to the center of the French empire, or Paris. The storytelling takes place in France, or on civilized ground, while both men head back to the focal point of that civilization. Therefore the tale, in the juxtaposition of a French train, or the actual location of the two men headed toward the center of the empire, with its story of an outpost on the extreme periphery of the colonies, seems as far as possible from life in France. The horrific colonial experience is shared by the narrator and his companion on safe ground and digested by radio audiences within the safety of their own homes.

The inner story itself took place in Indochina, or, as our storyteller calls it, "the bush of the empire." Before they journey there in sound, the narrator describes the area as "the land of the Mois and the Mouongs." Already the listeners hear the exotic sound of these tribal names and place the story outside of common and "civilized" experience. He continues, portraying these peoples as "savage like our ancestors, big guys, naked as jaybirds, with teeth filed to points and dirty daggers that they never go without." The group of savages that decapitates our hero is unclothed, therefore more uncivilized, and has evil habits that evoke inhuman tribal behavior. Their filed teeth show an inherent animalistic nature that displays itself in disfigured facial features. All of these traits make them the opposite of the two Frenchmen sharing the story on the train and distant and frightening to the radio audience.

Another link to the drastic difference between the periphery and the center was the treatment of the white wife throughout the play. Her behavior plays in opposition to the savagery of the outpost. According to Weber, she has no business being in the colonies at all. He says to Lechaume, "It's not really a place for the lady," and later to Sophie herself, "It's the first time I've seen a lady in a god-forsaken place like this." This stress on Sophie's qualities of a lady gives her the rank of being the most civilized (for who is more civilized than a lady?) in a completely savage land.[29] The comparison back to the savage natives was underlined with her presence.

The tale grows more frightening, and the conclusion more inevitable, when Sophie refuses to cede to the wild land around her. She has even brought along the accoutrements of her civilization in the body of a phonograph and Fragson records. She insists on playing Fragson songs all the time. Fragson, a Belle Epoque artist, helps to define the era of the story but also shows the distance the colonists had traveled from Paris, as the songs he sings represent the city's worldly culture and the opposite focus of "Greater France." Both men become annoyed at the constant phonograph music, but Sophie replies insouciantly to her husband's demands that she turn it off, "Ah my darling, who wanted me to come to this charming country? It wasn't me. . . . You think it's fun for a young woman like me?" Sophie misses the life of Paris, which she can but poorly reproduce in a record from the music halls of her beloved city. Sophie further complicates matters by hiking alone in the surrounding jungle, refusing to admit that where she resides is as far as she can be from the center of French civilization.

Sophie's Fragson recording also plays in aural opposition to the sound background of constant drumming coming from the jungle. The tribal drums remind the audience of the menace of the inhuman savages that surround the outpost. The drums also locate the story squarely in tribal lands far away from the metropole, where drum signals have no meaning. And when the drumming suddenly stops, the horror begins. The natives attack and kill the camp full of French and European colonists.

With his use of multiple layers, realistic sounds, and suspenseful horror, Denis convinced his listeners that these kinds of outrageous events were all too frequent in the early years of empire. The *Radio-Liberté* reviewer wrote in response, praising the heroic efforts of colonists like those in the play: "*K-247* . . . evokes some of the tragic hours lived by the pioneers to whom we owe, today, the train tracks that link to the city the most mysterious regions in the heart of our colonies. At the time in which these events occur, the French had no real colonial sense, something that is no longer true today." Weber, Lechaume, and Sophie were the heroes of the French colonial past, bringing civilization in the form of the railroad to the natives and understanding of mysterious Eastern cultures to Paris. For the French in the 1930s, the savage existed to be tamed by a better knowledge of France. The French, then, had a responsibility to sacrifice themselves to this cause.

This idea of wilderness in the colonies does not appear only in tales that were set during the Belle Epoque. On the radio, the French continued to sacrifice while working in the colonies, especially their links with the culture and manners from home. References to loneliness in the midst of savages appeared throughout the many plays (set in various time periods) that had colonial themes. This loneliness and lack of contact with France could eventually lead to degeneration and a return to savagery by the colonists.

In *Jekko the Malay* the Fammys complained to Brichet about their loneliness in Malaysia: "On this lost island in the Javanese archipelago visits between whites are as necessary as drinking eating and sleeping. . . . Ah, well, we, my wife and I who have lived here for so long, we're in the habit . . . of not seeing anybody and I confess that your being here amongst us, for these past few months, has given us back our taste for company."[30] Loneliness for Europeans dominated the Fammys' experience. As whites, they felt isolated and needed constant company. They did not classify natives as people. Society, or Europeans, had to be taken as and when they found them, which, in the far reaches of empire, was not very often, and in the case of Brichet, was the company of a man with bad manners.

Loneliness in the empire had strong costs as well. In *Calling Blima . . . From 283*, another of the plays in Jacques Cossin's series, solitude has terrible consequences. Like K-247, 283 is another numbered outpost, this time in the Sahara desert, too far from the center to be given an official French name. Our hero, Bernard, has been in the Sahara for two years and receives a new partner from France, François. Like Sophie in *K-247*, this new man brings along his phonograph, and together he and Bernard listen to jazz from France. The music makes Bertrand cry when he thinks about the consequences of staying away from France for too long: "I ask myself, deep down, if others, I mean those who live in civilized lands, if they feel what I do, if they really understand what music can bring to a person. No, of course not, they don't even think about it, they think it's all just in the natural order of things, they're caught up in the whirlwind of everyday life. Two years of this life have turned me into a primitive . . . *yes*, a primitive." The sound of jazz also helps to point to Bertrand's isolation. If jazz represents modernity and France, then listening to it brought on memories of the metropole. French listeners, too, could understand the contrast between the exotic sound decor of the desert winds and the familiar sounds of swing music.[31]

Another instance of degeneracy in the colonies comes in *Paramaribo*, another story that takes place in a colonial outpost in Guyana.[32] This time, Vlameke, a plantation agent, loses his head and has quite given up on Europe: "When you come here, you cut yourself off from the land of the living. Parents? I don't have any. . . . My friends have given up on me like I've given up on them. And as for the company, as long as the cocoa and sugar cane harvest isn't deficient, it couldn't care less about miserable little plantation agents." Too much time in the colony has left him degenerate, and Vlameke goes as far as to whip his servants and plantation workers. He destroys his wife, letting her die in from lack of medicine, convulsing to death in front of his eyes, and he is finally killed by another white man who is secretly in love with her. This time, instead of a silence surrounding the murder, native drums swell in the background, emphasizing the now totally primitive behavior of these two degenerated white men.

In the radio plays and songs, Bernard was not the only one to consider a lengthened stay in the colonies a route to degeneracy and primitiveness. When, in the play *The Last Act,* Simone Verigny saw the inconsistencies of her husband's old school friend who lived for years in Madagascar, she first asked if he had married a "negress" (he had not) and complained about his lack of manners.[33] Her husband replied, "Well, when one lives with savages for twenty years!" as if degeneracy of behavior were normal for one who left for the colonies. Would his marrying a native (and a black one at that) have been the last step in his degeneration from civilized European to savage? And this friend proved himself a degenerate, although not quite to the extent of marrying a woman from Madagascar—he became a dissipated cheater, who would even cheat his own country out of its rightful taxes from the profits he made from his plantation. In still other plays, characters call themselves "savages" after living for a while in the colonies, like Jean-Claude Dutillier in *The Caprice,* because, "In Kaolakh it's already the bush; you don't get any more unmannered than that." The French required the civilized atmosphere of their native land to retain their "civilized" characters.

In *Calling Blima* the *cafard,* or depression, that the colonies caused had an even worse end than simple degeneracy. Only Bernard had been able to withstand the oppressive heat and quiet of the colonial outpost. Of the other three companions he had, one shot himself, one purposely took off his hat in the desert sun, and one intentionally left his hat behind him. And François followed suit soon after his own arrival, leaving his hat conspicuously on his bed as he went out for observation. Suicide was the only answer for four out of five men at Outpost 283. The work in the colonies demanded the utmost sacrifice from the nation's citizens, and only the strongest survived the experience.

On the radio, most of the men who left for empire sacrificed themselves because they had failed in the metropole. They saw the empire as a chance to remake themselves in a place where nobody knew of their pasts. Many of these men, one is left to suppose, have departed for the colonies with nothing else left for them at home. François even admitted to Bernard, a week after he came to the Sahara, "I said to myself, with her gone, nothing really kept me alive . . . that's why I wanted to escape the world. I believed in the mirage of the faraway place."

This sentiment of using the colonies as a place to escape a lost love was common in the plays. Jean-Claude in *The Caprice* told his new sweetheart in France that he left for "the call of adventure," but she knew that it was instead because of a "lovesick heart." In Jacques Cossin's *Intelligence Service,* an Englishman leaves on a suicide mission to India because his girlfriend dumped him flat.[34] The songs about the Foreign Legion, like "My Legionnaire" and "La Fanion of the Legion," showed the desire that men had to leave France and their pasts behind them.[35] So it was with desperation that many of the fictional men left for the colonies, a desperation given to men by unfaithful white women who sent these men to horrific, lonely homosocial (since native women were off limits for serious relationships) places abroad.

Yet these men did not succeed in the colonies, and the empire became more of a hazard than an escape. Bernard committed suicide, Vlameke and Weber went insane, and the soldiers in the songs all die alone in the desert. Even Jean-Claude in *The Caprice* must find his happy ending back in France. On the radio, the escape route to the far reaches of empire proved illusory. The empire could not save those who journeyed there because it offered no solace and support. The problems that the men faced at home simply followed them to their posts in the colonies, and the colonies themselves posed graver problems than did France itself.

The authors of the plays and songs tried, however, to give the colonial men a heroic status. They often stressed the progress that France brought to its uncivilized "brothers and sisters" in its vast empire. The railroad appears in almost every colonial script, from its beginnings in the horrific *K-247* to its uses in *Two Men in Morocco*. In this play, the men admire the new city built by France, with "its banks, its train stations, its railroads, its bridges, its factories, its industrial works!" They have come to the colonies "for work"! They have brought the West with them, and during the economic crisis at home have found steady "Western" work in mines within the orientalist backdrop. The French have also brought plantations of rubber trees, coffee, sugar, and so on, as in *Jekko the Malay* or *The Caprice*. The quest to bring technology to the empire could even take on a ridiculous side, as in *Calling Blima*, in which two men manned a weather post in the Sahara, where the weather never seemed to change.

On the radio, the cultural benefits of empire were one-sided. Despite the remaining colonial architecture of the Colonial Exposition of 1931 and the artistic embracing of African "primitive" art, there was never a sense on the airwaves that the colonies had any place within the French metropole.[36] They were to rest in the periphery. In "The Color Line between the Lines: Racial Violence in France during the Great War," Tyler Stovall stresses that in spite of their valiant participation as soldiers in World War I, the colonial soldiers and factory workers were sent back home after the war.[37] Too many problems with race and assumed hierarchies arose between the colonial immigrants and the whites in France. In spite of generous behavior to American blacks (or certainly much more generous than what African Americans would find at home), there was no place in France for other people of color, especially those who came from the colonies.

The only repeated vision of the colonial in France is that of the imported African manservant or female domestic, usually with a funny-sounding name, who played the part of the ignorant, childlike foil to the narrator. Even this image was not a regular one for radio, instead appearing in radio publications, usually in comic strip form. *Ici . . . Radio-Cité*, the weekly newspaper of that private station, had a comic strip that depicted the ignorance of the one white man's black servant—especially toward whatever had to do with technology, like the radio.[38]

When it came to supposing the uncivilized technological ignorance and extreme exoticism of the African, the radio and its journals played straight into the stereotype. In a front-page spoof, *Radio-Journal* pulled out all the stops with a picture of a jovial thick-lipped African maid listening to her favorite station, "Radio-Cannibal." The accompanying story discussed the maid's love for her radio programs, which unfortunately her master couldn't understand as they aired in Bantu. The story gave African parallels to the kinds of programming found on French radio like soap operas, this time about the lives of blacks, the political news of the African kings, as opposed to French ministers, and the fashionable rage for tattoos on the thigh substituting for the silly vagaries in French fashion reports. The narrator forbade the maid to listen to "Radio-Cannibal" when he realized that the cooking shows had something of an anthropophagic nature! The exoticism of the African maid had gone one step too far and could prove dangerous to her employer.[39]

In *An Evening at the Chat Noir*, a play that depicts an evening in a Belle Epoque nightspot, a poem by MacNab is read aloud:[40]

> Did you see
> The six savages
> Who got off the ship
> In Paris yesterday?
> They were black
> Like tar
> From their heads
> To their toes.

The joke in the poem shows how it must have been a surprising sight to see blacks in Paris at all, and certainly those who came from Africa. The colonial subject in France had no accepted place on French radio.

In one hit song, "It's Zozo," written by André Hornaz and Paul Misraki for Ray Ventura, the barrier between France and the colonials is broken, as an African journeys to the International Exposition of 1937.[41] He is wide-eyed and happy, and he teaches the French how to lose their care in song. In minstrel-show singing, he meets with the distraught minister of finance and tells him:

> I've got what you need to save yourselves.
> It's not counterfeit money,
> It's not bars of gold,
> It's not government work programs,
> It's not even new taxes: No!
> It's Zozo! It's Zozo!
> With it everything's swell.
> It's Zozo! It's Zozo!
> With it everything becomes beautiful!

The song pokes fun at the idea that complex political and social issues could be repaired with a smile and a dance. The African is portrayed as ignorant and happy, and the French listener could smile at his simple suggestions for dealing with deep economic problems. The African provides amusement that can help the French forget about serious national troubles for a while.

Apart from the joking image of the hapless African on French metropolitan soil, any idea of mixing of cultures was anathema to the radio writers and producers. For them, the colonial influences on France itself could only be negative. Aside from harming the morale of the French who visited them, as we saw above, the colonies also brought death and destruction when they were imported into the metropole.

The Cossin crime drama *The Mystery of the Night of the Fourth* showed the fear of the entry of primitive and foreign culture onto French soil.[42] The story was a regular crime drama, with a murder to solve. A retired farmer dies in his cabin, strangled to death, with all the doors and windows locked from the inside. How he died and who killed him are the two questions that our fearless investigator, Lieutenant X, attempts to answer. The women of the nearby village claim that the farmer was killed by ghosts, since the gossiping group is very superstitious, as the writer believed most peasant women in France were. Everybody else has no idea. Our brave lieutenant, with no fear and under strong protest from his inferiors, spends the night in the cabin under the same conditions as the murdered farmer and quickly realizes who had done the murder. It was in fact not a human, but a boa constrictor that had entered into the house at night, found a warm body to sleep with, then accidentally strangled, and left the cold corpse behind in the morning, slithering out through a crack in the wall.

Cossin liberally borrows from a Sherlock Holmes mystery, *The Speckled Band*, in which an asp kills a man asleep in his locked room, but he radically alters the lessons of the tale. The lieutenant has a condescending relationship with both the village women and his inferior lackey, giving listeners an interesting view of French military and gender hierarchies. As a man with official army credentials, the lieutenant plays the voice of French reason and progress in the midst of a superstitious countryside full of chatty women. When he hears the gossip from the peasant women, he dismisses them outright, crying, "Enough absurdities!" and gets right down to the task at hand. At the same time, the male farmers of the countryside are the best of France and need his full respect. The farmer who dies was a good man, who made a living off the French soil and should have retired after a hard life at work. The lieutenant, to bring justice to the slain man, must bring the murderer to light. The lieutenant's assistant has no authority at all and listens to the unreasonable gossip and must be put in his place by his older and wiser boss.

The guilty party in the story is not really the snake, which after all is just an animal, but its owner, Madron, a man who also retired in the village, not from work on the soil, but from a plantation in Java. According to the villagers, he is a "good man, a native of this countryside." Yet he betrays his fellow French villagers. He brings back his snake with him, an exotic pet he did not want to leave behind in Java. This snake becomes a far-reaching evil from the uncivilized empire that kills a noble French peasant-farmer. Madron has learned too late the lesson that the culture of the colonies, even in the guise of a beloved pet, has no place in France.

Cossin sets up this unthinking colonial, who kills his snake after the fact, in opposition to our lieutenant, who, the listeners discover, also spent some time in Java. It is by this means that he can unravel the mystery. During the night, Madron uses whistles to call his snake to him, and the lieutenant recognizes these commands from his time in Malaysia. He received his army training overseas but, unlike the colonist, wisely brought nothing but rational knowledge learned from his army officers back with him to France. He admonishes Madron, "You brought a companion back with you, someone you had gotten accustomed to having around while you were over there, a terrible companion with whom you should have separated!"

We learn through this murder mystery that cultural objects and habits from the colonies had no place in the center of the French Empire. The radio taught its listeners that anything cultural brought back to France could only harm the civilization that already existed there. After hearing the solution to the murder, the lieutenant's helper cries out his alarm in a passion perhaps shared by radio listeners, "It's not possible! A boa! A giant snake in our peaceful little community!" The French had to maintain the distinction between the "primitive" colonies and the "civilized" metropole at all costs or the cream of French society, in the play a good French farmer, could be lost. Even the smallest object from the colonies, here a family pet, could spell disaster and death of the *patrimoine*.

The snake served as a metaphor for other nefarious and more realistic influences that the radio plays showed the colonies had on France. Another, more concrete problem that radio fiction revisited was the importation of drugs from the far reaches of the empire. Many characters get involved in the drug trade once they visit the East. For example, Roger, the hero in *The Viceroy of India's Daughter*, unwittingly aids an opium deal in Macao between French and Chinese merchants. In *The Crime on the Island*, one of the main characters is killed while trading heroin from Saigon off the coast of France.[43] Increasing drug use was one bad habit brought back from the colonies. The radio spread the idea that all cultural trade between France and its empire had to move outward, for the colonies could have no positive influence in the metropole.

Through the locales of the songs and the plays, the French expressed a desire for the exotic, in fabulous tales of mystery and strange difference. Yet the horrors of these tales displayed the great fear that listeners had of the not-French. How could listeners reconcile their desires and fears? The radio listeners worshipped the exotic but could not fall in love with it. To accommodate a desire for a European-exotic that fulfilled the need for true acceptance into French culture, all the stations played tangos from Argentina, rhythmic javas, and Hawaiian ukulele, all of which had a foreign flavor but contained strong European ties all coming from European cultures abroad.[44] Tango bands traveled from Argentina to play, while the Hawaiian groups came from the United

States. Many of the javas and tangos were written with French lyrics by local songwriters, including "The Most Beautiful Tango in the World" and "The Blue Java."[45] Radio programmers also created a sensation out of one singer, who represented both France and the exotic, a singer whom women could love with no guilt whatsoever—the Corsican crooner and heartthrob Tino Rossi.

The story and hits of the biggest singing star of the 1930s, Tino Rossi, help to show how the French appreciated the exotic while rejecting the overtly colonial. Since he was a Corsican, Frenchwomen could feel free to desire Rossi wholeheartedly, with no threat of miscegenation but with the perceived temptation of the exotic.[46] Tino Rossi was born and raised in Ajaccio in Corsica, one of the wildest departments in France. In the biography of his father, Rossi's son admits that for the French "a Corsican is an animal that is almost as exotic as a Pampan gaucho."[47] When he first appeared on a Parisian stage, in 1934, he sang at the Casino de Paris for a review entitled "French Parade." Representing Corsica, he dressed in native costume and became a citywide sensation.[48] Although wonderful on stage (always with a microphone), his light voice was destined for radio play. Marcel Bleustein-Blanchet, owner of the successful private station Radio-Cité, wrote in his autobiography: "The prototype of radio success was, incontestably, Tino Rossi, whom records made known, but whom the radio alone made a household name. [He] would never have seen such success without the radio, because [his] voice could not be heard without amplification."[49] As a crooner, Rossi needed the radio, where a microphone displayed the soft high tones of his tenor and made his Corsican accent easier to hear and interpret. His voice was also ideal for radio play, softer and more melodic than many stage singers, whose voices had to carry into vast theater halls.

Rossi's songs showcased his exotic background and turned him into a Mediterranean lover, sweet-voiced and dark, from across the sea, who wooed all the women of France. Vincent Scotto, the composer for Alibert, a Marseillais singer, became his writer, contributing to most of his 1930s hits. He never sang without a stress on the distinctions that made him not quite as French as his compatriots. He sang lovingly of Corsica, his home, in "Corsica, Island of Love":

> O Corsica, island of love,
> Land where I was born
> I love your cool streams,
> Your wild hills!

I have seen your enchanting places
And still, deep in my heart,
I will belong to you always, always
O Corsica, island of love![50]

Corsica in this song becomes both exotic, as an island apart from France with its own culture, and romantic. Tino Rossi explained his status as a heartthrob, having learned of love as a part of Corsican culture, on his "island of love." He also located his songs in other Mediterranean spots, such as Spain in "Tarantelle" and Italy in "Listen to the Mandolins."[51] He sang of love under a Mediterranean moon in "Marinella," where he implored his lover to dance the rumba (another exotic rhythm) with him until dawn. The instruments further established the scene, as all the songs were filled with the sounds of steel-stringed mandolins and plucked violins.[52]

Rossi also used language and lyrics to emphasize his exoticism. He sang, mixing French and Italo-Corsican, "Bella raggazina, piccola bambina, dans la nuit divina, viens tout près de moi!" in his hit "Bella Raggazina."[53] He used similar techniques in "Vieni, Vieni" and "Listen to the Mandolins."[54] The pseudo-Corsican that Rossi sang added romance and spice to the numbers, with a more fluid feel to the lyric than the typical French song. It also made the songs easier to croon, as Italian syllables float easier in the higher registers. In "Tchi Tchi," a song that has now become part of the French canon, he croons to his exotic lover, seducing her with both Corsican French and rhythmic sounds:

> O Katarinetta bella! Tchi, tchi!
> Listen, love is calling! Tchi, tchi!
> Why say no now? Ah! Ah!
> You must take advantage while you have time! Ah! Ah!
> Later, when you are old, Tchi, tchi!
> You will whisper to him, Tchi, tchi!
> "If only I had known back then," Ah! Ah!
> O my bella Katarinetta![55]

The rhythmic interpellations accentuate the sensuality of the song, perhaps reminding listeners of colonial and jazz syncopations.

Rossi became the biggest singing sensation France had ever seen, selling records in the millions through the 1930s. In 1935, he sold over fifty thousand records per month; by 1936, over eighty thousand. In comparison, other stars of the decade sold around eight thousand per month.[56] Rossi ten times outsold huge stars like Ray Ventura, Maurice Chevalier, and Edith Piaf. In the latter half of the decade, he was in a class by himself. Roland Dhordain, who would become a radio producer in the 1950s, wrote about the extreme appeal of Tino Rossi during his childhood and his own use of Rossi's appeal to attract the neighborhood girls to his apartment: "Tino Rossi's radio performances were always advertised well in advance, and when I found his name in *Mon Programme*, I would paste a sheet of paper on our apartment door announcing the date and time of the program. . . . And right on time, all of the girls in the building whose parents didn't own a radio would stop by to listen, in great ecstasy, to Tino."[57]

As women bought Rossi's hits in record numbers, many men complained of his popularity in letters to radio journals and editorials in daily newspapers (and probably also with friends who suffered the same problem). They preferred other stars to him, calling him a lightweight and expressing frustration at the time their wives and girlfriends spent mooning over him. Paul Reboux wrote a short diatribe about Rossi's voice in *Paris-Soir:* "I seem to always be listening to the wireless exhaling Tino Rossi's songs. These songs inspire disbelief in human intelligence. While listening to the program, I was thinking about Maurice Chevalier. I cannot express how much more I enjoy his friendly, jovial and lively style than that flood of fluids that Tino Rossi lets flow. I prefer Chevalier, the artist, to Tino Rossi, the faucet."[58] Despite this dislike and envy, other men imitated Rossi, especially on the amateur singing shows on private radio, hoping to follow his success on the radio and with women. Jacques Canetti, artistic director of Radio-Cité, commented in his autobiography that every male contestant on the amateur hour wanted to sing Tino Rossi's songs.[59] Rossi's popularity was so high that when *Le Petit Parisien* wrote of the 1937 radio elections, they printed a cartoon of a woman lounging on a sofa and listening to the radio who says, "Who to vote for? If only Tino was running!"[60]

Tino Rossi's success showed the French desire for the exotic but created no problems for the integrity of French radio culture. After all, Napoleon, too, came from Corsica. He proved the rule that any real cultural (or sexual!) contact between France and its empire was to be avoided. Had the French really desired the exotic in full, they might have chosen colonial musicians to be their stars. Tino Rossi brought the unknown into popular song, titillating women with his otherness. At the same time, he offered them an infatuation that did not cross racial lines, and he offered French music a new style of singing that, while exotic, remained wholly French.

An excellent comparison with Tino Rossi's radio and stage character can be drawn with the successful Parisian music-hall star Josephine Baker.[61] Like Tino Rossi, Josephine Baker exemplified the moderated exotic. On stage and in song, Baker represented the African and the colonial subject. She sang songs about experience as a French colonial's lover both in Indochina ("The Little Tonkinoise") and in Africa ("I Have Two Loves").[62] In reality she was African American and thus had the cover of Western civilization on top of her exotic African beauty. She may have danced with a banana skirt, strode the Champs-Elysées with a leopard, and warbled about experience under an African sky, but she sang with a strong, unmistakable American accent, rolling her "r"s and mispronouncing many of the words, making many of the lyrics practically unintelligible.[63] She, like Tino Rossi, owed her stardom to a French desire for a safe exotic.

French-Corsican Tino Rossi exemplified radio programmers' notion that colonial culture should have no more than a passing influence on French tastes. Radio stations had a responsibility to their listeners to keep the French home safe and intact, unaffected by outside forces. While the colonies were displayed as an ephemeral exotic vision, the tragic ends of most French and Europeans who ventured there quickly stripped away the appeal of faraway places. With sound images of restless and degenerate natives, horrible weather, and implicit loneliness, the colonies could offer only economic gain for France. It was the French heroes of the stories who could give the colonies the benefits of European civilization. On the radio, the mass medium of the family living room, the empire was a necessary evil, to be maintained at a distance, then exploited by radio playwrights and composers and enjoyed by French families as an evening's exotic entertainment.

CONCLUSION

In an ideal nation—for radio programmers, owners, and advertisers in the late 1930s who wanted expanding radio audiences—increasing numbers of French families came together around their radios every evening to listen to tales of adventure on colonial settings or to hear their neighbor compete in an amateur contest singing a rendition of Tino Rossi's "Marinella." During the day, housewives argued with the women they heard giving their opinions on *The Women's Forum* or received five minutes of beauty advice from an expert at Jean Prouvost's new women's magazine, *Marie-Claire*. Fathers came home and heard the news broadcast, listened to a radio family around the dinner table in *The Duraton Family* while eating with their own families, and then turned on a live concert by Ray Ventura and His Collegians or a retransmission of a play from a national theater. These fathers and families were encouraged to leave their radios on all day tuned to the programs that would appeal to whoever was presumed to be listening at each scheduled hour.

Radio programmers, owners, directors, and advertisers had to imagine these people on the other side of the ether, since they had no polls or record of who, exactly, was listening. To gain all-day, daily audiences, radio directors reified a notion of a traditional French family that used the radio as a fun, and sometimes educational, home appliance. Successful private station owners created an audience that they hoped would buy the wares their advertisers sold over the air. The listeners, in turn, appreciated radio as a break from their day and as entertainment they felt comfortable with inside their homes. The radio reminded listeners that foreign influences had no place in the metropole; the colonies offered France vast resources, but colonial culture itself soiled the nation. In the late 1930s, French families listened to radios knowing that, in their living and dining rooms, they were safe from politics, class strife, and foreign influences.

This programming was no accurate reflection of interwar society. Historians cannot look at plays, songs, and reality radio shows to give a realistic mirror of that world. It was, instead, a gauge of listener desires for themselves and that society—or perhaps, even more on point, a reflection of the imagined audience designed by those who made the programs. Certainly they hit a chord, and radio became more and more ubiquitous throughout the decades that followed. Yet the imagined radio world was one that did not foster much innovation beyond the technical. Although radio stations now had microphones as far away as Africa and radio antennae powerful enough to broadcast to audiences in New Zealand, the stations did not help generate new ways of thinking about the world. And in spite of competition between state and private actors, what was produced was strikingly hegemonic. Perhaps, as Marshall McLuhan wrote, "the medium is the message," or at least part of the message. It matters that this programming came by the airwaves into the domestic sphere. French interwar radio was programmed for an imagined home audience. So it could be that that imagined audiences' desires are the message. Programmers, advertisers, government officials, station owners, and all of those who shaped radio saw the viable audience in one way—as bourgeois (or desirous of the label), family-oriented, and regulated by a traditional daily schedule. In spite of radio's claims to democracy and inclusiveness, it was controlled by a conservative few and made for a captive audience that was increasingly seen as consumers. In spite of its technological innovation, radio programming was not truly original. In spite of its place in a new, modern world, the society reflected on air was traditional and rather stolid. In spite of the numerous women who had successful careers on the radio, the medium espoused the idea of separate spheres. Nineteen-thirties radio remained a paradox.

France's experiment with the mixture of private and public radio, with private interests leading the way, did not last, and so this story ends with the beginning of World War II. French private radio received a mortal blow in September 1939, when the radical government, now at war, began censoring and regulating private broadcasts in earnest. Most of the male engineers, actors, and producers were called to active army duty away from their stations. Private radio remained on the air but in a wounded state, no longer able to innovate and prosper, as its creative freedom and resources were severely damaged. Public radio, taken from the Ministry of the PTT and placed under the direct control of the Chambre des Deputés, became an organ of a nation at war. The government now strictly censored all production on every station, public or private.[1]

In June 1940, when the Nazis gained control of northern France, private radio was silenced for over five decades. In the German-occupied north, the Nazis and their collaborators took over the public stations and used the airwaves for propaganda. In the Free Zone, Vichy officials allowed some private stations to continue broadcasting, especially as two, Radio-Lyon and Radio-Toulouse, were owned by ministers in the new regime. Pierre Laval, the head of security and later titular head of Vichy, had control of Radio-Lyon, while Jacques Trémoulet, owner of Radio-Toulouse, became the vice-president of the Federation of Private Radio for the new government. With station owners in its government, Vichy could easily control the output of both private and public radio. Germans took control of French radio in the south when they occupied the area in late 1942, forcing owners of southern stations to liquidate their assets and turn over operation to the Nazis.[2] As historian Hélène Eck tells us, during the Second World War, whether in Paris or in Vichy, radio became another arm in the cause.[3]

Stars and staff positions would change both with the northern German occupation and the new dictatorial government in the south. Those who worked in radio would reflect the propaganda missions of the new fascist regimes. In one of the first moves the Germans made in their new control of the medium, the law of July 17, 1940, recorded all Jewish participation in radio in the Nazi and Vichy zones. In the summer of 1941, Jews were taken out of orchestras and removed from the studio altogether, including engineering positions as well as those on the microphone.[4] By November 1942, all station employees had to sign documents affirming their status as non-Jews, including disavowing the existence of one Jewish great-grandparent.[5] Radio was quickly Aryanized.

As many of radio's programmers, stars, and songwriters were Jewish, the ranks of radio employees changed quickly, and many of the radio stars went into hiding or fled the country. All the claims they made about inclusiveness and their place in the nation were for naught. Ironically, the hegemonic, assimilated vision of Frenchness that many espoused in their names, songs, and work would win out. In a few examples of the many stars and radio personalities mentioned in the body of this work, Mireille and her husband, former editor of the centrist weekly *Marianne* Emmanuel Berl, hid in a convent in Cahors. Ray Ventura and Paul Misraki and their families fled to Argentina from Toulon. Jacques Canetti, artistic director of Radio-Cité, went to South America as well, while his former boss, Marcel Bleustein-Blanchet, joined the Free French in London. Georges Mandel suffered the worst fate. The former minister of the PTT crossed the Mediterranean in the summer of 1940 to try to convince Morocco's resident-general Auguste Noguès to continue fighting against the Nazis from the colonies. Instead, Noguès turned him over to the German authorities when the general decided to back the Vichy regime. Mandel was incarcerated and later assassinated by the Nazis in August 1944 after the Allies invaded Normandy and were moving quickly through France.

Those who worked in radio had to choose between resistance and collaboration. In order to keep their positions, musicians, speakers, comedians, and engineers had to agree to use the radio for wartime propaganda and swear allegiance to the new French state. Many continued their work on the air, including stars like Maurice Chevalier, Charles Trenet, and Edith Piaf. All three performed for French POWs in Germany and enjoyed tours of Nazi Berlin while there. In the 1940 "Speaker Book" for German radio in Paris, Tino Rossi, Jean Tranchant, Damia, and songwriter Raymond Asso all made appearances in the first few months of the occupation. Jo Bouillon, jazz orchestra conductor at Radio-Paris before the war, continued his work apace.[6] Since Germans were now omnipresent in the north, and since entertainment was supposed to cater to their needs first, alongside these familiar broadcasts, however, could be heard a healthy dose of German classical music and opera, as well as shows for German soldiers who listened.[7]

Some stars and radio employees rejected work on German and Vichy-controlled radio and instead turned to resistance. For example, Jean Guignebert, formerly the program director at Radio-Cité, set up clandestine radio service in Paris, using both longwave and shortwave frequencies to broadcast to the burgeoning resistance movements across France. In 1943, one studio in Paris served the resistance by creating hundreds of hours of programming. Resisters broadcast these shows from four hidden antennae around Paris and its suburbs. From these emitters, the resistance could reach across France and to movements abroad. Some private radio stars and engineers helped with these programs, notably Maurice Bourdet, formerly a director at Poste Parisien, and Georges Brichet, a popular sports reporter for the station.[8]

After the war, many former supporters turned against private radio due to the Vichy government's continued exploitation of it, and especially the control of private radio by collaborators on trial or on the run. Jean Guignebert, now a resistance hero, became the minister of radio as the Fourth French Republic was set up. According to Marcel Bleustein-Blanchet, Guignebert told the former radio owner that the time for French private radio had ended. The resistance had made Guignebert a committed communist. "Capitalism is over," he said to Bleustein-Blanchet, and so then was private radio on French soil.[9] Bleustein-Blanchet would write *Sur mon antenne*, a history of his station Radio-Cité, in response to this decision. In a celebratory autobiography, he highlighted his radio's importance to free speech and democracy in the 1930s, especially with its public programs that included showed the station's commitment to audience participation. He also remarked on his experience flying bombing raids over Germany with the French resistance in London in 1943 and 1944. He wanted his profitable station back, but he would garner no sympathy from those in power. Radio-Cité was permanently off the air. With private radio's direct connections to Laval and Trémoulet, and with the success that private stations had over the state radio controlled by the Popular Front, commercial radio now had an irremovable stain of collaboration. Commercial radio would be broadcast into France from without, on stations like Radio-Luxembourg, which, in 1955 changed its name to Europe–No. 1 and became the private sector's answer to the public systems across western Europe, as well as the only commercial station broadcasting in French.[10]

Can private radio and its programming be blamed for Vichy as Jean Guignebert believed? Private radio owners had great success because they understood the rhetoric of family better than anyone. Even when broadcasting classical music concerts, Fernand Pouey, director of Radio-37, claimed, "We'll present them in a way that won't try the patience of the listener, but rather in a domestic and homey [*domiciliare et quotidien*] manner. . . . I can easily play Schubert if I announce it with a sound atmosphere of an animated, joyous family reunion."[11] Private radio stations understood that the feeling counted and that family mattered to French listeners, most of whom probably listened in family groups. A solid sense of a radio family, based on traditional values, brought listeners to the station and sold the advertisers' products.

But the Popular Front did not lose its audience because radio was inherently right-wing. The Popular Front chose to co-opt the styles and rhetoric of the right in early 1937. When the Popular Front listened to voters after the radio elections of 1937, the government had choices about how it would respond. The left-wing and democratic forces could have continued fighting, incorporating narrative styles familiar to the right, styles of narrative and story that could have had interesting characters in a left-wing or republican bent. If pathetic stories of prostitutes and adventurous tales of detectives were successful, there is no reason to believe that the left and center could not have created viable stories about successful working-class people and families. The Popular Front could have used messages in the same way that right-wing Catholic playwrights like Henriette Charasson and Suzanne and Cita Malard did: in narratives, not in public lectures and debates. Somehow, the blatant rhetoric of those plays worked for French listeners as academic speeches could not. Political rhetoric in the form of stories seemed acceptable to audiences, in spite of the overt messages they contained. But the Popular Front never used radio to its advantage and never really recognized the power of rhetoric about family in a medium that broadcast directly into millions of French homes. It never challenged the right or the private stations with a successful style of its own. In response to this failure, in 1945 the new postwar French government chose to face no competition in getting its message into the millions of French homes with radios.

The links between Vichy propaganda and the radio of the late 1930s would probably have been clear to most French people in the first half of the 1940s. Although some of the stars changed, the speakers changed, and control of the airwaves changed, the messages about family stayed the same. Ironically, much of the French music written by Jewish citizens continued on the radio. The Belgian occupation government even used the Ray Ventura hit, "Everything's fine, Madame la Marquise," as a propaganda tool to remind Belgians that Churchill's claims for victory during the Battle of Britain were quite exaggerated. In a poster with the song title, Churchill growls into a BBC microphone. Behind him, England, like the Marquise's chateau, is burning.[12] Ray Ventura's song had entirely lost its Jewish origins, becoming fully enveloped in the French cultural patrimony and serving as antiliberal jingoism.

In less ironic ways, considering the connections that radio programmers and advertisers made between notions of a French traditional family and the songs, plays, and public programs they broadcast, the Vichy slogan of "Work, Family, Nation" and the Nazi one of "Church, Kitchen, Children" could not have felt very foreign in tone. It was quite possible that for many French citizens, the 1930s vision of radio listeners meshed well with the Vichy and Nazi ideals about connections between family and the state.

In the 1930s, radio programmers and directors carefully chose programming that would maintain traditional ideas of the home, keeping shows comfortable and easy for listening audiences. Private radio and conservative interests controlled the content of radio and the vast majority of listeners. Private radio's life was, however, cut short by those who saw its power as a negative force on French culture and politics. It would not reappear until 1984, when President François Mitterrand and his socialist government allowed local private radio stations to operate using advertisements as revenue, once again giving private interests the ability to broadcast to French listeners.[13]

APPENDIX A
Educational Classes, Week of March 7, 1937

SUNDAY, MARCH 7, 1937

Radio-Paris
8:40, Beginning Italian
9:00, Continuing Italian
9:20, Continuing English
9:40, Beginning English
10:00, Beginning Accounting
10:20, Continuing Accounting
10:40–11:00, Spanish

Paris-PTT
8:40, Physical Fitness

MONDAY, MARCH 8, 1937

Radio-Paris
6:45–7:00, 7:45–8:00, Physical Fitness (Monday–Saturday)

Tour Eiffel
9:15–9:45, Secondary Education (Monday–Saturday)
10:00–10:15, Latin (Tuesday, Wednesday)
10:15–10:25, Secondary Education (continued) (Monday–Saturday)
14:30–15:00, Secondary Education (Monday–Saturday)
16:00–16:30, Educational Programming (Tuesday–Saturday)

19:00–20:00, Post–High School Education Programming (Monday, Thursday)

Strasbourg
6:45–7:00, Physical Fitness (Monday–Saturday)

TUESDAY, MARCH 9, 1937

Radio-Paris
17:00–17:20, First-Year English (Tuesday, Friday)

Limoges
15:15–16:00, Educational Programming

WEDNESDAY, MARCH 10, 1937

Paris-PTT
14:00–14:20, Esperanto, by M. Rousseau

THURSDAY, MARCH 11, 1937

Radio-Paris
8:00–8:20, German

FRIDAY, MARCH 12, 1937

Bordeaux-Lafayette
20:00–20:15, Spanish with M. de Maltes

Montpellier
18:15–18:30, English with M. Rubie

SATURDAY, MARCH 13, 1937

Tour Eiffel
15:00–15:45, Primary Education

Bordeaux-Lafayette
20:00–20:15, English with M. de Maltes

APPENDIX B

Lectures on Public Stations, Week of March 7, 1937

SUNDAY, MARCH 7, 1937

Radio-Paris
14:35–15:00, M. Sellier, "The Work of the Municipal Dispensaries"

MONDAY, MARCH 8, 1937

Radio-Paris
14:10–14:30, Leon-Pierre Quint, "Novelists Today"
15:30–15:45, Gabriel Reuillard, "The People's Poets"
15:45–16:00, Marcel Barrière, "The Esthetics of the Human Body: Colors"
17:00–17:10, "Historic Retrospective of the Week"
17:10–17:30, M. Chevaillier, "Pedagogical Lecture"
18:00–18:30, "The Artistic Half Hour"

Tour Eiffel
13:00–13:30, Lecture (Monday–Saturday)
13:50–14:10, Lecture (Monday–Saturday)

Paris PTT
14:00–14:05, M. Lutigneaux, "Grammar Mailbag"
14:05–14:10, Daniel Augé, "The Hemispheres of Magdeburg"
14:10–14:20, Dr. Hemmerdinger, "How to Make Up a Menu"
14:20–14:30, Etienne Buisson, "The Transvaal: Prodigious City"

Bordeaux-Lafayette
17:10–18:30, From the University of Bordeaux, M. Guillaume, "The Theater of Gascony"

Radio-PTT-Nord
17:30–18:00, "University Lecture," M. Duholt, "Lille's Tenements"
20:00–20:15, M. Lagache, "Lecture on Photography"
20:15–20:30, M. Waringhien, "Lecture on Literature"

Rennes-Bretagne
20:00–20:15, M. Lavoquer, "The Fiftieth Anniversary of Paul Feval's Death"

Strasbourg
20:00–20:15, Mlle Oulié, "The Women of Haiti"

TUESDAY, MARCH 9, 1937

Radio-Paris
14:00–14:15, Henri Bordeaux, "Literary Lectures: 'The Roquevillard Family'"
14:45–15:00, Jean Variot, "Popular Fables and Literature"
19:40–20:00, Jean-Richard Bloch, "France 1937: 'The Essay'"

Paris-PTT
14:15–14:30, M. Delphi-Fabrice, "Thirty Years of Montmartre and Elsewhere"
17:50–18:00, Mme Lavier, "Vegetable Tissue: Fundamental and Conductive Systems"

Radio-PTT-Nord
17:30–18:00, M. Hubert, "The Influence of Descartes in the XVIIth and XVIIIth Centuries"

Lyon-PTT
17:10–17:30, General Aviator Benoit, "Aerial Mountaineering"

Strasbourg
16:00–16:45, M. J.-A. Jeager, "On President Masaryk on His Birthday"
16:45–17:00, M. Nast, "Legal Questions: The Judicial Treasury"
17:15–17:30, M. Bergner, "Literary Chronicle: 'The Academy's Benjamin': M. Jacques de Lacretelle"

WEDNESDAY, MARCH 10, 1937

Radio-Paris

16:15–16:30, M. Petit, "Pascal"

17:00–17:15, M. Albert Ranc, "The Geology and Geochemistry of Helium"

18:30–19:30, From an article by Paul Dukas, "The History of Lyrical Theater in France from the Revolution to 1900: Edouard Lalo"

19:40–19:55, M. Fernand Gregh, "Poetical Theater in France since Beaumarchais"

Paris-PTT

16:00–16:10, M. Tuby, "Provincial Folklore"

17:40–17:55, Professor Besançon, "Pulmonary Tuberculosis in Adolescents"

Bordeaux-Lafayette

17:10–18:30, From the University of Bordeaux, M. Paul Courteault, "Ramond de Carbonnières and the Conquest of Mont-Perdu"

20:00–20:15, Lecture on Agriculture, "Family Allocations in Agriculture"

Rennes-Bretagne

20:00–20:15, Florian Le Roy, "The Sites and Traditions of Brittany"

Strasbourg

10:30–10:45, Mme Schisselé, "The Fresh Produce during Lent"

17:15–17:30, M. Ciad, "Algeria at the Exposition of 1937"

THURSDAY, MARCH 11, 1937

Radio-Paris

14:10–14:25, M. P. Rives and Mme Lise Daniels, "The Song of Work"

15:30–16:30, From the University of Paris, M. Boucher, "The Germanism of Richard Wagner"

19:10–19:25, Professor Gougerot, "Skin Problems and Puberty"

Tour Eiffel

17:30–18:30, M. Hourticq of the School of Fine Arts, "Flemish and Dutch Painting in the XVIIth Century"

Radio-PTT-Nord

18:00–18:30, M. Boulange, "The Legal Mechanisms behind Collective Organizations"

Nice-Côte d'Azur
17:30–17:45, Mme Marlo Vincent, "The Art of Interior Decoration"

Montpellier
18:00–18:15, "Raw Materials"

Strasbourg
17:15–17:30, Mlle Monteil, "The Eyes, Mirror of the Soul"

FRIDAY, MARCH 12, 1937

Paris-PTT
15:30–15:40, M. Jean Thomas, "Paris in French Literature: Paris in the XVIIIth Century Realist Novel; from the Abbot Prévost to Sebastian Mercier"
17:30–17:40, M. A. Silbert, "The Problems in the Far East"
17:50–18:00, Mme Edith Gerard, "African Magnetism"

Bordeaux-Lafayette
17:10–17:30, M. Rougerie, "The Poet Jean Lebrau"

Radio-PTT-Nord
17:30–18, M. le chanoîne David, "Eruthymos of Locre, Boxing Champion"

Montpellier
18:00–18:15, "Scientific Agriculture"

Strasbourg
17:15–17:30, In German, "History of French Culture"
18:15–18:30, M. H. Ley, "Artisans and Fiscal Reform"

SATURDAY, MARCH 13, 1937

Radio-Paris
14:00–14:20, M. Louis Sehcan, "Heroic Mythology"
14:20–14:35, M. J. Emile Bayard, "The Ministry of Public Works"
14:45–15:00, M. Rene Maran, "Dr. J.-C. Madrus and Our Knowledge of the Orient"

Paris-PTT
14:00–14:10, Dr. Gilbert Robin, Medical Lecture
14:10–14:20, Mme Charles Rabette, "The Art of Pleasing"

14:20–14:30, Mme Hélène Modiano, "Lecture on the Vulgarization of Philosophy"

19:35–19:50, M. Jose Germain, "The Seven Commandments of the Happy Man"

Bordeaux-Lafayette

19:45–20:00, M. Guillaumie, "Dialects"

Radio-PTT-Nord

16:30–16:40, M. Lequeux, "Japan and Its Expansion: Will Japan Remain an Island?"

20:15–20:30, Mlle Petit, "Lecture for Housewives"

Montpellier

16:10–16:30, Professor Palanque, University Lecture

NOTES

INTRODUCTION

1. Jacques Cossin and José de Bérys, *La Peur,* Radio-Paris, February 15, 1937.

2. Pierre Domène, "Avec Jean Guignebert," *Radio-Magazine,* February 27, 1938, 3.

3. Cécile Méadel, *Histoire de la radio des années trente: Du sans-filiste à l'auditeur* (Paris: Anthropos Economica, 1994), 203.

4. Vanessa Schwartz's work on the growth of visual culture in fin-de-siècle France was especially useful to me in conceiving new questions to ask about radio. Radio proposes new kinds of ideas that mirror visual cultural debates and turn those debates to audio culture and the 1930s. See Vanessa Schwartz, *Spectacular Realities: Early Mass Culture in Fin-de-Siècle Paris* (Berkeley: University of California Press, 1998); and *The Nineteenth-Century Visual Culture Reader,* ed. Vanessa Schwartz and Jeannene M. Przyblyski (New York: Routledge, 2004). For an insightful work on high and low Parisian culture as a whole during the 1930s, see Dudley Andrew and Steven Ungar, *Popular Front Paris and the Poetics of Culture* (Cambridge, MA: Harvard University Press, 2005).

5. There has been much excellent recent work on audio culture, especially in the American context. See, e.g., James Loviglio's study of interwar American radio, *Radio's Intimate Public: Network Broadcasting and Mass-Mediated Democracy* (Minneapolis: University of Minnesota, 2005); and Emily Thompson's excellent work on acoustic architecture in both symphony halls and radio studios, *The Soundscape of Modernity: Architectural Acoustics and the Culture of Listening in America, 1900–1933* (Cambridge, MA: MIT Press, 2004). For an overview of recent work in audio culture, see Michael Bull and Les Back, eds., *Audio Culture Reader* (Oxford: Berg, 2003).

6. For a good overview of the attempts to sell television to family audiences, see Lynn Spigel, *Make Room for TV: Television and the Family Ideal in Postwar America* (Chicago: University of Chicago Press, 1992).

7. There certainly were radios located outside of the household, in bars, in public squares, in businesses and factories. These public radios did not really take a large place in the listening spaces that programmers and station owners imagined for their audience. There is work done on public-sphere broadcasts of television, showing the impact that television had and has on our daily lives outside of our homes. See Anna McCarthy, *Ambient Television: Visual Culture and Public*

Space (Durham, NC: Duke University Press, 2001). This public sphere was not, however, a place that French critics thought about.

8. Kate Lacey, *Feminine Frequencies: Gender, German Radio, and the Public Sphere, 1923–1945* (Ann Arbor: University of Michigan Press, 1996). For work on the same issue in American radio, see Loviglio, *Radio's Intimate Public*.

9. For a look at crime literature, see Robin Walz, *Pulp Surrealism: Insolent Popular Culture in Early Twentieth-Century Paris* (Berkeley: University of California Press, 2000).

10. For fin-de-siècle reading habits and the popular classes, see Anne-Marie Thiesse, *Le Roman du quotidien : Lecteurs et lectures populaires à la Belle Epoque* (Paris: Chemin Vert, 1984).

11. Cécile Méadel, "Du local à l'universel: Les programmes de radio dans les années trente," in *Médias et villes, XVIIIè-XXè siècle,* ed. Christian Delporte (Tours: CEHVI, 1999), 91. Méadel also shows that although radios did not abound in rural France, this did not preclude the presence of radio stations. Early stations began with enthusiastic hobbyists who broadcast out of their own homes. Only when promoters wanted new stations in stronger markets did these radio enthusiasts often sell their right to their own stations. For example, Radio-37 and Jean Prouvost took over Radio-Beziers in order to obtain a license to broadcast commercially in Paris.

12. Elisabeth Cazenave and André-Jean Tudesq, "Radiodiffusion et politique: Les élections radiophoniques de 1937 en France," *Revue d'histoire moderne et contemporaine,* 1977, 530.

13. Lacey, *Feminine Frequencies*, 102. These radios cost only sixty-five Reichmarks. This put them in the range of almost every German household. The government also put radios up in public spaces so that even poorer Germans could hear the state message. The motto for radio by 1933 was "the Fuhrer's voice in every home and factory!"

14. Méadel, *Histoire*, 13.

15. This number assumed that all radio listeners were confined to their own households, an assumption that is, itself, very unlikely. Méadel assumes that the numbers were underestimated by at least twenty percent (ibid., 193). René Dhordain, in *Le Roman de la radio* (Paris: La Table Ronde, 1983), 49, claims that as his family was the only one in his working-class building to have a radio, they listened to their favorite programs with all of their neighbors.

16. Méadel, *Histoire*, 238.

17. Ibid.

18. Frank Tenot, *Radios privée, radios pirates* (Paris: Table Ronde, 1977). For information on regulation of actual pirate broadcasts, see the work of Derek Vaillant, "Sounds in the Shadows: The *Police de l'Air* and the Infra-Politics of Clandestine Radio in France, 1926–1940," *French Politics, Culture and Society* (forthcoming). Vaillant shows that, although concerned with pirate broadcasts, the interwar governments made little attempt to fully regulate transmissions from illegal radio users.

19. J. Reibel, "Il faut que M. Pivert," *T.S.F., Phono, Ciné,* October 10, 1936, 734.

20. Christine Bard claims that the 1930s began three decades of regression on women's issues in France. Certainly the prevailing notions of family and motherhood kept hopes for gender equality distant for active feminists of the day. Christine Bard, *Les Femmes dans la société française au 20ème siècle* (Paris: Armand Colin, 2001).

21. *Paris-soir,* February 15, 1939, 10.

22. Méadel, *Histoire*, 313.

23. *Radio-Magazine,* November 9, 1938, 8.

24. Lise Elina, *Le Micro et moi* (Paris: Pierre Horay, 1978), 52.

25. Charles Rearick, in his examination of interwar culture, ignores the radio completely. He misunderstands René Duval's analysis of French radio as intellectually boring as an excuse to leave radio out of his study. In fact, 1930s radio could be seen as television is today, often repetitive and stupid but clearly having a large impact on late twentieth-century culture. Charles Rearick, *The French in Love and War: Popular Culture in the Era of the World Wars* (New Haven, CT: Yale University Press, 1997).

26. Many of these records are catalogued in the Institut National de l'Audiovisuel in Paris. Perhaps when new conservation methods become available, these recordings will be more accessible to historians. For the moment, however, no one has listened to or rerecorded the vast majority of the French collection.

27. See Gerald Nachman, *Raised on Radio* (New York: Pantheon Books, 1998); and Ray Barfield, *Listening to Radio, 1920–1950* (Westport, CT: Praeger, 1996). Robert L. Mott, a sound engineer from 1930 to 1960, wrote a nostalgic memoir on foley: Robert L. Mott, *Radio Sound Effects: Who Did It, and How, in the Era of Broadcasting* (Jefferson, NC: McFarland, 1993). To date, the best histories of the radio have been social histories that analyze the makeup of the listening audience. Important to these works are the components that made radio a mass medium; as radios became less expensive, radio became a medium for all the classes and an especially important one for the working class, who could not afford many other daily entertainments. See Paddy Scannel and David Cardiff, *A Social History of British Broadcasting* (Oxford: Basil Blackwell, 1991); Robert J. Brown, *Manipulating the Ether: The Power of Broadcast Radio in Thirties America* (Jefferson, NC: McFarland, 1998). For a look at programming in the United States, see Susan J. Douglas, *Listening In: Radio and the American Imagination, from Amos 'n' Andy and Edward R. Murrow to Wolfman Jack and Howard Stern* (New York: Times Books, 1999).

28. For an excellent overview of the state of the field, see the recent *Auditory Culture Reader,* ed. Michael Bull and Les Back (Oxford: Berg, 2003). A similar edited work recently appeared on radio culture in the United States: Michele Hilmes and James Loviglio, eds., *Radio Reader: Essays in the Cultural History of Radio* (New York: Routledge, 2002).

29. See, in particular, Rebecca Scales, "Sounding the Nation: Radio and the Politics of Auditory Culture in Interwar France, 1921–1939" (PhD dissertation, Rutgers University, 2006). Scales's recent dissertation sees radio as a force for democracy in the interwar period. The focus on debates around radio and its uses for the public forms the center of her thesis.

30. See, e.g., René Duval, *L'Histoire de la radio en France* (Paris: Gallimard, 1980); and Tenot, *Radios privées, radios pirates.* See also Cécile Méadel's *L'Histoire de la radio des années trente: du sans-filiste à l'auditeur,* which covers the political history of the radio in the 1930s, tracing radio's years of rapid expansion. Méadel includes an in-depth study of programming hours for individual stations as well as a general overview of the programs featured on the air. Méadel posits that radio reached mass audiences and thus became a mass medium by 1935, when, as the title suggests, radio reached beyond the hobbyists and radios became widely available to a national listening public. Concurrently with the growth of their audience, stations began to program for the public and for advertisers, not for personal pleasure. Stations grew into fully functioning businesses with specific political and market agendas. Méadel's insightful analysis of the government's role

in establishing a radio network and the internal and governmental politics of establishing a new and vital electronic medium offers a starting point for this work on radio culture. She is joined by a group of historians concerned with the institutional history of the radio. The journal *Cahiers de l'histoire de la radio*, published by the Comité d'Histoire de la Radio, assesses each year of radio history, interviewing many of the major players in radio's past and shedding light on much of the legal and personnel history of the medium. See also Elizabeth Cazenave and Caroline Mauriat, "Les Auditeurs en France jusqu'en 1939," in *Histoire des publics à la radio et à la télévision*, Actes de la journée d'études du 20 mars 1992, ed. Michéle Bussierre, Caroline Mauriat, and Cécile Méadal (Paris: CHR, CHT, GEHRA, 1994).

31. This does not include the plays that took place in a colonial setting. I will discuss those sound backgrounds more specifically in chap. 6.

32. Henri Dorac, *La Revue des variétés*, broadcast between 1935 and 1940.

33. Rolain Gontrain, *Deux hommes au Maroc*, broadcast between 1935 and 1940.

34. Marshall McLuhan, *Understanding Media* (New York: McGraw-Hill, 1964).

35. Ibid., 299.

36. Ibid., 303.

37. See, e.g., Chantal Brunschwig, Louis-Jean Calvet, and Jean-Claude Klein, *Cent Ans de chanson française* (Paris: Editions du Seuil, 1981); André Sallée, *Music-hall et café-concert* (Paris: Bordas, 1985); Calvet, *Chanson et société* (Paris: Payot, 1981); Jean-Pierre Pasqualini, *100 ans de chanson* (Paris: Editions Atlas, 1996).

38. Most recent is Jean-Marie Planes's autobiographical essay that intertwines the history of popular songs of the twentieth century with personal anecdotes of how each song was reflected in his own memories of his past. Jean-Marie Planes, *Une Chanson qui nous ressemble: Petits essais sur quelques chansons françaises* (Bordeaux: Editions Confluences, 2001).

39. Pierre Saka, *Histoire de la chanson française de 1930 à nos jours* (Paris: Nathan, 1989).

40. The French like the storytelling nature of their classic songs. In a *New York Times* article that coincided with a Charles Aznavour concert in the city, Marcelle Clements wrote, "Like the blues, the chanson often takes the form of a lament. But unlike the blues, it is verbose." She admired chansons and the unique way that the French listened and remembered them: "When the French talk about the popular songs they grew up with, it isn't long before they tell you which ones made them cry." Marcelle Clements, "Sighing, a French Sound of Longing Endures," *New York Times*, October 18, 1998, 33.

41. One of the few recordings of 1930s radio still in the government's collection is of Edith Piaf singing three songs before a live audience in 1938: "Browning," "Madeleine qui avait du coeur," and "La Fanion de la Légion." Collection M. Ropiquet, Archives Diverses, 431.D.23 (196), Catalogue Avant-guerre, Fonds Sonores, L'Institut National de l'Audiovisuel (INA), Maison de la Radio, Paris. In other rare recordings, Tino Rossi sang as part of the "Journal sonore de la semaine." NS2806/KO00370, INA, L'Association des Archives de la Radio, Paris. Existing recordings of Maurice Chevalier include a 1938 comedy routine on Radio-Nîmes with fellow singer Charles Pélissier and a live performance in 1937 of "Je ne peux pas vivre sans amour" and "Quand il y a une femme dans un coin." "Fête des caf'conc' au vélodrome buffalo au profit de ris-orangis," September 30, 1938, NS04516/86INA08505PH0476, Archive Radio-Nîmes, INA, Paris; 1937, KO00144/X1086, INA, L'Association des Archives de la Radio, Paris.

42. Robert Desnos, "Les Disques," *Paris qui chante, Paris qui danse, Paris qui filme* March 1, 1939, 4.

43. Literary critic Richard Middleton theorizes that audiences found comfort in both rhythmic and song repetition. Listeners felt that they knew and "control[led] meaning and pleasure." Richard Middleton, "In the Groove, or Blowing Your Mind? The Pleasures of Musical Repetition," in *Popular Culture and Social Relations, ed.Tony Bennett, Colin Mercer, and Janet Woollacott* (Philadelphia: Open University Press, 1986). Desnos, then, misunderstood the French radio listeners. Instead of tiring of performers, they requested songs more frequently.

44. "Fernandel sous l'uniforme," *L'Ouest-Éclair,* December 10, 1937, 5.

45. *Le Petit Parisien,* 1937.

46. Histories of the Popular Front government and its culture are essential to my work in this chapter but not central to my argument as a whole. Pascal Ory, Henri Noguères, and Julian Jackson have all written excellent books about the Popular Front. Ory's almost encyclopedic cultural history of the production of the Popular Front has proved invaluable for comparisons of different government projects with that of the radio. The Popular Front took great pains to recreate France by involving itself in every aspect of high and popular culture, from national folk museums and international expositions to village dances and local theater. While Noguères celebrates the Popular Front, both Ory and Jackson determine that the coalition ultimately failed to create a socialist French culture. The government had neither the time nor the tacit support of enough French people to effect change on such a grand scale. See Pascal Ory, *La Belle Illusion: Culture et politique sous le signe du Front populaire, 1935–1938* (Paris: Plon, 1994); Julian Jackson, *The Popular Front in France: Defending Democracy, 1934–1938* (Cambridge: Cambridge University Press, 1988); Henri Noguères, *La Vie quotidienne en France au temps du Front populaire, 1935–1938* (Paris: Hachette, 1977).

1. THE PUBLICIS ANTENNAS

1. Christian Brochand, *Histoire générale de la radio et de la television,* vol. 1 (Paris: Documentation Française, 1994), 422.

2. I make this claim based wholly on anecdotal evidence. No ratings system was in place in France in the 1930s. In fact, Marcel Bleustein-Blanchet greatly admired Gallup polls when he visited the Gallup Institute offices on a trip to the United States in 1938. He had hoped to implement the same system in France, but World War II erupted before he could begin. Marcel Bleustein-Blanchet, *Sur mon antenne* (Paris: Editions Défense de la France, 1948), 93–96.

3. Other entertainment offered in cities could be quite expensive. While movies cost from two to fourteen francs for a ticket and were thus inside the budgets of the working class, who made an average of three hundred francs a week in 1936, music halls and concerts were quite out of reach. Only the bourgeoisie could enjoy these on a regular basis. Other evenings could be spent in bars or cafés, many of which may have had radios to entertain customers. Rural communities would have had village fairs and dances, as well as a local bar or café, but radio could offer farmers and peasants a daily evening entertainment suitable for the whole family. Brett Bowles, "Screening the Popular Front: The Sociology and Politics of Moviegoing," paper delivered at Historical Studies, Chapel Hill, NC, March 10, 2001.

4. Erik Barnouw, *The Sponsor: Notes on a Modern Potentate* (New York: Oxford University Press, 1978), 114–15.

5. The American context is excellent for comparison, as it was the only system in the West that also relied on advertising revenue. Susan Smulyan gives a fine analysis of the early effects of advertising on radio in the United States. Susan Smulyan, *Selling Radio: The Commercialization of American Broadcasting, 1920–1934* (Washington: Smithsonian, 1994), 9. It is important to remember, however, that the radio owners created a radio for an audience specifically. Although the United States system affected the choices owners made, notions of family and entertainment ultimately created a radio quite different from that of America. Marjorie Beale, in her analysis of French advertisers, stresses that advertising in France was particular to the nation in a battle of elite and popular culture. Marjorie A. Beale, *The Modernist Enterprise: Elites and the Threat of Modernity, 1900–1940* (Stanford, CA: Stanford University Press, 1999).

6. Article 109 or the "Loi du 31 Mai 1933," Archives Nationales de France (AN), F/43/1. To give a sense of what these sums of money may have meant to the populace in the late 1930s, the average hourly wage for men in France was seven francs an hour in 1936 (Georges Lefranc, *Histoire du Front Populaire* [Paris: Payot, 1965], 324). This made the tax expensive but affordable for most citizens, especially as it covered public radio fees for an entire year. By comparison, one movie ticket could cost anywhere between 2.5 and fourteen francs, depending on location and time of the showing (Bowles, "Screening the Popular Front").

7. The private stations were limited to the extant thirteen in the 1928 radio law that created the public stations. "Decret du 7 Juillet 1928," AN, F/43/1.

8. For an excellent overview of Mandel's career, see John M. Sherwood, *Georges Mandel and the Third Republic* (Stanford, CA: Stanford University Press, 1970).

9. Bertrand Favreau, *Georges Mandel: Ou la passion de la République, 1885–1944* (Paris: Fayard, 1996), 288.

10. Ibid.

11. Sherwood, *Georges Mandel*, 153.

12. Favreau, *Georges Mandel*, 290.

13. Paul Reboux, "La Gestion d'argent," *Paris-Soir*, October 17, 1936, 8.

14. Favreau, *Georges Mandel*, 291. Retransmissions of live theater performances became standard on public radio. This practice may have offered exposure for theaters during the hard recession years and may have given audiences the chance to hear major theater actors in performance. These shows, however, did not take the radio audiences' inability to see into account. Listeners probably had a difficult time following plays with a sound that was not well engineered and was without a sound background and the visual description of staged action.

15. André Sevry, "Les Projets de Radio 37," *Mon Programme*, October 10, 1938, 5.

16. Bleustein-Blanchet, *Sur mon antenne*, 16–17.

17. In her book *Irresistible Empire: America's Advance through 20th-Century Europe* (Cambridge, MA: Belknap Press, 2005), Victoria de Grazia notes that Marcel Bleustein-Blanchet was an innovator in many ways, especially in Americanizing the advertising industry. He was the first, in postwar France, to implement "social marketing" and "long-run perspective" on the national market (243).

18. Bleustein-Blanchet and Jean Maudet, *La Traversée du siecle* (Paris: Robert Laffont, 1994), 89; Publicis, *Les antennes de Publicis* (small and large formats) (Paris: Draeger, 1933).

19. Many of the owners knew Bleustein-Blanchet personally, being either cousins or friends of his Montmartre family.

20. *Les antennes de Publicis,* large format.

21. *Les antennes de Publicis,* small format, 13.

22. Ibid., 5.

23. Ibid., 31.

24. Ibid., 28; large format, 8.

25. Bleustein-Blanchet and Maudet, *La Traversée,* 89.

26. Johnny Hess and Charles Trenet would both become major singing stars in the 1930s. Hess had a hit in 1938 with "Je suis swing" and headed a swing band, while Trenet became one of the premier songwriters and performers of the century, with hits like "Je chante" (1938), "Y'a de la joie" (1936), and "La Mer" (1942).

27. These commercials were beloved by listeners, so much so that amateurs recorded them to listen to on their own time.

28. René Duval gives an excellent account of the machinations behind the creation of Radio-Cité in *Histoire de la radio en France* (Paris: Alain Moreau, 1980). Frank Tenot looks closely at the ways that private stations flouted French law in order to broadcast further and innovate on the radio. Marcel Bleustein-Blanchet was infamous for his attempts to give Radio-Cité a wider audience with a more powerful wattage (Tenot, *Radios privées, radio pirates*. Victoria de Grazia mentions the obvious fact that Radio-Cité was named after Radio City Music Hall, which Bleustein-Blanchet visited in an earlier trip to New York City. Whether the French listening audience would know of this is uncertain, but certainly Bleustein-Blanchet found inspiration in the American model (De Grazia, *Irresistible Empire,* 243).

29. *Le Petit Radio,* October 19, 1934, 5–27.

30. For a few weeks in 1936, *T.S.F. Programme: L'Illustration de la Radio* printed the scripts from "Les Amis de Mireille" toward the end of her run (from 1934 to 1936). Topics included "love" and "the automobile." *T.S.F. Programme: L'Illustration de la Radio,* April 24, 1936, 8–9, and May 7, 1936, 8–9.

31. *Le Petit Radio,* October 19, 1934, 9.

32. Ibid., 12.

33. The O'Cap theme was sung to "Avec Bidasse," by L. Bousquet and Mailfait.

34. *Les radios privées d'avant-guerre: Radio-Cité, Poste Parisien de 1935 à 1940* (Paris: EPM, 1994), track 10. It could be argued, that like the anthem of the Marines and Comet soap, the Monsavon theme became the meaning and memory of "Quand Madelon" for the interwar generation, adding another layer of meaning to Charles Rearick's analysis of why the song did not play well for World War II audiences. Rearick, *The French in Love and War,* 247, 249.

35. Louis Bousquet and Camille Robert, "Quand Madelon [When Madelon]" (1914).

36. Jean-Rémy Julien, *Musique et publicité: Du cri de Paris . . . aux messages publicitaires radio-phoniques et televisés* (Paris: Flammarion, 1989), 211.

37. Stars that appeared on the show included the comedy team of Jean, Jac, and Jo (*Petit Parisien,* October 5, 1937, 8), the crooner Réda Caire (*Petit Parisien,* October 13, 1937), songstress Annette Lajon (*Petit Parisien,* October 20, 1937), and Fréhel, the *chanson réaliste* singer (*Petit Parisien,* November 10, 1937).

38. The copy of the ad read "Milton also prefers Lévitan furniture!" and had photographs of him endorsing the product. *Petit Parisien*, March 9, 1939, 10.

39. *Paris-Soir,* July 20, 1939, 1. The advertiser for Lévitan was Publicis, Marcel Bleustein-Blanchet's company.

40. *Petit Parisien,* January 26, 1937, 6; *Petit Parisien,* October 16, 1937, 5.

41. *Paris-Soir,* November 17, 1938, 3.

42. *Le Petit Parisien,* March 13, 1936, 10.

43. *L'Intransigeant,* March 16, 1937, 11.

44. For example, *Paris-Soir,* June, 1, 1937, 6.

45. *Radio-Magazine,* December 12, 1937, 3.

46. Persil took out full-page advertisements each week in *Paris-Soir,* many of which plugged its show, *Le Kiosque à musique Persil* (*Paris-Soir,* November 3, 1938, 10, and November 9, 1938, 13). Palmolive's show was called *Cabaret Palmolive* and aired on Monday and Thursday nights (*Paris-Soir,* November 10, 1938, 10, and December, 16, 1938, 3). Lesieur offered free tickets to performances in their newspaper ads. The two-hour show also featured contests and prizes for those who listened (*Paris-Soir,* February 26, 1937, 13, and June 3, 1937, 9).

47. Clément Vautel, *Radio-Magazine,* April 16, 1933, 2.

48. "Qu'écoutez-vous?" *Radio-Liberté,* September 17, 1937, 1.

49. "Journal Officiel," July 16, 1938, AN, F/43/1.

50. Paul Clérouc's show on Paris, called *Les Ondes de Paris,* aired from June 1937 to August 1939 on Radio-Paris.

51. All of the plays that appeared on public radio between 1935 and 1980 are stored at the Bibliothèque de l'Arsenal in Paris in the ORTF files.

52. *France* was a fourteen-act, eight-hour miniseries celebrating the mythic history of France from the cave dwellers to Napoleon's death. It was broadcast on Radio-Paris over a four-week period (Marius Riollet, *France,* Radio-Paris, January 2, 9, 16, and 23, 1938). For more on this play, see Joelle Neulander, "Family Values and the Radio: The 1937 Radio Elections and the Miniseries *France,*" *French Politics, Culture, and Society* 24, no. 2 (2006): 26–45.

53. The *Intransigeant* wrote "Mr. George Colin and his group, because of their talent, have made listening agreeable" about a Dumas adaptation on Paris-PTT. *Intransigeant,* April 4, 1935, 10.

54. René Gerly, "La Radio," *Paris Qui Chante,* May 1, 1939, 7.

55. Louis Merlin, *J'en ai vu des choses,* 382–83.

56. *Choisir,* as quoted in *Radio-Famille Information,* December 1938, 2.

57. Marc Martin, "Le Marché publicitaire français et les grands médias, 1918–1970," *Vingtième Siècle* 20 (1988): 75–90, 81. Radio-Cité's success can be seen as even more extraordinary because the station could rely on local sources of advertising only, as its programs could reach only the Ile-de-France during the day. Evening broadcasts could sometimes be heard as far away as Marseilles and regularly as far as Dijon. Poste Parisien, on the other hand, with sixty kilowatts of power, could easily be heard across France and into North Africa, and sometimes even as far away as the United States and New Zealand.

58. Méadel, *Histoire,* 130.

59. The first diagram comes from Poste Parisien's publicity (*Poste Parisien* [Paris: Conseille

Générale d'Enérgie Radio-Electrique, 1936], 26). The second two diagrams are from Méadel, *Histoire*, 135, 138.

60. Richard Vinen argues that interwar businessmen were concerned with innovation over markets, as "the obsession with novelty, quality and diversity of product may actually have distracted business from the tasks of uniform production and mass marketing that were being undertaken by their American rivals" (Richard Vinen, *The Politics of Business, 1936–1945* [Cambridge: Cambridge University Press, 1991], 13). This innovative spirit may have worked quite differently for radio entrepreneurs, as novelty came with the creation of new programs and new economic markets.

2. OPENING UP THE STUDIO DOORS

1. Louis Léon-Martin, "L'Univers à domicile: Les secrets, la vie, les merveilles de la radio, un soir, à 7 heures au Poste Parisien," *Petit Parisien*, October 11, 1937, 1, 2.

2. One year earlier, in a promotional brochure, Poste Parisien located its place in the national cultural patrimony, including in its promotional literature the statement that "Poste Parisien represents . . . the creation of lively, strong work, destined to bring the rays of our musical artistry and French thought to the farthest reaches of the globe." The brochure promised that every employee and artist at Poste Parisien was French and that the station represented "the success of national industry." *Poste Parisien*, 2, 5.

3. Léon-Martin, "La Vie de la radio: Art et méchanique," *Le Petit Parisien*, October 23, 1937, 1, 2.

4. Léon-Martin, "La Radio et les artistes," *Le Petit Parisien*, October 20, 1937, 1, 4.

5. Léon-Martin, "La Radio et la vie: Autour d'un haut-parleur," *Le Petit Parisien*, October 28, 1937, 1, 2.

6. In another article in the series, Léon-Martin wrote, "There is the intimacy that I spoke of the other day, the way that the listener waits for the customary voice by the lamp, the place where we make room for the familiar *presence*." Here radio became part of the family, personified and brought into the home. Léon-Martin, "L'Univers à domicile: les échos de la radio," *Le Petit Parisien*, November 2, 1937, 5.

7. Léon-Martin, "Les Secrets, la vie, les merveilles de la radio: L'heure enfantine," *Le Petit Parisien*, October 18, 1937, 1, 5. Most other children's shows had uncles, aunts, and cousins who hosted, giving children a wealth of "family members" to listen to every Thursday off from school. In a trump, Poste Parisien was unique in including their character in the nuclear family and making Jaboune a brother figure.

8. In his autobiography, Bleustein-Blanchet claimed that Jean Prouvost wanted a station because he saw the benefits that *L'Intransigeant* received from its connection to Radio-Cité: "Our alliance, which was fruitful, disturbed the supreme power that was *Paris-Soir*. . . . *Paris-Soir* had to have its station" (Bleustein-Blanchet, *Sur mon antenne*, 79). In spite of this comment, it is not very clear what benefits Radio-Cité got from its association with *L'Intransigeant*. Unlike *Le Petit Parisien* and *Paris-Soir*, the paper never supported its radio station with articles or unsolicited advertisements. It seems that Radio-Cité was successful in spite of its partnership with a daily newspaper.

9. Marc Martin claims that the written press was quite worried about the success of private radios in gaining advertising revenue. In 1938 agreements were made between the printed press and the radio that limited the kind of news reporting that radio could do as well as the number of advertisements allowed in each hour of airplay. Martin, *Le Marché publicitaire français*, 82.

10. *Paris-Soir*, September 4, 1937, 5.

11. *Paris-Soir*, September 5, 1937, 1, 3.

12. Ibid., 4.

13. *Paris-Soir*, September 6, 1937, 1, 5.

14. Charles Trenet, "Y'a de la joie," 1937.

15. *Paris-Soir*, September 17, 1937, 3.

16. *Paris-Soir*, September 7, 1937, 5.

17. *Paris-Soir*, September 9, 1937, 10.

18. *Paris-Soir*, September 20, 1937, 11.

19. *Paris-Soir*'s daily back photo page regularly featured shots of the guests at *The Bar of the Stars* laughing and sharing toasts while participating in on-air conversations. For examples, see *Paris-Soir*, September 20, 1937, 12 (with singer Georgius and his wife); September 25, 1937, 13 (with Simone Vaudry, Paulette Conty, Pierre Renoir, Mady Berry, and Robert Le Vigan); October 1, 1937, 14 (with comedian Pierre-Dac).

20. *Paris-Soir*, September 17, 1937, 3.

21. Although there is some debate on the success of Radio-37 in entering the saturated Parisian market, the station did make quite a bit of money for its owner, Jean Prouvost. In the first five months of 1938, Radio-37 earned almost one and a half million francs in advertising revenue. Martin, *Le Marché publicitaire français*, 81.

22. Elena Razlogova researches the connections that American fan magazines gave radio listeners, making fans more loyal through the feeling that they could participate in shaping their favorite programs and stations. Elena Razlogova, "Radio, Politics and Scribbling Women: Gendered Accounts of Democracy in Letters to Radio Fan Magazines," paper presented at the American Historical Association, Boston, January 5, 2001.

23. André Sevry, "Du nouveau . . . sur les ondes à Radio-Cité," *Mon Programme*, September 11, 1938, 5.

24. Pierre Domène, "Avec Jean Guignebert," *Radio-Magazine*, February 27, 1938, 3.

25. David C. Goodman's work concentrates on the American forum series and the ways in which radio forums tried to create a historical past that included small-town democracy and participatory discussion and decision making across the United States. David C. Goodman, "Saving Democracy by Radio: The 1930s Radio Forum Movement," paper presented at American Historical Studies, Boston, January 5, 2001.

26. Bleustein-Blanchet, *Sur mon antenne*, 1948, 62.

27. Ibid., 63–64.

28. Ibid., 65.

29. Ibid., 69.

30. Ibid., 147–48.

31. *L'Ouest-Éclair*, October 17, 1934, 4. These ads usually appeared weekly, sometimes along with the newspaper section on the week's radio programs. A look through any daily paper of

the period will reveal countless radio advertisements for regional, national, and international companies.

32. Advertisement for *Radio-Pathé,* 1937. In author's collection.
33. *L'Ouest-Éclair,* October 17, 1934, 4.
34. *L'Ouest-Éclair,* February 26, 1937, 4.
35. *L'Intransigeant,* December 4, 1935, 14.
36. *L'Intransigeant,* March 18, 1937, 3.
37. Pierre Dubreuil, *Radio-Magazine,* March 19, 1933, 1.
38. Dagoussia, *Radio-Magazine,* April 21, 1935, 1.
39. Hermine David, *Radio-Magazine,* April 9, 1933, 1.
40. André Dignimont, *Radio-Magazine,* July 23, 1933, 1.
41. Dubreuil, *Radio-Magazine,* August 6, 1933, 1.
42. M. Maillies, *Radio-Magazine,* March 26, 1933, 1.
43. Many historians and music critics have written about the close relationship that the French created with jazz during the interwar years. See, e.g., Jeffrey Harold Jackson, "Making Jazz French: Music and Cosmopolitanism in Interwar Paris" (PhD dissertation, University of Rochester, 1999), and "Making Jazz French: The Reception of Jazz Music in Paris 1927–1934," *French Historical Studies* 25 (1): 149–70; A. David Franklin, "A Preliminary Study of the Acceptance of Jazz by French Music Critics in the 1920s and Early 1930s," *Annual Review of Jazz Studies* 4 (1988): 2–8; William H. Kenney, "'Le Hot': The Assimilation of American Jazz in France, 1917–1940," *American Studies* 1 (1984): 5–24. Tyler Stovall wrote of the success of interwar African American jazz performers in Paris in *Paris Noir: African Americans in the City of Light* (Boston: Houghton Mifflin, 1996). An African American woman named Bricktop opened a successful nightclub in Pigalle that featured the hottest jazz acts of the 1930s. In his autobiography, Jacques Canetti writes of introducing jazz to the French masses over the radio in a semiweekly "hot jazz" program on Poste Parisien beginning in 1933. At first letters came back to Poste Parisien full of racial hatred of the music, but soon the listeners began to enjoy it. Canetti brought performers like Duke Ellington and Louis Armstrong to Paris to give French audiences live shows of the music he played. He continued his show throughout the 1930s, switching to Radio-Cité when he was contracted as art director of that station (Jacques Canetti, *On cherche jeune homme aimant la musique* [Paris: Calmann-Lévy, 1978], 26, 73). In a scathing and racist review of jazz and radio written during World War II and published soon after, Sudré, a radio programmer and critic, while calling for a resurgence of traditional musical forms, had to grudgingly admit that jazz had become part of the French culture, "The accordion and the saxophone have become a national religion. They say people like them. Play light music if you want, but not vulgar music, incoherent and hysterical music like that Negro-American jazz that now poisons the country and which has turned us from our own popular musical traditions." Sudré, *Le Huitième Art* (Paris: Julliard, 1945), 168.
44. Other swing band leaders began with Ray Ventura before becoming successful with their own groups. Jo Boullion, who later becomes the leader of public radio's biggest swing band, played with Ray Ventura et Ses Collégiens in the early thirties.
45. For every three boxes of pasta, listeners could receive two tickets to a Wednesday-night performance. Listeners could either mail in the proofs of purchase with a self-addressed stamped

envelope or bring them to the Lustucru radio office themselves. The advertisement for that evening's performance was featured weekly on the back page of the Wednesday edition of *Le Petit Parisien*.

46. Ray Ventura's band played songs from the United States such as "I Like Bananas" (C. Yacich/Adaptation Paul Misraki, 1936), "The Leader Doesn't Like Music" from the movie "Honolulu" (G. Kahn, H. Warren/Adaptation Paul Misraki, 1939), and "Brother Bill" (J. Kennedy, W. Grosz, 1939). They also introduced France to "The Lambeth Walk," a popular English swing dance, in 1938 (D. Furber, N. Gay/Adaptation J. Gacon, M. Cab, H. Varna, 1938).

47. Hornez and Misraki, "Le Nez de Cléopatre," 1939; Maurice Vandaire, Charlys, and Raymond Legrand, "Toc, toc partout," 1936; Hornez and Misraki, "C'est dommage que j'puisse pas vous l'montrer," 1938; Max Blot and Misraki, "Les Chemises de l'archiduchesse," 1937.

48. Paul Misraki and Bach (pseud. of Henri Auguste Allum) and Laverne (pseud. of Charles Pasquier), "Tout va très bien, Madame la Marquise," 1935.

49. René Bizet, "Ray Ventura et ses Collégiens," *Radio-Magazine*, June 28, 1936, 4.

50. Hornez and Misraki, "Le grève de l'orchestre," 1936.

51. Hornez and Misraki, "Comme tout le monde," 1938.

52. Hornez, H. Decoin, and Misraki, "Ça vaut mieux que d'attraper la scarlatine," 1936.

53. Ironically, both Paul Misraki and Ray Ventura were Jewish. They seemed to understand that their own status as Jews denied them full entry into the family of France. Thus they changed their surnames and wrote antisemitic lyrics to this song.

54. Georgius and Rudolf Révil, "C'était de la publicité," 1938.

3. FAMILY VERSUS LIBERTY

1. Méadel, from *Histoire de la radio des années trente*, 94.

2. Extensive scholarship exists on radio in Great Britain and the British Broadcasting Company. Some of the most useful volumes for historians are Paddy Scannell and Dabid Cardiff, *A Social History of British Broadcasting*, vol. 1, *1922–1939: Serving the Nation* (London: Basil Blackwell, 1991); and Mark Pegg, *Broadcasting and Society, 1918–1939* (London: Croom Helm, 1983).

3. Kate Lacey's book on women and radio in Weimar and Nazi Germany also includes a brief summary of German radio history to World War II. She writes of Nazi programming, "Every program was carefully monitored to ensure that all radio output conformed with Nazi ideology. News and current affairs programs were most tightly coordinated, but entertainment was understood to perform an implicit political function and also came under close scrutiny." Kate Lacey, *Feminine Frequencies: Gender, German Radio, and the Public Sphere, 1923–1945* (Ann Arbor: University of Michigan Press, 1996), 101.

4. Ibid., 15.

5. Benjamin Huc and François Robin, *Histoire et dessous de la radio, en France et dans le monde* (Paris: Editions de France, 1938), 26.

6. Ibid., 28.

7. Ibid. In 1934, the Nazis implemented an industrial program in order to produce radios at half their normal price, enabling working-class families to buy their own machines. These radios

were the cheapest in the world, costing only seventy-six Reichmarks, or two weeks' average wages. Over five years, the Nazis sold three million radios under this program. Lacey, *Feminine Frequencies*, 102.

8. Méadel backs her basic thesis with close analyses of the numbers of radios in each French region that come from government lists of registered radios. She estimates that 10 to 20 percent of radio owners illegally did not report their radio purchases to the government.

9. Elisabeth Cazenave and André-Jean Tudesq look at the politics behind the elections, without a close analysis of the impact of the rhetoric used by candidates and their supporters. Elisabeth Cazenave and André-Jean Tudesq, "Radiodiffusion et politique: Les élections de 1937 en France," *Revue d'histoire moderne et contemporaine*, 1977, 529–55.

10. The government in power strictly controlled the two other Parisian stations, Tour-Eiffel, which served as the educational outpost, and Radio-Paris, the flagship French station that at one hundred kilowatts could easily be picked up across France and by neighboring countries as well.

11. Clément Vautel, "Radio-Chronique," *Radio-Magazine*, April 14, 1935, 2.

12. Vautel, "Radio-Chronique," *Radio-Magazine*, March 24, 1935, 2.

13. "Tous les auditeurs doivent voter," *Le Petit Radio*, April 26, 1937, 1.

14. Méadel, *Histoire*, 98.

15. Ibid., 99.

16. After two hundred postal workers in Nice struck the previous April, Mandel unceremoniously replaced them with Parisian workers and fired the leaders of the movement. With this action, Mandel made it clear to all the employees of his ministry that he would not support worker demands and strikes. Sherwood, *Georges Mandel*, 155–56.

17. Méadel, *Histoire*, 99. In an interwar editorial, Paul Reboux, the radio columnist for *Paris-Soir*, remarked that he liked Blum's radio delivery. He called it "a useful lesson of French style." Paul Reboux, "Leçon de style," *Paris-Soir*, September 9, 1936, 7.

18. Méadel, "La Gauche française et les médias de l'avant-guerre," *Cahiers d'Histoire de la Radiodiffusion* 40 (May 1994): 16.

19. For a much more extensive look at Popular Front programming and propaganda, see Joelle Neulander, "Broadcasting Morality: Family Values and the Culture of the Radio in 1930s France" (PhD dissertation, University of Iowa, 2001).

20. Pascal Ory, *La Belle Illusion: Culture et politique sous le signe du Front populaire, 1935–1938* (Paris: Plon, 1994). Ory's vast compendium of the culture of the Popular Front shows the all-encompassing program that the Popular Front envisioned. See also Julian Jackson, *The Popular Front in France*, 123. Many scholars have looked at the Popular Front's use of film (especially the films of Michel Carné and Jean Renoir) to teach the masses through entertaining stories that included scenes of the Popular Front goals and ideals. See Dudley Andrew, *Mists of Regret: Culture and Sensibility in Classic French Film* (Princeton, NJ: Princeton University Press, 1995); Elizabeth Grottle Strebel, *French Social Cinema of the Nineteen Thirties: A Cinematographic Expression of Popular Front Consciousness* (New York: Arno Press, 1980); and Jonathan Buchsbaum, *Cinema Engagé: Film in the Popular Front* (Chicago: University of Illinois Press), 1988.

21. Ory, *La Belle Illusion*, 344.

22. Huc and Robin showed the tax money for theaters as 50 million francs in 1937.

23. Sherwood, *Georges Mandel*.

24. "Art et Travail," *Vendredi,* March 26, 1937, 8.

25. Ory, *La Belle Illusion,* 380–82.

26. Carlos Larronde, *Le Théâtre Invisible* (Paris: Denoël, 1936), 56. Honegger was a member of the FMP, or the musical branch of the communist regional cultural organizations, the *Maisons de Culture.* Jackson, *The Popular Front,* 126.

27. Larronde, *Théâtre Invisible,* 99.

28. Ibid., 3. His work was published in 1936, just as the Popular Front took power in France. By 1938, Larronde would work for Radio-Paris, the flagship public station, interviewing writers. Jacques Amaire, "Notes d'écoute," *Vendredi,* January 28, 1938, 4.

29. A. Habaru, "De Sophocle à Jean Cocteau," *Vendredi,* June 18, 1937, 6; Jacques Amaire, "Notes d'écoute," *Vendredi,* February 4, 1938, 5; *Le Petit Radio,* February 11, 1938, 14.

30. Ory, *La Belle Illusion,* 381. The right and left fought fiercely over France's position on the Spanish Civil War. The right wing saw France's ties with the republicans as central to its condemnation of the Popular Front. Robert Soucy, *French Fascism: The Second Wave, 1933–1939* (New Haven: Yale University Press, 1995), 25.

31. Henri Noguères, *La Vie quotidienne en France au temps du Front populaire, 1935–1938* (Paris: Hachette, 1977), 217–18.

32. As an example, Blum gave his 1937 January address over the air, and it was reported in all the papers directly from the broadcast. Jean Zay gave a speech about education on January 5, 1937, calling for the installment of radios in every classroom in France. The speech itself was given over the airwaves and broadcast into available radios directly into classrooms across France. Yann Loranz, "Par radio, les écoliers entendent la voix de M. Jean Zay," *Paris-Soir,* January 5, 1937, 5.

33. A. Habaru, "L'Enseignement par les ondes," *Vendredi,* January 8, 1937, 8.

34. This information comes from the published weekly program guide in *Le Petit Radio,* March 5, 1937, 5–26.

35. Ibid.

36. As another example of the boring nature of state radio, Frank Tenot includes comparisons of a day's programming on public and private radio stations in 1938 to explain why private stations succeeded. Tenot, *Radios privées, radios pirates.*

37. *Le Petit Radio*'s program guide showed that Marseille-PTT planned daily lectures from 8:00 to 8:15 p.m. nightly but never gave specifics for each night (*Le Petit Radio,* January 10, 1936, 7–33). Many lectures seemed useful only as filler, such as the fifteen-minute talk by Fernand Depas on "The Monologue of Yesteryear" that filled a gap between two symphony concerts on Radio-Paris on January 13.

38. A. Habaru, "Emissions économiques et sociales," *Vendredi,* March 5, 1937, 8.

39. Paul Reboux, "Kiosques de musique," *Paris-Soir,* December 2, 1936, 11.

40. Méadel, *Histoire,* 171.

41. *Radio-Magazine* published over two hundred thousand copies each week. Alice Yaeger Kaplan, *Reproductions of Banality: Fascism, Literature and French Intellectual Life* (Minneapolis: University of Minnesota Press, 1986).

42. *Haut-Parleur: Hébdomadaire de vulgarisation radiophonique* (Paris).

43. The left would have to create its own organ of radio publicity, a monthly magazine called *Radio-Liberté,* after the radio party fashioned for the 1937 elections.

44. Whether women did or in what numbers has yet to be determined. I have found no evidence to point to how many women voted during the 1937 election.

45. In his memoir-history of the Popular Front, writer and journalist Daniel Guérin bemoans the inability of the Popular Front to push further in its social mission. He, as a communist, wanted a revolution that would overturn French society altogether, even if run through the bureaucracy of democratic, republican government. He blames the unions and the socialists for their willingness to turn power over to a government that would "fight against the working class" and discontinue the struggle along with the communist party. Daniel Guérin, *Front populaire: Révolution manquée* (Paris: Julliard, 1963), 200.

46. "Sans-filistes, il faut voter," *Vendredi*, February 5, 1937, 8.

47. *Radio-Liberté*, February 1936, 1–2.

48. Ibid.

49. *Radio-Liberté*, June 1937, 1.

50. Robert Soucy, *French Fascism: The Second Wave, 1933–1939* (New Haven, CT: Yale University Press, 1995), 29. Soucy gives an excellent account of the growth and decline of fascism during the rise and fall of the Popular Front. In the book he argues that French fascism was tied to the fate of left-wing politics, gaining widespread support only when its counterpart did as well.

51. Ory, *La Belle Illusion*, 814.

52. "Les Eléctions radiophoniques," *Radio-Magazine*, February 7, 1937, 12.

53. *Le Figaro*, October 15, 1937, 11.

54. "Révélations . . . pour quelques uns," *Radio et Famille*, Lille, December 10, 1936, 13.

55. *Radio et Famille*, February 10, 1937, 7.

56. "Eléctions Radiophoniques," *Radio-Magazine*, February 21,1937, 15.

57. G. Nicolai, "Consultation éléctorale," *Le Petit Radio*, January 29, 1937, 2.

58. "Auditeurs, pour une bonne radio groupez-vous autour des *Radio-Familles*," *Choisir*, January 17, 1937, 2; A. Forèze, "Les *Radio-Familles* n'ont rien à craindre si tous ceux qui doivent les aider font leur devoir," *Choisir*, January 24, 1937, 1.

59. Henri David, "Un Devoir familial à remplir," *Choisir*, February 14, 1937, 2.

60. "Aux sans-filistes," *Choisir*, February 21, 1937, 2.

61. Henri Hennon, "Sans-filistes, contre la politique, unissez-vous," *T.S.F.-Revue*, January 27, 1937, 10–11.

62. Philippe Roland, "Les Eléctions radiophoniques," *Le Figaro*, February 6, 1937, 3. In the 1936–37 radio season, *Radio-Magazine* ran weekly advertisements in the paper's radio column. *Le Figaro*, January 8, 1937, 6.

63. "Les Eléctions radiophoniques," *Le Figaro*, February 22, 1937, 4.

64. "Aux sans-filistes" *Choisir*, February 21, 1937, 2.

65. Jean Morienval, "Nous nous tiendrons sur le terrain de la radio," *Choisir*, January 31, 1937, 1. *Radio et Famille*, Lille's paper for the group Radio-Famille, also alerted its readers that the radio was being used a communist tool: "They are creating a red army out of France." *Radio et Famille*, December 10, 1936, 7.

66. "La Semaine du 20 au 27 février sera la semaine du vote," *Choisir*, February 14, 1937, 1.

67. C.-M. Savarit, "Le Mois radiophonique," *T.S.F.-Revue*. February 20. 1937, 1–2.

68. Nicolai, "Consultation éléctorale," 2.

69. G. Nicolai, "Aux Urnes," *Le Petit Radio,* February 19, 1937, p.2, "Page d'histoire sur les éléctions radiophoniques de 1937," *Le Petit Radio,* February 12, 1937, p.2, and "Encore 24 heures!" *Le Petit Radio,* February 26, 1937, 2. In spite of Nicolai's insistence on radio's neutrality, the newspaper did not always have the view that politics had no place on the airwaves. One year before, during the election campaigns, Lucien Luluc, another editor of the journal commented on the usefulness of the radio as a political tool. He felt that it helped the French public to hear the candidates (Lucien Leluc, "D'un micro à l'autre," *Le Petit Radio,* March 13, 1936, 7). Clément Vautel, too, had varying opinions on politics and radio. In 1933, for example, he had two columns that contradicted one another on the necessity of politicians using the airwaves. In the first, he wonders why French politicians didn't use the radio as Franklin D. Roosevelt did in the United States. In the other, he worries about the use of propaganda on the radio and the problems that it means for a republic. Clément Vautel, "Radio-Chronique," *Radio-Magazine,* March 26, 1933, 2, and January 15, 1933, 2.

70. "Servir la radio ou s'en servir?" *Choisir,* January 17, 1937, 1.

71. Vautel, "Radio-Chronique," *Radio-Magazine,* January 10, 1937, 2.

72. C.-M. Savarit, "Le Mois radiophonique," *T.S.F.-Revue,* January 20, 1937, 1–2.

73. Jean Reibel, "Tous les auditeurs honnêtes," *T.S.F., Phono, Ciné,* August 26, 1937, 12, and "Les Eléctions," *T.S.F., Phono, Ciné,* February 10, 1937, 13.

74. "Fascisme radiophonique," *Le Petit Radio,* January 15, 1937, 2.

75. Forèze, "Les *Radio-Famille*s n'ont rien à craindre," 1.

76. C.-M. Savarit, "Le Mois radiophonique," *T.S.F.-Revue,* February 20, 1937, 1–2.

77. *L'Echo de* Radio-Famille *de l'Ouest,* Rennes, February 1937, 4.

78. *Radio-Famille Information,* Paris, December 1938, 6.

79. *Radio-Famille Information de la Loire Inferieure,* Nantes, November 1938, 3. This article condemned six plays heard on public stations during a three-week period (*Radio-Famille Information,* March 1939, 4). Also included were other songs, all about love. On that page as well was a critique of the play "The Duel," which was deemed "an attack on religion, on government, on morality."

80. *Radio-Famille Information,* January 1939, 4.

81. Méadel, *Histoire,* 168–69.

82. Jean Morienval, "Eléctions difficiles," *Choisir,* February 14, 1937, 1.

83. L. Jude, "Des Eléctions en janvier?" *Choisir,* January 10, 1937, 1.

84. "Eléctions radiophoniques," *Choisir,* January 24, 1937, 1.

85. "Pour une Radio saine, libre, familiale, votez et faites voter *Radio-Famille,*" *Choisir,* February 21, 1937, 1.

86. "A la dernière minute," *Le Figaro,* February 5, 1937, 1.

87. Philippe Roland, "Le Premier Jour des éléctions radiophoniques," *Le Figaro,* February 21, 1937, 1, 3. In the article, Roland visits a polling place and converses with the staff and voters. He reports on a conversation in which a man said, "I overheard, sir, your conversation with that administrator. I just voted against Radio-Liberté with the national list of Radio-Famille. I have a peaceful conscience, but how can I be sure that the elections will be held in a fair manner?"

88. "On veut fausser les résultats des éléctions radiophoniques," *Le Figaro,* February 24, 1937, 4.

89. Philippe Roland, "En assistant au dépouillement du scrutin dans un désordre édifiant," *Le Figaro,* March 1, 1937, 1, 3.

90. "Ce qu'il faut savoir pour voter aux élections radiophoniques," *Choisir*, February 21, 1937, 1; "Listes des candidats des Radio-Familles," *Choisir*, February 14, 1937, 18; "Une Radio bienfaisante pour tous est une nécessité nationale: que chacun travaille pour elle aux élections prochaines," *Choisir*, February 7, 1937, 1–2.

91. "Auditeurs de T.S.F.: Votez et sachez comment voter contre la liste d'inspiration communiste," *Le Figaro*, February 9, 1937, 6.

92. H. Frederic Pottecher, "Aux urnes, auditeurs," *Paris-Soir*, February 18, 1937, 1, 3; "On vote cette semaine," *Mon Programme*, February 20, 1937, 3.

93. Brochand, *Histoire générale de la radio et de la télévision*, vol. 1, 303.

94. The statistics in this table come from ibid., 302. This information is also readily available from any of the radio guides printed after the election. The calculations of percentage are my own.

95. C.-M. Savarit, "Le Mois radiophonique," *T.S.F.-Revue*, March 20, 1937, 1–2, "Les Eléctions radiophoniques," *Le Petit Radio*, March 5, 1937, 2, and "Enorme succès des Radio-Familles," *Choisir*, March 7, 1937, 1.

96. "Notre 'Crochet' radiophonique," *Le Figaro*, March 6, 1937, 1. The newspaper named its poll after "Le Crochet radiphonique" on Radio-Cité, a show in which audience members could verbally harass bad singers off the air, ostensibly controlling which acts aired on the radio.

97. "Le Crochet radiophonique des lecteurs du 'Figaro,'" *Le Figaro*, April 13, 1937, 1, 4. I will deal more with the realist songs, in both their risqué and their conservative elements, in chap. 5.

98. Paul Reboux, "Politique des airs," *Paris-Soir*, February 24, 1937, 11.

99. "Les Eléctions radiophoniques," *Le Petit Parisien*, February 23, 1937, 1.

100. These two newspapers may have had another reason to ignore the public radio elections as *Le Petit Parisien* had its own private station, Le Poste Parisien, and *Paris-Soir* was looking to acquire one of its own, as it would do several months later and call it Radio-37.

101. Certainly women could vote and probably did. The radio critics, though, clearly saw fathers and men as the voters, and their references to the election reflect that bias. There has been excellent work on women's participation in the postwar elections, including Christine Bard, *Les Femmes dans la société française au 20è siècle* (Paris: Armand Colin, 2001), and Janine Mossuz-Lavau, "Le Vote des femmes en France (1945–1993)," *Revue Française de Science Politique* 43, no. 4 (1993): 673–89.

102. Julian Jackson points out that the Popular Front could not understand the public's dismissal of their larger cultural program. He concludes, however, "Opening the doors of culture to the people did not guarantee that they would select the culture being offered." Jackson, *The Popular Front in France*, 131.

103. Clément Vautel, "Radio-Chronique," *Radio-Magazine*, February 14, 1937, 2. He also writes, "The real elections, oh dear listeners, they took place last May." He understands that the Popular Front has legitimate political power. Only national elections can truly change the course of state radio. A year later Vautel would comment on the lack of power of Radio-Famille to make significant changes to the radio. In this column, comparing the programmers to Louis XIV, he wrote, "'Le radio c'est moi,' says the state." Vautel, "Chronique sans fil," *Radio-Magazine*, January 23, 1938, 2.

104. "La Radio française sera-t-elle libérée des influences antinationales?" *Le Figaro*, March

2, 1937, 1; "Radio-Famille triomphe de Radio-Liberté," *Le Figaro,* March 4, 1937, 1, 3; Philippe Roland, "Le Succès des listes de Radio-Famille va-t-il nous procurer des émissions radiophoniques neutres et impartiales?" *Le Figaro,* March 5, 1937, 1, 3.

105. J.-G. Poincignon, "Voix populi: Le genre ennuyeux est condamné," *Mon Programme,* March 13, 1937, 4.

106. G. Nicolai, "Juste retour," *Le Petit Radio,* April 20, 1937, 2.

107. "La Question du jour," *Radio-Liberté,* July 2, 1937, 2.

108. *La Semaine Radiophonique* praised Cossin's show, noting the expertise of his entourage of writers. Of his popularity they wrote, "Each time he goes further in his choice of plays to correspond to the tastes of the crowd of listeners." Marcel Bertrand, "Livrets et partitions," *La Semaine Radiophonique,* July 25, 1937, 5.

109. This information comes from a sample week's programming from *Le Petit Radio,* February 11, 1938, 6–29.

110. Jacques Amaire critiqued every popular program that public stations aired, including the jazz orchestra led by Jo Bouillon (Amaire, "Notes d'écoute," *Vendredi,* January 7, 1937, 5), and a show with comedy sensation Fernandel (Amaire, *Vendredi,* December 10, 1937, 5). He hated variety shows of all sorts and criticized their already common appearance on private stations and their new appearance on government radio, "There are already enough general stores on the radio. That means that our national stations need not sell candy suckers and almond syrup."

111. Jacques Amaire, "Notes d'écoute," *Vendredi,* February 11, 1938, 5.

112. Listeners were quite dissatisfied with public radio and turned to private stations for much of their radio time. For example, in "Au Radio-Club de Nantes," *Radio-Magazine,* April 18, 1937, 13, appeared this comment, "The Nantes Radio-Club regrets the fact that all of its members have stopped listening to public radio between 6:30 and 8:30 p.m. They prefer Poste Parisien and Radio-Toulouse."

113. A. Habaru, "Humaniser les ondes," *Vendredi,* March 19, 1937, 8.

4. AROUND THE CRADLE

1. Radio schedules placed children's programs at hours of children's leisure, concentrating almost solely on Thursday afternoons, a time when schools were closed and children were at home. The radio could babysit children on their day off, with mothers continuing housework and errands as their children listened to special programs on the radio. Evening radio plays rarely had youthful child characters who spoke. Audiences had to assume their presence in the conversation and actions of their parents in the house.

2. Susan B. Whitney shows that the communists created women's clubs in order to recruit members and to fall in line with Popular Front policies (Susan B. Whitney, "Embracing the Status Quo: French Communists, Young Women and the Popular Front," *Journal of Social History* 30, no. 1 [1996]: 29–53). Christine Bard and Jean-Louis Robert add that Stalin's own policies changed, and thus the PCF was simply falling in line with international communism when it abruptly changed tacks in 1935–36 (Christine Bard and Jean-Louis Robert, "The French Communist Party and Women, 1920–1939," in *Women and Socialism, Socialism and Women: Europe*

between the World Wars, ed. Helmut Gruber and Pamela Graves [New York: Berghahn Books, 1998], 321–47).

3. Léon Blum was one of the few politicians not to speak out in favor of pronatalism and separate spheres. Other members of his party were outspoken about the issue, calling for the responsibility of women to become nurturers and mothers for France.

4. See Charles Sowerwine, "Women and the Origins of the French Socialist Party: A Neglected Contribution," *Third Republic* 3–4 (1977): 105–27. Sowerwine points to the hopes that many feminists placed in socialism to defend and fight for their political rights, hopes that remained unfulfilled as the party searched for changes in labor policy and not for gender equality. See also Charles Sowerwine, "Le Groupe feministe socialiste, 1899–1902," *Mouvement Social* 90 (1975): 87–120.

5. Two of the three women were appointed to positions that underscored their maternal qualities and the fact that they came from all three of the parties in the Popular Front coalition. Socialist Suzanne Lacore oversaw "the protection of children," while radical Cécile Brunschwig became the undersecretary of education. The third, communist Irène Joliot-Curie, on the basis of her famous parents, Marie and Pierre Curie, was appointed undersecretary of scientific research. Sian Reynolds, "Women and the Popular Front in France: The Case of the Three Women Ministers," *French History* 8, no. 2 (1994): 196–224.

6. For an excellent overview of the politics of the radicals and the radical-feminists, see Sian Reynolds, *France between the Wars: Gender and Politics* (New York: Routledge, 1996); and Paul Smith, *Feminism and the Third Republic: Women's Political and Civil Rights in France* (Oxford: Clarendon Press, 1996).

7. Marie-Monique Huss writes about the problem of low conscription rates in an article that summarizes the problems of the birthrate in the interwar period (Marie-Monique Huss, "Pronatalism in the Inter-war Period in France," *Journal of Contemporary History* 25 [1990]: 39–68). Cheryl A. Koos analyzes the rhetoric of the fascists, which differed from most in that it called for a strong paternal influence in the family with the family vote. Antoine Redier, one of the fascist leaders of the pronatalist movement, wanted a new distribution of the vote, giving fathers of large families more weight than single men and fathers of small families (Cheryl A. Koos, "Fascism, Fatherhood, and the Family in Interwar France: The Case of Antoine Redier and the Legion," *Journal of Family History* 24, no. 3 [1999]: 317–29). For a general demographic look at the rise of pronatalism, see C. Alison McIntosh, "The Rise of Twentieth-Century Pronatalism," *International Journal of Politics* 12, no. 3 (1982): 42–80. In "Gender, Anti-individualism, and Nationalism," Koos shows how the "new women" became the scapegoat for conservative rhetoric about the family. My next chapter will look closely at the part that the radio played in attacking the independent French woman (Cheryl A. Koos, "Gender, Anti-individualism, and Nationalism: The Alliance Nationale and the Pronatalist Backlash against the Femme Moderne," *French Historical Studies* 19, no. 3 [1996]: 699–723). Helmut Gruber blames the policies on an "obsession with demography" in interwar France. He claims that "in France, maternalist welfare measures were aimed at enhancing an unlimited maternity" (Helmut Gruber, "French Women in the Crossfire of Class, Sex, Maternity, and Citizenship," in *Women and Socialism, Socialism and Women: Europe between the Wars*, ed. Helmut Gruber and Pamela Graves [New York: Berghahn, 1998], 301, 308).

8. Paul Reboux, *Paris-Soir,* September 17, 1937, 3.

9. *Radio-Magazine,* December 12, 1937, 3.

10. See Mary Louise Roberts, *Civilization without Sexes: Reconstructing Gender in Postwar France, 1917–1927* (Chicago: University of Chicago Press, 1994).

11. François Jardy, "Le Psychologie de l'auditeur," *Le Petit Radio,* February 1936, 1.

12. Germaine Blondin, "La Femme et la radiophonie," *Le Petit Radio,* March 25, 1938, 7.

13. Germaine Blondin both wrote regular criticism for radio and recited stories and poetry over the airwaves. Fellow critic Paul Reboux wrote of her radio performances, "We know that in *Radio-Magazine* Germaine Blondin appreciates radio productions with a laudable sense of modernism and wisdom. She has just shown us that she is not one of those critics to whom you can say, 'See if you can do as well!' She is one of those who has the right to say, 'I'll do it better.'" Paul Reboux, "Poésie," *Paris-Soir,* January 20, 1937, 10.

14. Urdes's column appeared in only four issues of *Radio-Magazine,* September 4–25, 1938.

15. Isabelle d'Urdes, "La Femme et la radio," *Radio-Magazine,* September 4, 1938, 12.

16. Paul Reboux, "Voix de femmes," *Paris-Soir,* December 25, 1936, 9. In a flash of feminist consciousness rarely seen from radio critics, Reboux claimed that these women programmers should have had more opportunities to program because they understood the ways that listeners used their radios, "Yes, I'll repeat it. Women have a sense of the right moment. We should let them program more often."

17. *Mon Programme,* November 6, 1938, 22, 34.

18. *Marie-Claire* was in the Radio-37 family, connected by the daily newspaper *Paris-Soir.* Jean Prouvost promoted all of his publications through advertisements and connected articles and programs that linked them together and encouraged the readers and listeners to subscribe and listen to all of his media outlets.

19. Radio programming week, February 11–17, 1938. In *Le Petit Radio,* February 11, 1938, 6–29.

20. Helmut Gruber points to a lack of connection between the Popular Front and feminists. Feminists and socialists had different agendas, as most feminists were bourgeois, and the socialists working class. Of the socialist feminists and suffrage, Gruber writes, "Virtually all the leading women socialists—Suzanne Buisson, Marthe Louis-Levy, Germaine Picard-Moch, Andrée Marty-Capgras—denounced male socialist opponents of women's suffrage, but none were prepared to challenge Blum or the rest of the SFIO leadership about the party's failure to organize real campaigns or to use organized public pressure against the Senate during the popular front." He later continues, "In reviewing the relationship between the French working-class movement and women in the inter-war years, one is almost forced to conclude that neither party nor trade union made any real effort to advance the position of women." Gruber, "French Women in the Crossfire of Class, Sex, Maternity, and Citizenship," 293, 308.

21. See Karen Offen, *European Feminisms, 1700–1750: A Political History* (Stanford, CA: Stanford University Press, 2000). For a discussion about the differences between individual and relational feminism, see her chapter "Contextualizing the Theory and Practice of Feminism in Nineteenth-Century Europe (1789–1914)," in *Becoming Visible: Women in European History* (3rd ed.), ed. Renate Bridenthal, Susan Mosher Stuard, and Merry E. Wiesner (New York: Houghton Mifflin, 1998), 327–56.

22. Joan Scott, *Only Paradoxes to Offer: French Feminists and the Rights of Man* (Cambridge, MA: Harvard University Press, 1996).

23. Suzanne Cilly, "Les Femmes à la radio," *Radio-Liberté,* June–July 1936, 3.

24. This was important because most radio listeners tuned into private stations only. We could perhaps compare their listenership to our own television watching. Most Americans watch network and cable rather than PBS. Those who do watch PBS usually have a grasp or interest in the issues already. Like PBS, French public radio had fewer listeners and often preached to the already converted.

25. For a closer look at Netter's accomplishments, see Christine Bard, "Yvonne Netter (1889–1985): Itinéraire d'une avocate féministe et sioniste dans la première moitié du siècle en France," in *Sexe et race: Discours et formes nouvelles d'exclusions du XIXème au XXème siècle,* ed. Rita Thalmann (Paris: Centre d'études et de recherches gérmaniques [CERG], 1990), 142–71. On Netter's legal work in the context of the work of other French feminist lawyers, see Sara Kimble, "Justice Redressed: Social Uses of the Law and Citizenship in France, 1890–1945" (PhD dissertation, University of Iowa, 2002).

26. Yvonne Netter appeared on *The Women's Forum* in the first week of June 1939. Her appearance sparked a number of response letters in the following week's issue of Radio-Cité's radio guide. *Ici . . . Radio-Cité,* June 14, 1939, 5.

27. Hubert Bourgin, "L'Opinion d'un journaliste sur 'La Tribune de la Femme,'" *Ici . . . Radio-Cité,* July 14, 1939, 2.

28. Hubert Bourgin wrote numerous works, including, *Cinquante ans d'expérience démocratique, 1874–1924* (Paris: Nouvelle librairie nationale, 1925); *De Jaurès à Léon Blum: L'école normale et la politique* (Paris: A. Fayard, 1938); *La Guerre pour la paix* (Paris: M. Rivière, 1915); *Quand tout le monde est roi: La crise de la démocratie* (Paris: Les Presses Modernes, 1929).

29. Paul Reboux, radio critic in *Paris-Soir,* had criticized this notion the year before *The Women's Forum* aired. He remarked that the stations were wrong when they claimed that "for the considerations of sound technology, the service must only give employment to men, because their voices respond better to the exigencies of the microphone" and referred to the "numerous comments made by listeners" about the sound of high voices over the air. Reboux disagreed and called for action on the part of public stations to remedy the situation. Paul Reboux, "Voix de femmes," *Paris-Soir,* May 22, 1936, 12.

30. Some of the letters to the station complained about Jean Guignebert's unwillingness to enter into the conversation. These listeners wanted the debates to have more structure and wanted to limit the opinions that women expressed over the air.

31. Paul Reboux, *Paris-Soir,* September 25, 1936, 9.

32. Roberts, *Civilization without Sexes,* 1994.

33. Movies, too, attacked single women on all fronts, as films portrayed young single women as sexual predators and women beyond child-bearing years as shrewish gossips. Geneviève Sellier, "Le Cinéma des années 1930," in *Un Siècle d'antiféminisme,* ed. Christine Bard (Paris: Fayard, 1999), 205–14.

34. Raymond Asso and Marguerite Monnet, "Mon Légionnaire," 1936; Asso and Monnet, "La Fanion de la Légion," 1936.

35. Jacques Cossin, *Allô Blima . . . Ici 283,* Radio-Paris, March 23, 1936.

36. Studies from the Belle Epoque and the Vichy period assess the notions of masculinity in those eras, noting the fears of "demasculinization" that some French writers (notably Drieu la Rochelle of *Je Suis Partout*) had. In both the Belle Epoque and during Vichy, these ideas were often linked to the population decline in France, especially as compared to Germany. See particularly Michael D. Sibalis, "Defining Masculinity in Fin-de Siècle France: Sexual Anxiety and the Emergence of the Homosexual," *Proceedings of the Annual Meeting of the Western Society for French History* 25 (1998): 247–56, on the Belle Epoque; and Joan Tumblety, "Revenge for Fascist Knights: Masculine Identities in *Je Suis Partout*," *Modern and Contemporary France* 7 (1999): 11–20.

37. For a close look at honor codes and dueling, see Robert A. Nye, *Masculinity and Male Codes of Honor in Modern France* (New York: Oxford University Press, 1993). Nye argues that the aristocratic honor code met its end after World War I, when fighting duels seemed out of place in a world of modern warfare and a new, less honorable Europe. More study of masculinity in the interwar period remains to be done.

38. Nonn's plays have no redeemable women characters at all. In fact, women cause most of the destruction in his stories. See plays like *Rencontres Immortelles: Adam et Eve*, French radiodiffusion 1935–40, and *Markus*, French radiodiffusion 1935–40.

39. The first show aired in October 1938 (*Ici . . . Radio-Cité*, October 21, 1938, 4). The show was based on a similar show that Marcel Bleustein-Blanchet, owner of the station, saw on a trip to New York made the summer of 1938 (Bleustein-Blanchet, *Sur mon antenne*, 143).

40. Bleustein-Blanchet, *Sur mon antenne*, 144.

41. "Les Huit inconnus de Verdun" aired on November 11, 1938, to commemorate the twentieth anniversary of the armistice of World War I. *Ici . . . Radio-Cité*, November 11, 1938, 1.

42. For a moving account of the battle at the Fort de Vaux, see Allistair Horne, *The Price of Glory: Verdun 1916* (New York: St. Martin's Press, 1963).

43. Bleustein-Blanchet, *Sur mon antenne*, 144.

44. Ibid., 145.

45. Louis Jean Lespine, *Hélène, divine parmis les femmes*, Radio-Paris, February 14, 1937.

46. Lucien Leluc, "D'un micro à l'autre," *Le Petit Radio*, March 6, 1936, 3.

47. *La Famille Duraton*, originally titled "Autour de la Table," aired from 1936 to 1939 on Radio-Cité. For the 1936–37 season it aired at 1:30 p.m.; in 1937–38 it moved to the evenings, at 7:30. After World War II, the program was picked up by Radio Luxembourg, where it aired until 1953.

48. The years after 1945 were broadcast on Radio-Luxembourg, the private station that aired in France after the war.

49. Lise Elina, *Le Micro et moi* (Paris: Pierre Horay, 1978), 49.

50. "Les 'Duraton' peints par eux-mêmes," *Ici . . . Radio Cité*, January 8, 1938, 1.

51. Ibid.

52. Germaine Blondin, "La Famile Duraton," *Radio-Magazine*, February 13, 1938, 3. In contrast to this image, in another interview with Blondin, Jean Nohain, star at Poste Parisien, loved his job and never saw his own four children at home (Germaine Blondin, "Au Service de la fantaisie radiophonique," *Radio-Magazine*, April 30, 1939, 3, 5).

53. Galli was one of the featured announcers and hosts on Radio-Cité, co-hosting *Le Crochet radiophonique* and conducting interviews with other celebrities.

54. See n. 7 of this chapter.

55. Although much radio fiction after 1936 stressed the patriotic responsibility of women to become mothers, early radio critics wanted more airtime on the subject. Lamenting the lack of air play of pronatalist beliefs, J. Reibel reminds his readers about the National Conference on the Birthrate in Lyon from September 25 to September 27, 1936. J. Reibel, "La Question de natalité," *T.S.F., Phono, Ciné,* September 25, 1936, 719.

56. Cita Malard and Suzanne Malard, *Les Survivants,* Radio-Paris, February 14, 1937. In a review of the play in the Catholic radio journal *Choisir,* a critic wrote, "It is one of the most moving radio plays written by Cita and Suzanne Malard.... A surprising sense of tragedy, a superior sense of feeling and a strange nobility are born from the action in which the simplicity of feeling equals the greatness of mind." *Choisir,* February 14, 1937, 3.

57. In an interview with Germaine Blondin, the Malards appeared as the perfect image of mother-daughter felicity. They wrote together, lived together, and shared each other's thoughts. Germaine Blondin, "Avec Cita et Suzanne Malard," *Radio-Magazine,* April 17, 1938, 3.

58. Henriette Charasson's family guides include, among others, *Les Heures du foyer* (Paris: Laguy, 1926); *Le Livre de la mere* (Paris: Flammarion, 1944); *La Mère* (Paris: Nouvelle Société d'Edition, 1931); with André Thibaut, *Le Livre du nouveau né* (Paris: Société Parisenne d'Edition, 1928).

59. Henriette Charasson, *Les Mères de Paris: Autour d'un berceau,* Bordeaux-Lafayette, July 9, 1939.

60. Henriette Chaudet, *L'Epoque,* June 4, 1939.

61. These poems were collected in Charasson, "Ballade à Marie," in *Le Livre de la Mère* (Paris: Flammarion, 1944).

62. Hugues Nonn, *Markus,* French radiodiffusion, 1935–40.

63. Lespine, *Hélène, divine parmis les femmes.* The next chapter will focus on single working-class men and women, showing their negative depiction in radio fiction.

64. Suzanne Normand, *Portraits d'honnêtes femmes dans le roman français: 1) Henriette de Montsauf, 2) Elmire,* French radiodiffusion, 1935–40.

65. Louis Gratias, *Les Voix de l'ombre,* Radio-Paris, July 10, 1938.

66. Raoul Praxy, *Dollars,* Lyon-PTT, June 1. 1939. Praxy was also the vice-president of the Societé des Auteurs et Compositeurs Dramatiques. For a complex look at the attack on the "new woman," see Roberts, *Civilization without Sexes.*

67. Charles Oberfeld and C.-L. Pothier, "La Femme est faite pour l'homme," 1934.

68. Gabriel Timmory, *La Soiree d'hier,* Radio-PTT-Nord, March 17, 1938.

69. Yvonne Guilbert, *Venus Justifiée,* French radiodiffusion, 1935–40.

70. Charles Oberfeld, R. Pujol, and C.-L. Pothier, "C'est pour mon papa," 1930.

71. Roger Bernstein and George Van Parys, "C'est lui," 1934.

72. Henri Garat, "Serait-ce un rêve?" 1931.

73. Frank Churchill, "Un Jour mon prince arrivera," French adaptation by F. Salabert, 1938.

74. H. Christiné and A. Willametz, "Elle est épatante cette petite femme-là," 1933.

75. Bleustein-Blanchet, *Sur mon antenne,* 70.

76. The median wage for men in 1936 was about eight francs per hour. Georges LeFranc, *Histoire du Front Populaire* (Paris: Payot, 1965), 324.

77. Bleustein-Blanchet, Sur mon antenne, 72.

78. Ibid., 70.

79. Ibid., 71.

80. Ibid.

81. Ibid.

82. A good contemporary comparison can be made with ABC's show "Extreme Home Makeover," which each week rewards a fully redesigned and furnished house to "deserving" families. The shows and all the contents of the house are sponsored by Sears, and the hosts visit the store each week and purchase all of the appliances and decorations there. The builders are often from national contracting companies, like Beazer Homes. Since the show's debut, its host, Ty Pennington, has had his own home-decorating line established at Sears department stores. In spite of this obvious marketing, the show still retains its claim on the heartstrings of its viewing public. It is the modern-day equivalent to Radio-Cité's public programs, something that probably would have pleased Marcel Bleustein-Blanchet.

83. Louis Merlin, *J'en ai vu des choses* (Paris: Julliard, 1962), 420–21.

5. THE PERILS OF THE SINGLE LIFE

1. In this sense, Ray Ventura may have shown a more realistic vision of working-class women than the standard song or play did. Paulette works as a store clerk, a standard position for working-class women in the city. No other play or song places women in the store, even though a job there would have been quite expected at the time (Louise A. Tilly and Joan W. Scott, *Women, Work, and Family* [New York: Routledge, 1978], 182–83). Even Zola recognized the ubiquitous placement of the shop girl by the end of the nineteenth century, focusing on the life of a woman who worked in a department store in *Au Bonheur des Dames*.

2. In their work, Adrian Rifkin and Kelley Conway show how this fascination with working-class life and criminality extended far into French culture. Adrian Rifkin depicts the liminal part of Paris in photographs, songs, crime reporting, and film as one of the central themes of popular culture in the first half of the twentieth century (Adrian Rifkin, *Street Noises: Parisian Pleasure, 1900–1940* [Manchester: Manchester University Press, 1993]). Kelley Conway analyzes the gendered implications of music hall and film, especially in women performer's use of the realist song to create their own vision of France (Kelley Conway, "The *Chanteuse* at the City Limits" [PhD dissertation, University of California, Los Angeles, 1999]).

3. As we saw in chap. 1, Jean Nohain parlayed his success with Mireille into a fruitful radio career, performing as "Jaboune" for the station's Thursday afternoon children's programs.

4. Marie-Claire, April 30, 1937, 3.

5. Mireille, *Avec le soleil pour temoin* (Paris: Robert Laffont, 1981), 52.

6. Ibid., 73.

7. The show *(Les amis de Mireille)* featured conversations around the microphone with invited celebrity guests. The group would chat and then break out into Mireille's songs as they fit into a directed conversation.

8. Mireille and Jean Nohain, "A cause du comptable," 1934.

9. Mireille and Jean Nohain, "Presque Oui," 1933.

10. Mireille and Jean Nohain, "Couchés dans le foin," 1933.

11. Adrian Rifkin looks closely at Maurice Chevalier's autobiography and the ways in which Chevalier categorizes himself as part of the Parisian (and particularly Ménilmontant) working class. Here, instead of looking at the Paris landscape, I will try to fit Chevalier's work into radio's larger depiction of the working-class man and the ways that Chevalier became the powerful representative of his class.

12. The biographical information on Chevalier comes from three rather celebratory texts: James Harding, *Maurice Chevalier: His Life, 1888–1972* (London: Secker & Warburg, 1982); Michael Freedland, *Maurice Chevalier,* (New York: Morrow, 1981); and David Bret, *Maurice Chevalier: Up on Top of a Rainbow* (London: Robson Books, 1992).

13. Chevalier writes of his success in America with some surprise. He assumes that it is his innate ability that wins him his fame. In his autobiography, he often writes of the positive responses he gets from other entertainers after they see his show. He sees himself as an exotic, but friendly, commodity. Maurice Chevalier, *Ma Route et mes chansons* (Paris: Flammarion, 1998).

14. Maurice Chevalier must have suggested this character to Rodgers and Hart, who then created the song around his depiction. The "apache" fitted his tailor perfectly because it revealed his working-class roots in a dance number performed as a baron to his wealthy audience.

15. Bret, *Maurice Chevalier: Up on Top of a Rainbow,* 92.

16. Nostalgia for the Belle Epoque and a time prior to World War II may also play a role in the song's popularity. Other artists used nostalgia to promote themselves, including Polaire, who gained her fame from a whole show sung with songs and costumes from the Belle Epoque. She was written up favorably in *Paris-Midi,* a daily paper in Paris, which also had a photo of her in her 1900s garb. "Polaire," *Paris-Midi,* December, 1934, from Fonds Bouglé, Manuscripts (Press Cuttings/Variety), Bibliothéque de l'Histoire de la Ville de Paris, Paris.

17. Bret, *Maurice Chevalier: Up on Top of a Rainbow,* 101.

18. For work on paraliterature, see Robin Walz, *Pulp Surrealism: Insolent Popular Culture in Early Twentieth-Century Paris* (Berkeley: University of California Press, 2000). On *fait divers,* see Schwartz, *Spectacular Realities,* and on apaches and *fait divers,* Dominique Kalifa, *L'Encre et le sang: Récits de crimes et société à la Belle Époque* (Paris: Fayard, 1995), *Les Crimes de Paris: Lieux et non-lieux du crime à Paris au XIXe siècle* (Paris: BILIPO, 2000), and *Crime et culture au XIXe siècle* (Paris: Perrin, 2005).

19. Patricia C. Nichols reviews the literature of English studies of language and class in "Networks and Hierarchies: Language and Social Stratification," in *Language and Power,* ed. Chris Kramarae, Muriel Schulz, and William M O'Barr (Beverly Hills, CA: Sage, 1984), 23–42. In their work, Lars Andersson and Peter Trudgill, two English linguists point out that "bad language" has direct links to perceptions of class status and that by using slang and bad language, people can transcend class, lending themselves allures of "toughness and strength." Lars Andersson and Peter Trudgill, *Bad Language* (Oxford: Blackwell, 1990), 8–9.

20. Geo Koger and Vincent Scotto, "Ma Pomme," 1935.

21. Rifkin, *Street Noises,* 79–85.

22. Sullivan, Willemetz and Pothier, "La Petite Dame de l'Expo," 1938; Willemetz, René Toché, and Charles Borel-Clerc, "Ah! Si vous connaissiez ma poule!" 1938; Van Parys and Jean Boyer, "Appelez-ça comme vous voulez," 1939.

23. See chap. 2.

24. Mistinguett made only one sound film in 1932 and found the transition to radio very difficult. In spite of lucrative contracts with Radio-37 and Poste Parisien, her constant appearances on the air inspired only disgust from most radio listeners. For example, in *Notes d'écoute*, *Vendredi*'s weekly column on the radio, Mistinguett is berated for appearing too frequently on Radio-37. "On Radio 37 Mistinguett continues to prolong her stay. We will admit one thing: she still has beautiful legs. Too bad that you can't see them on the radio." Jacques Amaire, "Notes d'écoute," *Vendredi*, May 20, 1938, 7.

25. Fernandel, "Pour que vous m'eussiez dit oui," 1941. The original, unattractive-sounding, and snobby French is sung as follows:

> Pour que vous m'eussiez dit oui
> Il eu fallu que je vous le demandasse
> Pour que je vous le demandasse
> Il eu fallu d'abord que je l'osasse
> Que nos mains se mélassent
> Que vous frissonassiez
> Que je vous sérmonasse
> Que vous sympathissiez
> Ah! Mais je n'ai pas osé, zosé, zosé!

26. Paul Misraki and Andre Hornaz, "C'est dommage que j'puisse pas vous l'montrer" (ed. Ray Ventura, 1938).

27. Eugen Weber, *The Hollow Years: France in the 1930s* (New York: Norton, 1994).

28. Tilly and Scott estimate that 55 percent of working women worked in the industrial sector. Tilly and Scott, *Women, Work, and Family*, 152.

29. Suzanne Cordelier, *Femmes au travail: Etude pratique sur dix-sept carrières féminines* (Paris: Plon, 1935). Cordelier also uses the paradoxical argument that female difference should lead to their equality. She claims that these careers are specifically suited to women because of the "natural" female character, with "finesse, delicacy, sense of nuance and inward psychology" (3). Sara Kimble, in her University of Iowa dissertation, "Justice Redressed" (August 2002), shows that many bourgeois women entered the professions, including law, and made more of their lives than Suzanne Cordelier thought possible.

30. Susan Bachrach, *Dames Employées: The Feminization of Postal Work in Nineteenth-Century France* (New York: Haworth Press, 1984).

31. Catherine Omnès, *Ouvrières Parisiennes: Marchés du travail et trajectoires professionelles au 20è siècle* (Paris: Editions de l'Ecole des Hautes Etudes en Sciences Sociales, 1997), 167.

32. Nonn, *Marcus*, 1935–40.

33. Tilly and Scott, *Women, Work, and Family*, 152. Tilly explains that by the 1930s working women would choose almost any career over domestic service. Many families had to fire servants. While the percentage of women in the workforce remained stable over the first half of the twentieth century, the number of women in domestic service dropped. Over the first half of the decade, the age of the domestic servant rose, as well (ibid., 155). Radio plays do not reflect this change.

34. The trope of the "French maid" runs through centuries of farce and tale, from the innocent victim of an evil count in Mozart's *The Marriage of Figaro* to Jean Genet's ferocious pair in *Les Bonnes*. On 1930s French radio, the maid appeared frequently and always as a sexual(ized) victim of circumstance and assumption.

35. Jean A. Dauven, *Samedi soir*, Radio-Paris, May 13, 1936.

36. André-Micho, *Bijoute*, Radio-Paris, February 2, 1936.

37. In opposition to the images of the working girl were repeated images of happy family life. The successful families on French radio were always the middle-class families, with a working husband and a wife in the private sphere. *La Famille Duraton*, a daily soap that featured a "typical" French family around the dinner table showed the "natural" family portrait. Over the years, the daughter moves from the bosom of her family directly into marriage. In other radio plays where virtuous women are featured, their hopes always ride around marriage and children. Some good examples are Henriette Charasson, *Autour d'un berceau*, Bordeaux-Lafayette, July 9, 1939; André Deleaze, *La Femme qui épousa le diable*, Strasbourg, March 12, 1937; Suzanne Normand, *Portraits d'honnêtes femmes dans le roman français: 1. Henriette de Montsauf, 2. Elmire*, 1936.

38. Henriette Charasson, *Le Théâtre Express: La Femme de ménage (III)* (1935–40).

39. It is no surprise that even the unattractive, barren Marie becomes a mother in this play. Henriette Charasson, as we saw in chap. 4, was a Catholic pronatalist activist who saw motherhood as the only option for patriotic French women.

40. Cossin and de Bérys, *La Peur*.

41. The idea that women were emotionally unstable was another stereotype propagated by French radio fiction. See, e.g., Théo Bergerat, *Souvent femme varie*, Lille (Radio-PTT-Nord), December 24, 1938.

42. Léon Lemmonier and Jacques Cossin, *La Démarche*, Radio-Paris, October 30, 1938.

43. Mireille and Jean Nohain, "C'est gentil," 1935.

44. Mireille and Jean Nohain, "27, rue des Acacias," 1933.

45. Paul Misraki and Jean Féline, "Pas de tout d'argent," 1936.

46. Mireille and Jean Nohain, "Ma Grandmère était garde-barrière," 1935.

47. Again, this notion of crime was not new to French listeners. They had literature, newspapers, stage plays, and cinema that all featured the criminal element. See nn. 19 and 22.

48. J. Vaillard and Raymond Asso, "Browning," 1938; J. Delanney and Suzy Solidor, "Dans un port," 1937; Raoul Le Peltier and A. Valsien, "Mon Vieux Pataud," 1936; Robert Malleron, "L'Etranger," 1936.

49. J. Manse and C. Oberfeld, "Un Dur, un vrai, un tatoué," 1938.

50. In all of the radio plays I have read, I have found none that focus on positive images of working-class families. Working-class families are either absent altogether from the stories of working people's experience or they are portrayed as linked to ultimate criminal behavior in the children they produce. Bourgeois families, on the other hand, appear in both positive and negative images of French life.

51. Roger-François Didelot, *Le Retour dans la nuit*, Radio-Paris, March 13, 1938.

52. Georges Avryl, *Cellule 29*, Strasbourg, September 10, 1937.

53. André de Lorde, *L'Enfant*, Lille (Radio-PTT-Nord), April 15, 1939.

54. The literal translation is "sidewalk song," but because *faire le trottoir* ("do the sidewalk")

in slang means to be a prostitute, the use of the term "prostitute's song" would be more correct. These songs belong to a larger group of songs called *chansons réalistes* that depicted every aspect of life on the streets—from senseless killings to drug use. Kelley Conway attempts to give the female realist performers agency in the creation of realist songs on film and on the music-hall stage, where women artists embodied these characters and gave them life (Kelley Conway, "Les 'Goualeuses' de l'écran," in *Le Cinéma au rendez-vous des arts: France, années 20 et 30*, ed. Emmanuelle Toulet [Paris: Bibliothèque Nationale de France, 1995]). René Baudelaire breaks down the basic forms of this song trope in *La Chanson réaliste* (Paris: L'Harmattan, 1996).

55. The necessity for easy recognition reflects Elizabeth Tonkin's ideas about "genre" and the importance of communication between audience and performer in *Narrating Our Pasts: The Social Construction of Oral History* (Cambridge, Cambridge University Press, 1992). Tonkin claims that audiences need to understand the type of story they listen to, in order to fully comprehend its meaning. Stories thus fall into types, or genres, that share styles and themes. She focuses on oral performance and oral history, but I believe her ideas can be equally applicable here. Performance in the *chanson du trottoir* is exceedingly important, as the lyrics themselves could not fully express the image in each song. Voice, background, and tempo all played fundamental roles in these songs.

56. Although these songs were sung by women, they were always written by men. The most famous lyricists who specialized in these songs were Raymond Asso, who wrote for Edith Piaf and Marie Dubas, and Borel-Clerc, who wrote for many of the singers.

57. Elizabeth K. Menon, "Images of Pleasure and Vice: Women on the Fringe," in *Montmartre and the Making of Mass Culture*, ed. Gabriel P. Weisberg (New Brunswick, NJ: Rutgers University Press, 2001), 37–71.

58. Ibid., 37.

59. Kelley Conway, *Chanteuse in the City: The Realist Singer in French Film* (Berkeley: University of California Press, 2004).

60. M. Monnot, A. Rhegent, and R. Malleron, "Maison louche," 1935; R. Dumas and E. Rocagno, "Le Tango des filles," and "Fleur de joie," 1932.

61. J. Delettre and M. Aubret, "En maison," 1934.

62. H. Ackermans, Polgé, and Noyelle, "La Catin du village," 1933.

63. Prostitution was legalized in France because manhood was directly linked to sexuality and the need for and ability to have sex. In her dissertation, Michele Rhoades explores the ways that doctors justified legalized prostitution during World War I as providing a service for male soldiers—a service that often ended with both sex partners getting and spreading syphilis (Michele Rhoades, "'No Safe Women': Prostitution, Masculinity, and Disease in France during the Great War" [PhD dissertation, University of Iowa, 2001]). For an excellent general history of the relationship between prostitution and the state, see Alain Corbin, *Women for Hire: Prostitution and Sexuality in France after 1850* (Cambridge, MA: Harvard University Press, 1990). Corbin shows that by the interwar years the public brothel had nearly disappeared and most prostitutes worked on the streets (as they did in the songs) rather than in houses.

64. R. de Buxeuil and Suzanne Quentin, "Les Poupées de minuit," 1932.

65. J. Delettre and P. Bayle, "Le Tango des filles," 1936.

66. J. Boyer, M. Audret, and Léo Lelièvre *fils*, "Les filles qui, la nuit . . . ," 1936.

67. J. Boyer, M. Audret, and Léo Lelièvre fils, "Ecoute-donc, chéri . . . ," 1936.

68. Kelley Conway shows how, often, these singers' lives reflected the pain they sang of in their songs, including Frehel, Piaf, and others. Conway, "The Chanteuse at the City Limits," 32.

69. Interestingly, Chevalier, too, was born in Ménilmontant and used his connection to that neighborhood in much of his music, including the song "Ménilmontant" about his continued love for his childhood neighborhood.

70. Adrian Rifkin does an excellent analysis of Piaf's early years and their effect on Piaf's career (Rifkin, *Street Noises*, 74). He also looks at how Piaf's association with Léplée almost destroyed her career when he was brutally murdered by someone Piaf may have known. Because of its connection with the seedy side of Parisian life, including male prostitution, *Detective*, one of the 1930s tabloids picked up the story and published it nationwide. It was only through her tremendous talent as a performer that Piaf was able to continue working (ibid., 76).

71. The biographical information on Edith Piaf comes from several sources, including *Femmes et arts: Sarah Bernhardt, Edith Piaf, Simone Signoret, Agnès Varda* (Ramorantin: Editions Martinsart, 1980); Joelle Montserrat, *Edith Piaf et la chanson* (Paris: Editions PAC, 1983; and Monique Lange, *Histoire de Piaf* (Paris: Editions Ramsay, 1979). These biographies are all rather celebratory and never call into question Piaf's shady past or early death. The latest homage to Piaf came in the 2007 film *La Môme* (*La Vie en rose*), directed by Olivier Dahan and starring, to rave reviews, Marion Cotillard as Piaf and the ubiquitous Gérard Départdieu as Louis Léplée. The film runs the standard biopic story on one of France's favorite singing stars. Success in her career only leads to trouble in her personal life. Piaf's story seems fairly staged for this movie adaptation.

72. In his autobiography, *On cherche jeune homme aimant la musique*, Jacques Canetti tells us that he also signed Piaf to Polydor Records to record her first songs.

73. *Femmes et arts*, 379. Raymond Asso was one of the most prominent lyricists of the 1930s, and Marie Dubas and Edith Piaf competed for his songs. Piaf's voice and characterization fit the prostitutes' songs better than did Dubas's. Piaf's voice was huskier and much more expressive. Her recording of "Mon Légionnaire" has become part of the French cultural patrimony, while Dubas's version appears only on "retro" CDs. Because of her greater success, Edith Piaf won Asso's favor, and the lyricist began writing songs specifically for her, choosing her as his muse. Between 1936 and 1940, Piaf recorded seventeen songs with lyrics by Asso. This is a testament to the importance of performance in the success of French song. Damia performed both comedy numbers and the occasional realist song. Piaf exclusively performed realist songs. Songs had much more power when they were performed in an appropriate style.

74. Raymond Asso and Marguerite Monnot, "Mon Légionnaire," 1936.

75. Jacques Simonot and Pierre Bayle, "Reste," Polydor Records, 1937.

76. How much these marginal characters affected bourgeois values is debatable. Women may have felt empowered by Piaf's sexual escapades. By the 1940s, Piaf, fed up with the *chanson du trottoir*, sings about love won and kept in songs like "La Vie en rose" and "Je ne regrette rien." She claimed to want to sing about "simple loves, health and the joy of living." Rifkin, *Street Noises*, 33.

77. Adrian Rifkin writes about Piaf's problems with the tabloids. As she started her career, her manager was murdered by one of his young gay lovers. Her connection with him nearly

ruined her. She overcame this by meeting her audiences face to face on a national tour. Within a few months, audiences reclaimed her as a true star. Ibid., 76.

78. Raymond Asso, "Elle fréquentait la rue Pigalle," 1936. This insistence on the return to the shady streets harkens back to a trope in French literature, when prostitutes, dumped by lovers, move back into the old neighborhood, often as a semimoral punishment for explicit sexual behavior.

79. Mary Lou Roberts, in *Civilization without Sexes*, analyzes the impact of Margueritte's book as an attempt to temper the phenomenon of the "garçonne," or genderless woman, that was a prevalent figure in the jazz age in France. It is no surprise that the 1937 movie featured Piaf, who, in her stage personality, was seen as sexually active. In a switch on Piaf's stage character, however, in the film, the sexually active woman is tamed and placed back into the patriarchal household.

80. In her book, Roberts looks at the "new woman" of the 1920s and analyzes how culture reflected a desire to restrain her and conform her to an idealistic view of prewar women. She claims that postwar male anxiety contributed to this desire to return women to their idealized past roles.

6. BOA CONSTRICTORS, MAN-EATERS, AND *LE CAFARD*

1. Jacques Cossin, *L'Enigme da la nuit du 4*, Radio-Paris, December 13, 1936.

2. This is in contrast to cinema, in which the colonies offered heroes an escape from French poverty and a chance for the future.

3. Edward Said, *Orientalism* (New York: Vintage, 1978).

4. These reports came on Radio-Paris and were listed in the weekly program guides. Because the state was overwhelmingly positive in its colonial propaganda, it is doubtful that the reports contained much realistic news about independence struggles and colonial organization.

5. Weber, *The Hollow Years*, 180.

6. "Allô allô Poste Parisien," *La Semaine Radiophonique*, March 20, 1938, 8.

7. Antoinette Roland, "La Semaine passée: Notes d'écoute," *La Semaine Radiophonique*, April 24, 1938, 7.

8. This sound "view" and inherent ownership from description could be compared to the travelogues composed in the late nineteenth century by African explorers who, in seeing the landscape, conquered it. For an excellent analysis of the implications of travel writing, see Mary Louise Pratt, *Imperial Eyes : Travel Writing and Transculturation* (London ; New York : Routledge, 1992).

9. Timothy Mitchell uses the colonial and world expositions as a way of analyzing the structures of how Europeans saw the world around them. Every view became an exhibition, and the world conformed to the museums Europeans created: "They took semiosis to be a universal condition, and set about describing the orient as though it were an exhibition." Timothy Mitchell, *Colonising Egypt* (Berkeley: University of California Press, 1991), 14.

10. François de Teramond, *La Fille du Vice-Roi des Indes*, French radiodiffusion, 1935–40.

11. René-Paul Groffe, *L'Histoire du Prince Ahmed et de la fée Pari-Banou*, French radiodiffusion, 1935–40.

12. Jacques Tem, "René-Paul Groffe," *Le Petit Radio*, April 5, 1935, 1.

13. Rolain Gontrain, *Deux hommes au Maroc,* Radio-Paris, 1935–40.

14. Two of the rousing colonial songs were "Abd El Kader: Marche triomphale du Centenaire de la conquête de l'Algérie" (A. Evrard and L. Boyer, 1930) and "Qu'est-ce que t'attends pour aller aux colonies" (C. Oberfeld and A. Dahl, 1931).

15. Anne Stoler deals with this idea in "Making Empire Respectable: The Politics of Race and Sexual Morality in 20th-Century Colonial Cultures," *American Ethnologist,* November 1989, 634–60.

16. Teramond, *La Fille du Vice-Roi des Indes,* 1935–40. It is interesting to note that the only organized rebellion depicted in radio fiction occurred in India, or under the auspices of the British, not French, empire. This gave an impression that no organizations to fight for independence were forming in the French colonies, authorized the continuation of the French system, and offered a favorable comparison to be made against the British, who could not control the colonies they had.

17. Jacques Cossin, *Jekko le Malais,* Radio-Paris, April 10, 1938.

18. Maurice Zeller Denis, *Taipan,* Radio-Paris, August 12, 1938. About 70 percent of the radio plays on public radio were classics and current fiction rewritten for the radio.

19. Jacques-Jean Clément, *Le Caprice,* Radio-Paris, 1935–40.

20. André de Lorde, *L'Enfant,* Lille (Radio-PTT-Nord), April 15, 1939.

21. Colette Vivier, *Didine et Jacquot,* French radiodiffusion, 1935–40.

22. Raymond Asso and R. Cloerec, "Le Grand Voyage du pauvre nègre," 1939.

23. Jacques Cossin, *Allô Blima . . . Ici 283 . . . ,* Radio-Paris, March 23, 1936. This play was also part of a festival of Jacques Cossin's work on Radio-PTT-Nord, April 5, 1938. Many of the radio journals mention this event, as Cossin's plays were quite admired by French audiences.

24. R. Sarvil and Vincent Scotto, "Viens dans ma casbah," 1933.

25. Georgius and A. H. Poussigues, "Chez les bédouins," 1925; L. Montagné and Parissé, "Le Radabi-Nacou-Naha," 1935.

26. Paul Mizraki and André Hornez, "La Marquise Voyage," 1937.

27. Marc Denis, *K-247,* Paris-PTT, September 17, 1937.

28. *Radio-Liberté,* August 8, 1937, 7.

29. In an analysis of colonial gender relations, Ann Stoler shows how unwelcome women were in the colonies at the outset of empire (Stoler, *Making Empire Respectable*). Sophie, like the women in the late nineteenth-century empire, causes great problems with her presence in a land not yet ready for white women.

30. Cossin, *Jekko le Malais.*

31. It is interesting to note that jazz represents the metropole here, and not African American music. Jazz, by the 1930s, is no longer an exotic musical form.

32. Georges Avryl, *Paramaribo,* Strasbourg-PTT, May 24, 1938.

33. René Lemarchand Charmel, *Le Dernier Acte,* Radio-Paris, July 3, 1938.

34. Jacques Cossin, *Intelligence Service,* Radio-Paris, July 17, 1938.

35. Raymond Asso and M. Monnot, "Mon Légionnaire," 1935, and "La Fanion de la Légion," 1936.

36. The reality was quite different, as Gwendolyn Wright points out in her book *The Politics of Design in French Colonial Urbanism* (Chicago: University of Chicago Press, 1991). Colonial architectures directly affected building styles in Paris and throughout France throughout the nineteenth and twentieth centuries.

37. Tyler Stovall, *Paris Noir,* and "The Color Line between the Lines: Racial Violence in France during the Great War," *American Historical Review* 103, no. 3 (1998): 737–69.

38. *Ici . . . Radio-Cité,* 1938–39. The weekly comic strip, about a Monsieur Moustique, a Frenchman who loved the radio, also featured his black manservant, Bouboula, doing foolish things because of what he hears on the radio.

39. Jean Topsy, "Ici Radio-Cannibal," *Radio-Journal,* December 1, 1935, 1.

40. Georges Chepfer, *Une Soirée au Chat Noir,* Radio-Paris, January 15, 1935.

41. Paul Misraki and André Hornez, "C'est Zozo" (ed. Ray Ventura), Paris, 1937.

42. Jacques Cossin and André Charpentier, *L'Enigme de la nuit du 4,* Radio-Paris, December 13, 1936. The play was rebroadcast at least once at a Jacques Cossin festival on Lille (Radio-PTT-Nord), April 5, 1938. "Gala Jacques Cossin," *La Semaine Radiophonique,* April 3, 1938, 42.

43. Roland Mane, *Le Crime de l'îlot,* Radio-Paris, June 27, 1937.

44. Hours of tangos from Argentina, javas (or exoticized waltzes) from Java, and Hawaiian ukulele music can be found in the program minutes. Although they were not nearly as popular as swing, it was clear that the listeners enjoyed all of these styles. In the week of November 6, 1938, the radio program listings showcased multiple Argentine orchestras, including Mario Melfi's on Poste Parisien, Osvaldo Fresedo's on Radio-Paris, and Géno Aubry's on Ile-de-France. Lille-PTT and Bordeaux-S.O. played French and Argentine recordings of hit tangos. Strasbourg-PTT, Radio-Toulouse, and Radio-Agen each programmed over half an hour of Hawaiian ukulele music into their schedules. *Mon Programme,* November 6, 1938, 8–47.

45. Vincent Scotto, Robert Sarvil, and Alibert, with Gaby Sims, "Le Plus Beau Tango du monde," 1935; Scotto, Georges Koger, and N. Renard, "La Java bleue," 1938.

46. In a similar bar to the temptation of miscegenation, coordinators of the beauty pageant at the International Exposition of Paris in 1937 that was to crown "Miss France d'Outremer" chose as contestants all biracial women. In this way, "Miss France," the embodiment of colonial beauty, would not be wholly non-French but would rather display the qualities of Frenchness within a colonial body. Ironically, of course, though more desirable for their French traits, these women (unlike Rossi) were products of miscegenation themselves and countered notions of racial protection. They "proved" to audiences of the pageant, however, that French beauty had to come from France. See Elizabeth Ezra, "Colonialism Exposed: Miss France d'Outre-mer, 1937," in *Identity Papers: Contested Nationhood in Twentieth-Century France,* ed. Steven Ungar and Tom Conley (Minneapolis: University of Minnesota Press, 1996), 50–65.

47. Laurent Rossi, *Tino Rossi: Mon père* (Paris: Flammarion, 1993), 56.

48. Ibid., 60.

49. Bleustein-Blanchet, *Sur mon antenne,* 68.

50. Vincent Scotto and Georges Koger, "O Corse, île d'amour," 1935.

51. Scotto, Jean Rodor, George Koger, and Emile Mariús Audiffred, "Tarantelle," 1937.

52. Scotto, Koger, Pujol, and Audiffred, "Marinella," 1936.

53. Scotto, Koger, and H. Vendresse, "Bella raggazina," 1936.

54. Scotto, Koger, Rodor, and Audiffred, "Ecoutez les Mandolines," 1936; Scotto, Koger, and Henri Varna, "Vieni, vieni," 1934.

55. Scotto, Koger, Pujol, and Audiffred, "Tchi Tchi," 1936.

56. Rossi, *Tino Rossi,* 66.

57. Roland Dhordain, *Le Roman de la radio* (Paris: La Table Ronde, 1983), 53.

58. Paul Reboux, "Le Robinet," *Paris-Soir*, October 13, 1936, 9. *Ici . . . Radio-Cité*'s letter page had letters about Rossi almost every week. As we saw in chap. 3, the *Petit Parisien* made fun of the women who loved Rossi by claiming that they had no sense to vote for anyone else in the 1937 radio election. "Les Eléctions radiophoniques," *Petit Parisien*, February 23, 1937, 1.

59. Canetti, *On cherche jeune homme aimant la musique*, 53.

60. "Les élections radiophoniques," *Le Petit Parisien*, February 23, 1937, 1.

61. Josephine Baker did not figure much on the radio because she did not like the studio or microphone. It was rare for anyone to hear her over the airwaves. She gave an interview to *Le Petit Radio* in early 1935, but she never really capitalized on her fame by becoming a radio star. Jacques Tem, "Josephine Baker," *Le Petit Radio*, February 22, 1935, 1.

62. Scotto, H. Christiné, and Villard, "La petite Tonkinoise," 1930; Scotto, Koger, and Henri Varna, "J'ai deux amours," 1931. "J'ai deux amours," originally about an African girl who falls in love with her French colonial master, became Baker's theme song, speaking about her American heritage and her love of her adopted city of Paris:

> I have two loves
> My country and Paris.
> My heart will always be
> In love with them.

63. For an excellent race analysis of Baker's experiences in Paris during the 1930s, see Phyllis Rose, "Queen of the Colonies," chap. 5 in *Jazz Cleopatra: Josephine Baker in Her Time* (New York: Bantam Doubleday, 1989), 142–80.

CONCLUSION

1. The "Official Journal" of the government lists a decree on September 1, 1939, that reads, "The decree . . . placed the administration of national radio under the direct authority of the prime minister, in order that in grave situations, the government control the powerful instrument of moral defense." "Journal Officiel," September 7, 1939, 11.178, AN, F/43.

2. Brochand, *Histoire générale de la radio et de la télévision*, vol. 1, 585. For a detailed account of radio under Vichy, see Hélène Eck, *La Guerre des ondes: histoire des radios de langue française pendant la Deuxième Guerre Mondiale* (Paris: Communauté des radios publiques de langue française, 1985).

3. Hélène Eck, "A la recherché d'un art radiophonique," in *La Vie culturelle sous Vichy*, ed. Jean-Pierre Rioux (Paris: Editions Complexe, 1990), 270.

4. "Loi du 17 juillet 1940, Artistes/musiciens juifs" AN, F43/170; "Notes (Marseille) du chef de la section," August 9, 1941, AN, F43/170.

5. "Note au Directeur des programmes," November 5, 1942, AN, F43/170.

6. Bouillon would later marry Josephine Baker, who spent the war aiding the resistance in North Africa.

7. Sprecherbuch, Livre du Speaker, August 1940. AN, F/43/59.

8. Christian Brochand, *Histoire générale de la radio et de la télévision,* vol. 2, 29–30.

9. Bleustein-Blanchet, *La Rage de convaincre* (Paris: Laffont, 1970), 248.

10. Denis Maréchal, *Radio Luxembourg, 1933–1993: Un media au Coeur de l'Europe* (Nancy: Presses Universitaires de Nancy, 1994), 133.

11. André Sevry, "Les Projets de Radio 37," *Mon Programme,* October 10, 1938, 5.

12. Laurent Gervereau and Denis Peschanski, eds., *La Propagande sous Vichy, 1940–1944* (Nanterre: Bibliothèque de documentation contemporaine, 1990), 244.

13. Brochand, *Histoire générale de la radio et de la télévision,* vol. 2, 670.

INDEX

Page numbers in italics refer to illustrations.

Adison, Fred, 36, 63, 70, 96
advertising, 8; and endorsements, 36; jingles, 33; for programs, 34, 35, 36; of programs, 50; and radio sponsorship, 30–31, 38; of radio sets, 58–59; of radio stations, 15, 50; revenue, 25
Alibert (Henri), 170, 181
Allô Blima . . . Ici 283 (Cossin), 113, 169, 174, 175, 176
Alpes-Grenoble-PTT, 7, 94
Amaire, Jacques, 96
anti-arab sentiment, 169–70
anti-semitism: depiction of, 68–69; on radio during Vichy and occupation, 187–89
"apaches," 132–33
Arletty (Léonie Marie Julie Bathiat), 10, 120–21
"Art and Work," 76, 96
Aslan, Coco (Grégoire Aslanian), 63
assimilation of Jewish names, 63, 130, 188, 190
Asso, Raymond, 154, 188
At Least Fifteen Years (Radio-Cité), 37, 55, 57, 124–127
audience participation: as live audiences, 55–56; on the microphone, 54–55, 108–12; and radio-clubs, 53–54; sharing their stories, 39, 113–14

Baker, Josephine, 123, 184
The Banania Wake-Up (Poste Parisien and Radio-Toulouse), 36
The Bar of the Stars (Radio-37), 50, 51–52
Bijoute (André-Mycho), 141–42
Bizet, René, 65
Bleustein-Blanchet, Marcel: and advertising revenue, 44; and advertising slogans, 31–32; and Antennes de Publicis, 28–31; and competition for advertising, 46; and founding of Publicis, 27; and Free French, 188; and iron lung, 57; and launch of Radio-Cité, 27, 33; and public programs, 56; and Publicis, 16; and sponsorships, 70; and staffing of Radio-Cité, 9; on Tino Rossi, 181
Blondin, Germaine, 37, 102, 103, 107, 115
Blot, Max, 63
Blum, Léon, 9, 75, 78, 101
Bordeaux-Lafayette-PTT, 7, 79, 94
Bouillon, Jo, 63, 188
Bourdet, Maurice, 188
Bourgin, Hubert, 110
Boyer, Lucienne, 34
Brichet, Georges, 188
Brown, Al, 52

le cafard, 160, 168, 175, 184
Canetti, Jacques, 9, 54, 154, 188
The Caprice (Clément), 168, 175, 176

Catholic plays, 117–18
Cellule 29 (Avryl), 148
chansons du trottoir, 150–53, 156, 157–58
chansons réalistes, 113, 146–47, 150–53
Charasson, Henriette, 10, 117–18, 139
Chevalier, Maurice: available recording, x; during the occupation, 188; and the founding of Radio-37, 49–51; as a frequent radio personality, 14; and Jacques Canetti, 56; with Misinguett, 155; songs as relevant to today's audience, 13; success versus Tino Rossi, 183; as working-class icon, 130, 132–36, 146
Choisir, 40, 81, 87, 91
Clérouc, Paul, 39
Clevers, Lyne, 52
Cocteau, Jean, 10, 76, 77
Code de la Famille, 101
Colin, Georges, 10, 39–40
Colonial Exposition of 1931, 161
colonies, depiction of on radio, 166, 172–75
Compargue, Paul, 83
Conseils de Gérance, 73–74
Cordelier, Suzanne, 138
Cossin, Jacques, 1, 4, 39, 160
Cot, Pierre, 83
crime drama, 2, 9, 39, 95, 113, 143, 146, 178, 180
criticism of programming, amateur, 110–11
criticism of programming, professional: by left-wing press, 77, 80, 96, 106–7; by Paul Reboux, 27, 51, 53, 102, 104–5, 112, 183; reviews of radio plays, 118, 173; reviews of *La Tribune de la Femme,* 110; by right-wing press, 87, 89, 90, 118
criticism of women as listeners, 102–4
Le Crochet radiophonique (Radio-Cité), 35, 55, 57

Daladier, Edouard, 9, 83
Damia (Marie-Louise Damien), 113, 152, 153
David, Henri, 87
La Démarche (Cossin and Lemonnier), 143

depictions of Africans as primitive, 168–69, 176–78
depictions of Asian stereotypes, 166–68
Desnos, Robert, 14
Dollars (Praxy), 119–20, 121
Domène, Pierre, 54
domestic labor, 140–44
Dubas, Marie, 154
d'Urdes, Isabele, 104–5

educational programming, 27, 75–80
Elina, Lise, 10, 15, 116
L'Enfant (De Lorde), 148, 168
The Enigma of the Night of the Fourth (Cossin), 160, 178–80
Esbly, Mirane, 152
An Evening at the Chat Noir (Chepfer), 177–78

La Famille Duraton, 10, 35, 115–16, 185
fashions of the Belle Epoque, 40, 113, 132, 136, 172, 173, 177
Fear (Cossin and de Berys), 1, 4, 143
Fernandel, 10, 13–14, 137, 147
Fernandel and Company, 137
Ferrié Plan, 25, 71, 73
Les Fiancés de Byrrh, 55, 57, 124–27
Le Figaro and the radio elections, 86, 91, 92, 94
Flandin, Pierre Etienne, 25
foley, 12, 162–65
Frehel (Marguerite Boulc'h), 152–53
A French Imperial Voice: From North Africa to Black Africa through the Sahara Desert (Décharme), 162–63

Galli, Yvonne, 35, 115–16
La Garçonne (film and novel), 156–57
Georgius (Georges Auguste Charles Guibourg), 69
Germany: and comparisons to French radio, 3–5, 6, 72, 75; language instruction of French schools, 78; radio under occupation of, 187–88; threat of war with, 117

Germinet, Gabriel, 77
Gershwin, George, 96
Goebbels, Joseph, 72
Gorki, Maxim, 76
Great Britain: colonies of, 166; and comparisons to French radio, 4–5, 6, 72, 75; histories of radio of, 10; interpretation of swing music of, 63–64; language instruction of French schools, 78; and World War II, 190
Grunebaum, Jean, 43, 47, 70
Guignebert, Jean, 54, 188–89
Guitry, Sacha, 52

The Half Hour about the Home, (Radio-Paris), 104
Harvey, Lilian, 123
Haut-Parleur, 81
Helen, Divine among Women (Lespine), 114, 118
Hess, Johnny, 33
homophobia, depiction of, 68–69
Honegger, Arthur, 76, 77
Hornez, André, 63, 69, 128, 178
Huc, Benjamin, 72

Ici . . . Radio Cité, 53–54, 110–11, 177
Intelligence Service (Cossin and Coolus), 175–76
intermedia relationships, 23–24, 33–34, 46–49, 50, 53, 59
International Exposition of 1937, 48, 84, 61–63, 125, 136, 161–62, 178
L'Intransigeant, 37; and partnership with Radio-Cité, 53, 59

Jacques Cossin's Half Hour of Crime Drama and Adventure (Radio-Paris), 2, 95, 113
Jardillier, Robert, 80, 91
Jardy, Francois, 102–3
javas, 181
jazz as French music style, 63, 95, 174, 188
Jekko the Malay (Cossin), 166–67, 173–74, 176

Le Jeu des questions (Radio-Cité), 34, 51
Jude, L., 91

K-247 (Denis), 170–73

Larronde, Carlos, 77
The Last Act (Charmel), 175
Laval, Pierre, 31, 187, 189
lectures on radio, 78–80
Lefèvre, René, 52
Léon-Martin, Louis, 46–49
Limoges-PTT, 7, 94
The Little Friends' Club (Poste Parisien), 48–49
Lustucru Theatre (Radio-Cité, Radio-Ile-de-France, Radio-Luxembourg, and Radio-Toulouse), 36, 63
Lyon-PTT, 7, 94, 105, 107

Malard, Suzanne and Cita, 117, 139, 190
Mandel, Georges: appointment to the PTT, 5; assassination of, 188; and collection of radio tax, 26; and elimination of advertising on public radio, 33, 71; and extension of Ferrié Plan, 74; and increase in tax revenue, 26; and retransmission of radio plays, 26, 76; and strikes of 1936, 75; work at the PTT, 25–27
Marcus (Nonn), 139
Marseille-PTT, 7, 94
Mathieu, M., 47
"May 36," 76–77, 96
Merlin, Louis, 40
Milton, Georges, 36, 122
Ministry of Post, Telegraph and Telephone (PTT), 5, 9, 24, 25, 42, 74–75, 80, 91, 186, 188
Minute of Beauty (Radio-Cité), 105
Minute of Good Sense (Radio-Cité), 105
Minute for the Perfect Housewife (Radio-Cité), 105
Mireille (Hartuch), 13; bourgeois upbringing of, 130, 132, 138; change of last name,

Mireille (Hartuch) *(continued)*
  130; and *Mireille and Friends,* 34, 131; sexual and social freedom of, 130–32; success due to the microphone, 47; teams with Jean Nohain, 34, 131; and Vichy, 187; and working-class sexual promiscuity, 144–46, 158
Mireille and Friends (Poste Parisien), 34, 131
miscegenation, fear of, 166, 168, 181
Misraki, Paul (Mizrachi), 63, 69, 128, 178, 187
Mistinguett (Jeanne Bourgeois), 132, 135
Mon Programme, 81, 92, 95
Montmartre, 150–51
Montpelier-PTT, 7, 94
Moreno, Marguerite, 47
multi-station programs, 36
"Muse of the Radio," 115
Le Music-Hall des Jeunes (Radio-Cité), 55, 56, 154

Netter, Yvette, 152
Netter, Yvonne, 109
Nice-PTT, 7, 73, 94
Nicloai, G., 87, 88, 95
Noël-Noël (Lucien Noël), 36, 56, 63
Nohain, Jean: as Jaboune, 48–49; praised by *Le Figaro,* 86; teams with Mireille, 34, 130–31

occupation, radio during the, 187–89
On a Bench (Radio-Cité), 40
L'Ouest-Éclair, 59

Paramaribo (Avryl), 174
Paris-PTT, 6; left-wing criticism of programming on, 107; and Parisian regional Conseil de Gérance, 73; programming hours, 6; radio election results for, 94; right-wing criticism of programming on, 90; women's programming on, 107
Paris-Soir: and advertising for programs, 36; and radio elections, 92, 93; and Radio-37, 46, 49, 50, 52, 53; and Tino Rossi, 93, 183
Le Petit Parisien and Poste Parisien, 33–34, 46–49, 59

Le Petit Radio, 4, 102, 115
Piaf, Edith, 14; activities during the occupation, 188; and African stereotypes in song, 169; as archetypical single working-class girl, 153–57; and *chansons réalists,* 146–47, 154–57; hoarse vocal timbre of, 150; and Jacques Canetti, 56; male heroism in songs, 113; and *Le Music-Hall des Jeunes,* 56; as Raymond Asso's muse, 154; and success on the radio, 15; training of, 154; as Victor Margueritte's *garçonne* in film, 156–57
Pierre-Dac (André Isaac), 38
Pills and Tabet, 34, 130, 131, 144
Piot, Jean, 83
Poincignon, J.-G., 95
Popular Front, 17; candidates for radio elections, 90; and conservative ideals, 189–190; creation of left-wing radio programming, 70; criticism of in radio guides, 73–74, 81, 84, 86–90, 95, 96; criticism of commercial radio by, 23, 38; depicted in swing music, 65; and depictions of family, 127; desire to use radio for education, 71, 75, 94; limitations in use of radio, 73, 83; and paid vacations, 125; programming on radio, 76–80; and Radio-Liberté, 83–84; use of other national radio systems as models, 72; use of radio elections, 82; and women, 101; and women's programming, 106
popular song: and advertising, 35–36, 69; Africans in, 178; airtime of, 33; anti-Arab sentiment in, 170; anti-semitism in, 68; and *The Bar of the Stars,* 52; and *chansons réalistes,* 150–58; criminality in, 132–33, 137, 147, 150–58; and *Le Crochet radiophonique,* 57; domestic labor in, 144; during the occupation, 188, 190; exoticism in, 181–82, 185; and film, 15; and founding of Radio-37, 51–52; history of, 13; homophobia in, 68; live audiences for, 56–57; and masculinity, 132–33, 134–35; methodol-

ogy for, 13; misogyny in, 120–21, 122, 133; and *Le Music-Hall des Jeunes,* 56; politics in, 64–65, 67; and Popular Front, 64–65, 78, 95–96; promiscuity in, 131, 137, 144, 145–46, 150–58; prostitution in, 128, 137, 150–58; racism in, 168–69, 178; relevance to present day of, 13–14; right-wing criticism of, 65, 90; romance in, 123, 124, 131; and swing music, 63–70

Porter, Cole, 96

Portraits of Honest Woman in the French Novel (Normand), 118

Poste Parisien, 6; and *Academy of Silliness,* 38; and advertisers, 38; and advertising revenue, 40; audience for, 48–49; and *The Banania Wake-Up,* 36; and colonies, 162–63; early years, 33–34, 46; employees, 40, 44; expenses, 40; flow chart, 43; left-wing criticism of, 23; and *The Little Friends' Club,* 48; and *Lustucru Theatre,* 36; Max Regnier on, 34; and *Mireille and Friends,* 34, 131; programming on, 36; and Publicis, 28; relationship with *Le Petit Parisien,* 33–34; 46–49; reputation of, 45; and resistance, 188; versus public radio, 79; wattage of, 33

Pouey, Fernand, 27, 189

Prouvost, Jean: and baptism of Radio-37, 136; and *Marie-Claire,* 185; and radio advertising, 70; and reasons for founding Radio-37, 49; and use of *Paris-Soir* to promote Radio-37, 52

public programs at Radio-Cité, 54–55, 56, 73, 108–10, 124

Publicis: and *Antennes de Publicis,* 28–32; and Charles Trenet, 33, 56; creation of, 16, 27–28; and in-house recording studio, 33; and jingles, 33, 35; and "Quand Madelon," 35; and success of, 44

radio election results, 92–94

radio guides, description of, 81–82

radio plays: acting troupes of, 40–41, 76–77, 96, 113; adultery in, 114–15, 118–19, 121, 141, 142; Africans in, 168; anti-feminism in, 119–20; Arabs in, 169; Asians in, 164; 166–68, 171–173; crime drama, 1, 39, 95, 143–44, 160, 178–80; criminality in, 1, 143–44, 147–50; criticism of, 118, 173; domestic labor in, 140–44; fees for writing, 39; left-wing ideals in, 77; marriage in, 114–15, 119, 121, 141, 142–43; masculinity and heroism in, 39, 112, 113–14, 119; motherhood in, 115, 117–18; nationalism in, 117–18, 160, 171–74; orientalism in, 164–65; stage direction for, 11–12, 77; versus retransmission of theater, 26, 76

radio tax, 2, 24–25, 26, 82, 89

Radio-37: advertising on, 50, 70; criticism of, 51–52, 53; founding of, 46, 49–52, 136; and Maurice Chevalier, 49–50, 136; programming on, 52–53, 105, 189; relationship with *Paris-Soir,* 49, 52, 53; reputation of, 45–46, 53

Radio-Agen, 6, 37, 38

Radio-Beziers, 5, 6, 28

Radio Bordeaux-Sud-Ouest, 6, 37, 38

Radio-Cité, 6; and advertising revenue, 40; audience participation on, 54–58, 114; audience response to, 1, 10, 53; celebrities on, 14–15, 35, 36, 37, 39, 96, 115, 137; as charitable organization, 57–58; criticism of, 23; and Edith Piaf, 56, 154; and employees, 9, 40, 54; on film, 15; founding of, 27, 33, 49; growth of, 6, 8; and *Ici . . . Radio-Cité,* 53, 177; and live audiences, 55; and newspaper advertising, 15, 36; and partnership with *L'Intransigeant,* 53; and postwar experience of employees, 188–89; and programs, 14, 35, 38, 40, 51, 54–57, 63, 105, 108–11, 113, 115–16, 124–27, 137, 183; and radio-club, 53–54; reputation of, 8, 45; response of other commercial stations to, 33, 46; sponsorship of programs on, 15, 35, 38; staffing of, 8–9, 40, 44

The Radio-Cité Forum, 108
radio-clubs, 53–54
Radio-Ile-de-France, 6; advertising on, 36, 37, 38; founding of, 49; programming on, 36, 37, 38, 63; Ray Ventura on, 63; reputation of, 45
Radio-Family: and anti-communism, 87–88; appeal to voters, 99; and candidate lists, 91; election results, 101; and political neutrality, 89; and political speeches, 88; and program content, 90; and relationship with Catholic radio guides, 86, 87, 88, 89, 91, 92; tenets of, 85–87
Radio-Journal, 177
Radio-L.L., 6, 33
Radio-Liberté: and criticism, 171; election results, 94; loss of elections of, 91–92; membership of, 83; response of right to, 85–91; tenets of, 83–84; and women's programming, 106
Radio-Liberté (journal), 83–84, 106
Radio-Luxembourg, 6; advertising on, 37, 38, 40; left-wing criticism of, 23; and postwar broadcasting, 189; programming on, 37, 38, 40, 63; Ray Ventura on, 63
Radio-Lyon, 28, 31, 37, 38, 187
Radio-Magazine: and advertising on the radio, 38; Clément Vautel in, 38, 73–74, 89; on Conseils de Gérance, 73–74; cover images of radio listeners, 60–63; criticism of programs, 37, 89; Germaine Blondin in, 37, 103; on jazz as French style, 65; politics of, 81; and programming for women, 103–4; on radio election results, 94; on Radio-Famille, 87; on Ray Ventura, 65; relationship between audience and station, 54; on women on radio, 116
Radio-Méditerranée (Montpelier), 6
Radio-Nice-Côte d'Azur, 6, 29–31, 37, 38
Radio-Nîmes, 6, 29–30
Radio-Normandie, 6, 31–32, 33, 37, 38
Radio-Paris, 7; broadcast hours, 6; crime dramas on, 9; as flagship station, 5–6;

and Georges Mandel, 26; lectures on, 79; Paul Reboux on, 104; and the Popular Front, 23; and the PTT, 26; signal power of, 26; and swing music, 188; women's programming on, 104, 105, 107
Radio-PTT-Nord, 7; popular music on, 96; radio election results for, 94; regional Conseil de Gérance, 73; Tino Rossi on, 96; women's programming on, 108
Radio-Toulouse: advertising on, 36, 37, 38; advertising revenue of, 40; and Antennes Publicis, 28; celebrities on, 38; programming on, 36, 37, 38, 63, 78; Ray Ventura on, 63; Vichy and, 187
Radio-Tour Eiffel, 7, 28, 107
Ray Ventura et Ses Collégiens: and anti-semitism, 68, 187; assimilation to France of, 63; and *chansons du trottoir*, 128, 130, 145, 157–58; and colonies, 170, 178; during the occupation, 187; fees for, 40, 96; Frenchness of music of, 65; and Great Depression, 65, 67; homophobia, 68; *Lustucru Theatre*, 36; performance in drag of, 64; popularity of, 14, 185; radio programs for, 36, 63; reflection in audience of, 63–70; relevance today of, 13; and songs during the occupation, 190; and strikes by Popular Front, 65; success versus Tino Rossi, 183; and working-class sexuality in songs of, 128, 130, 137, 145, 158
Reboux, Paul: and column in *Paris-Soir*, 27, 51–2, 53, 93, 102, 104, 112; on family listeners, 102, 112; and *Le Jeu des Questions*, 51; on men's programming, 112; on radio elections, 93; on Radio-37, 51–52, 53; on radio tax, 27; on Tino Rossi, 183; on women's programming, 104–5
Regnier, Max, 34, 37, 102
Rennes-Bretagne-PTT, 7, 73, 94
Le Retour dans la nuit (Didelot), 147
retransmission of stage plays, 40, 76
The Lesieur Review (Ile-de-France, Radio-Luxembourg, and Radio-Toulouse), 38

Robin, François, 72
Roland, Pierre, 95
Rossi, Tino: as candidate for radio elections, 93; as Corsican, 181; criticism of, 183; and *Le Crochet radiophonique*, 183, 185; as crooner, 47, 78; during the occupation, 188; exoticism of, 18, 181–84; female audiences of, 183–84; and Italo-French lyrics, 182; Paul Reboux on, 183; and Popular Front, 78; programs for, 96; record sales versus other singers, 183; relevance today, 13; use of microphone amplification, 14, 15

Sablon, Germaine, 154
Sablon, Jean, 40, 47, 137
Saillard, Roger, 43, 47
Saint-Granier (Jean de Granier de Cassagnac): catchphrase of, 15; celebrity endorsement of, 15, 36; cross-gender appeal of, 105–6; as host of radio programs, 56, 125; lack of notoriety of, 10; and *The Minute of Good Sense*, 105–6; and relationship with Radio-Cité, 15, 36, 105–6, 125
La Salle Pleyel, 55, 56, 63
Samedi soir (Dauven), 140–41
Savarit, C.-M., 88, 89
Scotto, Vincent, 181
La Semaine Radiophonique, 81, 163
Simon, Michel, 124
slang (terms), 134–35, 151
social Darwinism and race, 168
Solidor, Suzy, 169
The Song of the Spheres (Larronde), 77
Souplex, Raymond, 40
Sourza, Jane, 125
Soviet Union: and comparisons to French radio, 6, 72, 75; and international exposition, 84; and Radio-Liberté, 84; rightwing fears of influence of, 85, 88, 91
speaker/*speakerine*, 1–2, 12, 115–16
Strasbourg-PTT, 7, 94

The Survivors (Malard and Malard), 117
swing bands: criticism of, 65; expression of French identity with, 174; fees for, 40; increase in public programming of, 95; newspaper advertising with, 36; programs featuring, 36; reflection of audience make up in, 45, 63–70; sexuality in songs by, 68, 128, 137; and songs by Ray Ventura et Ses Collégiens, 63–70, 128; and studio audiences, 63
Sylva, Berthe, 152

Taipan (Denis), 165, 167
tango, 180–81
Le Théâtre Express: La femme de ménage III (Charasson), 142–43
Le Théâtre du Peuple, 76
Toulouse-PTT, 7, 94
Tranchant, Jean, 187
Trémoulet, Jacques, 187, 189
Trenet, Charles: as composer for Maurice Chevalier, 51; during the occupation, 188; as jingle-writer for Publicis, 33; on *Le Music-Hall des Jeunes*, 56; popularity of, 14
True Stories, 39, 113–14
The Twelfth Gong of Midnight (Larronde), 77
Two Men in Morocco (Gontrain), 12, 165, 166, 176

ukulele, 180
United States: African Americans from, in France, 177, 184; and *chanson réaliste*, 147; and comparisons to French radio, 4, 6, 72; and histories of the radio, 10–11, 24; immigration of French to, 147; and influence on French swing, 63–64, 95–96; Maurice Chevalier in, 132–33; Mireille in, 130; in popular song, 147, 170; radio programming in, 55, 57

Vaillant-Couturier, Paul, 83
The Variety Review (Dorac), 12
Variot, Jean, 39

Vautel, Clement: on advertising and the radio tax, 38; on the Conseils de Gérance, 74, 94; and critique of left-wing programming, 89; right-wing ties of, 74
Vendredi, 76, 78, 80, 93, 96
Ventura, Ray. *See* Ray Ventura et Ses Collégiens
The Viceroy of India's Daughter, (Teramond), 164, 166
Vichy, radio under, 187–89
The Voice from the Shadows (Gratias), 119

The Women's Forum (Radio-Cité), 108–11, 127, 185
Women's Hour (Lyon-PTT), 107
women's programming: criticism of, 106–7; and feminism, 107–12; lectures, 105–6; *The Women's Forum,* 108–12

Yesterday Evening (Timmory), 121
The Youth Forum (Radio-Cité), 108

Zay, Jean, 78